DA 110 .025 2006
Oakland, John.
British civilization

 **W9-DET-398**

RIVIER COLLEGE

3 4670 00212 9930

British Civilization

Reviews of the previous editions:

'John Oakland is the doyen of civilization studies.' *British Studies Now*

'This is a first rate, lucidly written text.' *G.E.C. Paton, Aston University*

'Suitable above all because it covers so many areas of contemporary institutions . . . a useful reference work.' *Patrick Leech, University of Bologna*

'Strikes a balance between providing up-to-date information and being a source of general reference.' *Anne K. Bjørge, Norwegian School of Economics and Business Administration*

'An excellent presentation of the British economic and political/institutional system.' *J. Condriou, Université de Provence*

'A perfect tool and source for class activities.' *Borek Sousedik, Tobos ELT, Czech Republic*

British Civilization provides a comprehensive introduction to a wide range of aspects of contemporary Britain, including its country and people, politics and government, education, the economy, the media, arts and religion.

It includes:

- discussion of recent developments and areas of topical interest in British society such as immigration, asylum seekers, the war against terror, the changing welfare state and Britain's relationships with the US and the EU
- new illustrations, maps, diagrams and graphs, and tables
- expanded chapters
- a companion website.

British Civilization is a vital introduction to the crucial and complex identities of Britain.

For supplementary exercises, questions and tutor guidance, go to **www.routledge.com/textbooks/0415365228**.

John Oakland is Senior Lecturer in English at the Norwegian University of Science and Technology and the author (with David Mauk) of *American Civilization* (now in its 4th edition), *Contemporary Britain* and *British Civilization: A Student's Dictionary* (now in its 2nd edition).

British Civilization

An introduction

Sixth edition

John Oakland

Routledge
Taylor & Francis Group

LONDON AND NEW YORK

First published 1989

Second edition 1991
Third edition 1995
Fourth edition 1998
Fifth edition 2002
Reprinted 2004, 2005

Sixth edition published in 2006
by Routledge
2 Park Square, Milton Park, Abingdon, Oxon, OX14 4RN

Simultaneously published in the USA and Canada
by Routledge
270 Madison Avenue, New York NY 10016

Routledge is an imprint of the Taylor & Francis Group, an informa business

© 1989, 1991, 1995, 1998, 2002, 2006 John Oakland

Typeset in Berling and Futura by
Keystroke, Jacaranda Lodge, Wolverhampton
Printed and bound in Great Britain by
TJ International Ltd, Padstow, Cornwall

All rights reserved. No part of this book may be reprinted or reproduced or utilised
in any form or by any electronic, mechanical, or other means, now known or hereafter
invented, including photocopying and recording, or in any information storage or
retrieval system, without permission in writing from the publishers.

British Library Cataloguing in Publication Data
A catalogue record for this book is available from the British Library

Library of Congress Cataloging in Publication Data
Oakland, John.
    British civilization : an introduction / John Oakland. – 6th ed.
        p. cm.
    Includes bibliographical references (p.) and index.
    ISBN 0–415–36521–X – ISBN 0–415–36522–8 (pbk.) 1. Great Britain–Civilization.
    I. Title.
    DA110.O25 2006
    941–dc22   2005036378

ISBN10: 0–415–36521–X (hbk)
ISBN10: 0–415–36522–8 (pbk)
ISBN10: 0–203–01662–9 (ebk)

ISBN13: 978–0–415–36521–5 (hbk)
ISBN13: 978–0–415–36522–2 (pbk)
ISBN13: 978–0–203–01662–6 (ebk)

REGINA LIBRARY
RIVIER COLLEGE
NASHUA, NH 03060

Contents

Plates

Figures

Tables

Preface and acknowledgements

This book examines central structural features of British society, such as politics and government, international relations, the law, the economy, social services, the media, education and religion. Chapters on the country, the people, arts, sports and leisure are also included to illustrate the geographical, human and cultural diversity of British civilization. Each chapter attempts to assess the attitudes of British people to the social conditions in which they live and operate.

Methodologically, the book combines descriptive and analytical approaches within a historical context. Each chapter has its own historical perspectives and provides information on debates and recent developments in Britain. The book is intended to allow students to organize their own responses to British society and to encourage critical discussion. Essay and term exercises at the end of each chapter direct readers to central issues and can be adequately approached from material contained in the text. Further information may be found in the suggested further reading and relevant websites. Recommended introductory dictionaries for terms are Oakland, J. (2003) *British Civilization: A Student's Dictionary*, London: Routledge and Crowther, J. and Kavanagh, K. (1999) *Oxford Guide to British and American Culture*, Oxford: Oxford University Press.

A book of this type is necessarily indebted for many of its facts, ideas and statistics, to a range of reference sources, which cannot all be mentioned here, but to which general acknowledgement is gratefully made (see also Further reading in each chapter). Particular thanks are due to *UK: The Official Yearbook of the UK* and the *Annual Abstract of Statistics* (both published by the Office for National Statistics and Palgrave Macmillan: London); *British Social Attitudes* (London: Sage Publications); newspapers of record such as *The Times* (London) and public opinion poll sources, such as *Market and Opinion Research International* (*MORI*), *Gallup, ICM, Populus* and *Yougov*.

The websites included in this book are mainly those of public institutions. Although these may present official and standard views, they are often more permanent, up-to-date and informative than many independent websites, which can quickly change their addresses and content or simply disappear.

The term 'billion' in this book refers to 'a thousand million'.

Chronology of significant dates in British history

Prehistory:	British Isles and Ireland originally part of European land mass: warmer conditions alternated with severe Ice Ages
700,000 BC:	butchered animal bones and stone artefacts indicate hominid activity
500,000 BC:	earliest human bones found in southern England (Boxgrove Man)
c. 250,000 BC:	nomadic Old Stone Age (Paleolithic) peoples arrived
50,000 BC:	warmer climate encouraged arrival of ancestors of modern populations
10,000 BC:	end of Ice Ages. Population consisted of hunter-gatherers and fishers
5,000 BC:	contemporary islands gradually separated from Continental Europe
c. 3,000 BC:	New Stone Age (Neolithic) peoples populated the western parts of the islands. Farming introduced; stone and earth monuments built
c. 1,800 BC:	Bronze Age settlers (Beaker Folk) in southeast and eastern England; traded in gold, copper and tin
c. 600 BC:	settlement of the Celts (Iron Age) from Austria and Switzerland began
c. 200 BC:	invasions by Belgic tribes, mainly in eastern England
55–54 BC:	Julius Caesar's exploratory expeditions
AD 43:	Roman conquest of England, Wales and (temporarily) lowland Scotland by Claudius began. Christian influences
200–400:	the Scots from Ireland colonized western Scotland
122–38:	Hadrian's Wall built between Scotland and England
c. 409:	Roman army withdrew from Britain; wars between the Celts
c. 410:	Germanic (Anglo-Saxon) invasions began
c. 450–600:	Eight Anglo-Saxon kingdoms (the Heptarchy) gradually created in England. Mainly Celtic peoples in Wales, Ireland, Scotland and Cornwall
430:	existing Celtic Christianity in Ireland later spread by St Patrick (from 432) and other missionaries in Ireland, Scotland, Wales and northern England

597:	St Augustine preached Christianity (Roman Catholic church model) to Anglo-Saxons of southern England. Establishment of ecclesiastical capital in Canterbury, Kent
664:	Synod of Whitby chose Roman Catholic church model for British Christianity
789–95:	Scandinavian (Viking) raids began
800:	Cornwall conquered by Anglo-Saxons
820:	Anglo-Saxon kingdoms dominated by Wessex; union of the Heptarchy
832–60:	union of Scots and Picts in Scotland under Kenneth Macalpin to form most of the eventual kingdom of Scotland
860s:	Scandinavians controlled much of northern and eastern England (East Anglia, Northumbria and eastern Mercia – the Danelaw)
871–99:	reign of Alfred the Great of Wessex
878:	Scandinavians defeated in England by King Alfred of Wessex and confined to the Danelaw
954:	the Kingdom of England formed; recovery of the Danelaw
1013–4:	Sven of Norway/Denmark conquered England
1014:	Scandinavians defeated in Ireland
1018:	Scotland came under English rule

The early Middle Ages

1066:	September; King Harold defeated Norwegian army at Stamford Bridge, October; William I (the Conqueror) defeated King Harold at Hastings and ascended the English throne. The Norman Conquest: feudalism introduced
1072:	William I invaded Scotland
1086:	*Domesday Book* (tax and land records) compiled for whole of England by the Normans
1169:	Henry II invaded and controlled the east coast of Ireland
1200s:	first Oxford and Cambridge colleges founded
1215:	King John signed Magna Carta at Runnymede near Windsor, which protected English feudal (aristocratic) rights against royal abuse
1258 and 1264:	first English parliamentary structures
1282:	much of Wales controlled by England under Edward I
1295:	the Model Parliament (first regular English Parliament)
1296:	the Scots defeated by Edward I
1297:	first Irish Parliament
1301:	Edward of Caernarvon (later Edward II) named as first Prince of Wales
1314:	Scottish victory at battle of Bannockburn regained Scottish independence
1326:	first Scottish Parliament

The late Middle Ages

1337:	Hundred Years War between England and France began
1348–9:	plague (Black Death) destroyed a third of the islands' population
1362:	English replaced French as the official language
1381:	Peasants' Revolt (popular rebellion) in England
c. 1387–c. 1394:	Geoffrey Chaucer wrote *The Canterbury Tales*
1400–10:	Failed Welsh revolt by Owain Glyndwr against English rule
1406:	Earl of Derby bought Isle of Man from Scotland
1407:	House of Commons became responsible for taxation
1411:	first university in Scotland founded (St Andrews)
1415:	Battle of Agincourt; England defeated France
1455–87:	Wars of the Roses between Yorkists and Lancastrians
1469:	Orkney and Shetland transferred to Scotland by Norway
1477:	first book printed in England, by William Caxton

Towards the nation state (Britain)

1509:	accession of Henry VIII
1513:	Henry VIII defeated the Scots at Flodden
1534–40:	Henry VIII broke with Papacy and became Head of the English Church (Roman Catholic); beginning of the English Reformation
1536–42:	Acts of Union led to legal and administrative integration of England and Wales
1547–53:	Protestantism became official religion in England under Edward VI
1553–58:	Catholic reaction under Mary I: Roman Catholicism restored
1558–1603:	Elizabeth I: Protestantism established
1558:	Calais, England's last possession in France, lost
1560:	creation of Protestant Church of Scotland by John Knox: the Scottish Reformation
1585–90:	first tentative English colonizing ventures in North America
1587:	Mary Stuart, Queen of Scots, executed in London
1588:	defeat of Spanish Armada
c. 1590–c. 1613:	plays of William Shakespeare written
1600:	East India (trading) Company founded
1603:	dynastic union of England and Scotland under James VI of Scotland (James I of England); Union of the Two Crowns
1607:	Plantation of Ulster (Northern Ireland) with Scottish and English Protestant settlers: establishment of first permanent English colony in North America at Jamestown (Virginia)
1611:	the Authorized (King James) Version of the Bible issued

1628:	monarch's power restricted by the Petition of Right
1641:	rebellion in Ireland
1642–48:	Civil Wars between King and Parliament
1649:	execution of Charles I; monarchy abolished
1653–58:	Oliver Cromwell ruled England as Lord Protector
1660:	monarchy restored under Charles II (the Restoration)
1665:	the Great Plague in England
1666:	the Great Fire of London
1679:	Habeas Corpus Act passed. Party political system gradually initiated
1686:	Isaac Newton proposed laws of motion and gravitation
1688:	The Glorious Revolution: accession of William III and Mary II to the throne
1689:	the Declaration of Rights
1690:	Irish defeated by William III at the Battle of the Boyne

The eighteenth century

1707:	Acts of Union joined England/Wales and Scotland (Great Britain): unification of Scottish and English Parliaments
1715:	Scottish Jacobite rebellions crushed
1721:	Robert Walpole became Britain's first prime minister
1739:	War with Spain
1742:	War with France
1745:	Failed Scottish rebellion under Bonnie Prince Charlie to restore the British throne to the Stuarts
1756:	the Seven Years War
1750s–1830s:	Industrial Revolutions
1759:	war with France; Canada won from French
1761:	opening of the Bridgewater Canal began the Canal Age
1765:	Isle of Man purchased by British Crown
1769:	the steam engine and the spinning machine invented
1775–83:	American War for Independence; loss of the Thirteen Colonies
1793–1815:	Revolutionary and Napoleonic Wars

The nineteenth century

1801:	Act of Union joined Great Britain and Ireland (United Kingdom)
1805:	Battle of Trafalgar: Nelson defeated the French navy
1807:	abolition of the slave trade in the British Empire: ending of slavery in 1833
1815:	Napoleon defeated by Wellington at Waterloo

1825:	opening of the Stockton and Darlington Railway, the world's first public passenger railway
1829:	Catholic emancipation (freedom of religious worship)
1832:	First Reform Act extended the male franchise (vote) by 50 per cent
1837–1901:	reign of Queen Victoria
1838:	the People's Charter and the beginning of trade unions
1839:	The Durham Report on dominion status for some colonies, such as Canada
1845:	disastrous harvest failure in Ireland
1851:	first organized trade unions appeared
1853–6:	The Crimean War
1868:	Trade Union Congress (TUC) established
1870:	compulsory elementary state school education introduced in England. Canada became first dominion state
1871:	legal recognition of trade unions
1899:	The Boer War (South Africa)

The twentieth century

1901:	death of Queen Victoria
1904:	Entente Cordiale with France
1910–36:	the British Empire reached its global territorial peak
1911:	political veto power of the House of Lords restricted
1914–18:	First World War
1916:	Easter Rising against Britain in Dublin
1918:	all men over twenty-one and women over thirty receive the vote
1919:	League of Nations created
1921–2:	Irish Free State established by Anglo-Irish Treaty; Northern Ireland remained part of the United Kingdom with its own devolved parliament
1924:	first Labour government
1926:	the General Strike
1928:	votes for all women over 21
1930s:	economic depression, poverty and high unemployment: Jarrow March 1936
1931:	British Commonwealth of Nations emerges
1936:	abdication of King Edward VIII
1939–45:	Second World War (W. Churchill, Prime Minister 1940)
1940:	the Battle of Britain
1944:	Butler Education Act: state education compulsory to 15
1945:	United Nations formed
1947:	Independence for India and Pakistan; beginning of large-scale decolonialization

1948:   National Health Service created; free medical care for all

1949:   Irish Free State became the Republic of Ireland. NATO created. The modern Commonwealth emerged

1952:   accession of Elizabeth II

1956:   the Suez Canal Crisis

1960:   Britain joined European Free Trade Association (EFTA)

1965:   death penalty (by hanging) for serious crimes abolished

1965–9: oil and gas discoveries in the North Sea

1968:   protest and violence erupted in Northern Ireland

1969:   vote extended to all persons over eighteen

1971:   decimal currency introduced

1972:   direct rule from Westminster in Northern Ireland

1973:   Britain left EFTA and entered European Economic Community (now EU)

1975:   referendum affirmed Britain's continued membership of EEC

1979:   Margaret Thatcher: Britain's first woman Prime Minister

1981:   Social Democratic Party (SDP) formed

1982:   the Falklands War with Argentina

1984:   Miners' strike

1985:   Anglo-Irish Agreement allows the Irish Republic an input in the running of Northern Ireland

1988:   SDP merged with Liberal Party; becomes known as the Liberal Democrats

1994:   Channel Rail Tunnel between France and Britain opened

1997:   Referendums on devolution for Scotland and Wales. Sovereignty of Hong Kong transferred to China

1998:   Belfast (Good Friday) Agreement; endorsed by referendums in both parts of Ireland; election of devolved Northern Ireland Assembly

1999:   devolution structures in Scotland (a Parliament) and Wales (an Assembly)

The twenty-first century

2000:   number of hereditary peers entitled to sit and vote in the House of Lords reduced from 750 to 92

2003:   Gains for Democratic Unionist Party and Sinn Fein in Northern Ireland Assembly elections; Assembly suspended

2005:   Labour party achieves third successive victory in UK general election; Northern Ireland Assembly remains suspended; IRA orders members to cease 'military operations'; international decommissioning body reports that IRA weapons have been 'put beyond use'; some Unionist paramilitaries move to disarm

Chapter 1

The British context

- Historical growth
- Structural change
- Contemporary conditions
- British attitudes to Britain
- *Exercises*
- *Further reading*
- *Websites*

This chapter introduces four aspects of British civilization (historical growth, structural change, contemporary conditions and British attitudes to Britain) which will be treated later in more specific detail according to chapter topics (such as government, education or religion). All will be placed within historical perspectives in order to show how Britain has evolved to its contemporary position.

Historical growth

The historical context is important in any attempt to understand British society today, whether by Britons or overseas students. But a research survey by *Encyclopaedia Britannica* in November 2001 found that most school-leavers in Britain were ignorant of some of the key events in their history and that a quarter had no interest in bygone days. Other recent opinion polls show that historical knowledge and an adequate awareness of the country's past are lacking among many Britons of all ages.

These findings clash with stereotypical international perceptions about Britain, which are revealed in answers to research surveys such as those by the Royal Society for the Arts (November 2004) and the British Council/MORI (November1999). Respondents tended to see British people as conventional and backward-looking and having an exaggerated and outdated respect for their history, traditions and institutions. The country is often perceived from abroad through images of monarchy, kilts, castles, aristocracy, quaint behaviour and a stagnating, risk-averse economy.

Such stereotypes do not accurately describe the complex and diverse reality of contemporary Britain with all its strengths and weaknesses. Within Britain itself, critics call for more teaching of British history in schools to combat public ignorance; the Labour government has introduced courses on citizenship into the curriculum so that pupils may learn what constitutes a British civic culture; and official bodies at all levels attempt to counter negative overseas images.

Britain, whose constitutional title is the United Kingdom of Great Britain and Northern Ireland (UK), today comprises a collection of large and smaller islands off the north-western European mainland, which are totally surrounded by sea (the North Sea, the English Channel, the Irish Sea and the Atlantic Ocean). It shares the second-largest island with the Republic of Ireland, with whom it has a land border. In pre-history, these areas were visited by Old and New Stone Age nomads, some of whom later settled permanently. From about 600 BC–AD 1066 the islands were subjected to successive settlement and invasion patterns from peoples who came mostly from mainland Europe, such as Celts, Belgic tribes, Romans, Germanic tribes (Anglo-Saxons), Scandinavians and Normans. These groups were added to in later centuries by immigration movements, particularly in the twentieth century, to produce the present multi-ethnic British population with its mixed identities of origin. Today, there are still substantial differences between the peoples of England, Wales, Scotland and Northern Ireland, and competing allegiances within the four countries themselves.

The early settlers and invaders contributed between the ninth and twelfth centuries to the building-blocks on which were gradually established the separate nations of England, Wales, Scotland and Ireland (with England and Scotland gaining stronger individual identities by the tenth century). All these countries underwent very varied internal experiences, abrupt political changes and periodic violence as well as external conflicts with each other in their historical growth to nationhood.

Their later individual developments within the islands were greatly influenced first by the expansionist, military aims of English monarchs and second by a series of dynastic and political unions. Ireland and Wales had been effectively under English control since the twelfth and thirteenth centuries respectively, while Scotland in 1603 was joined dynastically to England. Movement towards a more recognizable British state structure (with its Parliament power base in London) occurred with political unions between England, Wales and Scotland (Great Britain) in 1707 and between Great Britain and Ireland in 1801. In 1921, the southern part of Ireland left the union to later become the Republic of Ireland. The present United Kingdom consists therefore of Great Britain (England, Scotland and Wales) and Northern Ireland.

These historical developments involved political and constitutional issues and encouraged the gradual creation of a centralized British (or UK) state, which owed much to English models and dominance. State structures (such as monarchy, government, Parliament and the law) evolved slowly, unevenly and often pragmatically (rather than by revolutionary change) to provide an umbrella organization for the four component countries. But there have also been periods of upheaval and ideological conflict (such as royalist and tribal battles, Civil Wars, nationalist revolts by the Scots, Welsh and Irish against the English, lasting struggles with European powers, religious ferment, social dissension and political quarrels).

Nevertheless, it is often argued that the supposed evolutionary characteristics of the modern British state are attributable to the insular and conservative mentalities of island peoples, with their preference for traditional habits and institutions and distrust of change for change's sake. Some influences have come from abroad in the long historical process. But the absence of any successful external military invasion of the islands since the Norman Conquest of AD 1066 has allowed the individual nations of England, Scotland, Wales and Ireland to develop internally in distinctive ways, despite frequent struggles among and within them.

Meanwhile the social organizations and constitutional principles of the larger British state, such as parliamentary democracy, government, law, economic systems, a modern welfare state and religious faiths, have also developed slowly although often accompanied by fierce disputes. The structures and philosophies of this emerging British statehood have sometimes been imitated by other countries, or exported overseas through the creation of a global empire from the sixteenth century and a commercial need to establish world markets for British goods.

The British Empire may be seen as an extension of English monarchs' internal military expansionism within the islands and in mainland Europe. Following some early reversals in Europe, they sought raw materials, possessions, trade and power overseas. This colonialism was aided by an increasing military might (achieved by later victories over European and other nations) into the twentieth century. Internally, substantial agricultural revolutions in England from the New Stone Age and Anglo-Saxon period onwards added appreciably to the country's wealth, exports, prestige and international trade. Britain also developed an early manufacturing and financial base. It became an industrial and largely urban country from the late eighteenth century because of a series of industrial revolutions and inventions. Throughout its history, Britain has also been responsible for major scientific and medical advances.

PLATE 1.1 The Norman Conquest 1066.
The 11th or 12th century Bayeux tapestry, Bayeux, France represents the story of the Battle of Hastings and the Norman Conquest of England.
(*Roger-Viollet/Rex Features*)

PLATE 1.2 Oliver Cromwell (1599–1658).
English general, politician and Puritan who led the Parliamentarian army against King Charles I in the English Civil War 1642–51. Became Lord Protector of England (1653–58) after the King's defeat and execution in 1649. The period from 1649–1660 constitutes the only break in the English monarchy's continuous history.
(*Rex Features*)

The development of the British state and its empire historically was aided by economic, industrial, maritime and military strength, so that by the nineteenth century the country had become a dominant industrial and naval world power. It was a main player in developing Western ideas and principles of law, property, business, liberty, capitalism, parliamentary democracy and civil society.

Political union within Britain itself (despite continuing tensions) had also gradually encouraged the idea of a British identity (Britishness), in which all the component countries of the UK could share. This was tied to Britain's imperial position in the world and to an identification with the powerful institutions of the state, such as the monarchy, law, Parliament, the military and Protestant religion. But national identities in the four nations of the union persisted and became stronger as Britain's international standing declined and competing forces arose in the twentieth century. Pressure for constitutional change eventually resulted first in the partition of Ireland in 1921 and second devolution (transfer of some political power from London to elected bodies in Scotland, Wales and Northern Ireland) by 1998–9. Such changes also encouraged fierce debates about the nature of Britishness, individual national identities in the component countries and the future constitutional structure of the UK, which are still being addressed in contemporary Britain.

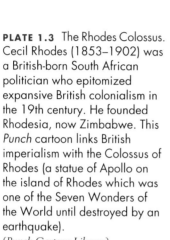

PLATE 1.3 The Rhodes Colossus. Cecil Rhodes (1853–1902) was a British-born South African politician who epitomized expansive British colonialism in the 19th century. He founded Rhodesia, now Zimbabwe. This *Punch* cartoon links British imperialism with the Colossus of Rhodes (a statue of Apollo on the island of Rhodes which was one of the Seven Wonders of the World until destroyed by an earthquake).
(*Punch Cartoon Library*)

THE RHODES COLOSSUS
STRIDING FROM CAPE TOWN TO CAIRO.

The British state has seen many other internal reforms over time, such as the extension of the vote in the nineteenth and twentieth centuries, the diminishing power of the aristocratic House of Lords, the increasing authority of the popularly elected House of Commons in the parliamentary structure and the decline of executive monarchy. It underwent substantial collectivist social changes in the twentieth century, such as nationalization (with the state becoming the owner of public industries and services) and the creation of a welfare state. Later in that century, these emphases changed as government economic policies effectively shifted British society, collectively and individually, along free market lines.

The country has thus experienced significant change (as well as relative decline) in the twentieth century. Its social and economic strength was seriously reduced by the effects of two world wars in the first half of the century and by the dismantling of its earlier imperial global power in the second half. Its ethnic composition, state structures, social policies, religious beliefs and economic institutions have all been affected by profound domestic developments and external pressures. Traditional notions of Britain's place in the world, the nature of its society and hopes for its future have been subjected to debates, re-evaluation and pressures on many levels. These continued as the country entered the twenty-first century.

Since the Second World War (1939–45), Britain has had to adjust with difficulty to the results of a withdrawal from empire (which was judged as inevitable in the face of growing nationalism and self-determination in the colonies); a reduction in world status; global economic recessions; a relative decline in economic power; increased foreign competition; internal social change; a geo-political world order of the dominant superpowers (the USA and the Soviet Union); international fluctuations and new tensions after the break-up of the latter; and a changing Europe following the destruction of two world wars.

Britain has been forced into a reluctant search for a new identity and direction, both internationally and nationally, which some critics argue it has not yet achieved. While maintaining many of its traditional worldwide commercial, cultural and political links, such as the so-called 'special relationship' with the United States of America, it has nevertheless moved from empire and its successor Commonwealth towards an avowed economic and political commitment to Europe, mainly through membership of what is now the European Union (EU).

In recent centuries, Britain rarely saw itself as an integral part of mainland Europe. It sheltered behind the sea barrier of the English Channel and its outlook was westwards and worldwide. Today the psychological and physical isolation from Europe is slowly changing, as illustrated by increased cooperation between Britain and other European countries and by the opening (1994) of a Channel rail

PLATE 1.4 Edward Heath signing EEC agreement, Belgium, 1972.
Edward Heath (1916–2005) who, as British Conservative Prime Minister (1970–74), led Britain into the European Economic Community (now European Union) by signing the EEC Agreement in 1972.
(*PUBLI PRESS/Rex Features*)

tunnel between England and France. But the relationship between Britain and
Europe continues to be problematic and new associations have been forced by
events and circumstances, rather than wholeheartedly sought. The historical
impulses to national independence and isolationism still appear to condition many
British people in their dealings with and attitudes to the outside world, despite
their reliance on global trade and international relationships.

Critics (and British politicians) argue that isolationism is not a viable option
in a globalized world. Britain has been involved, not without significant public
protest, in recent overseas military action in Bosnia, Kosovo, two Iraq wars,
Afghanistan and other trouble spots worldwide as a partner in the North Atlantic
Treaty Alliance (NATO) and the American-led 'War against Terror'. Britain
has attracted terrorist threats itself (arguably for some critics as a result of such
commitments and alliances), culminating in suicide bombings against the London
public transport system by British-born individuals on 7 July 2005 and further
failed attempts on 21 July. These terrorist attacks have raised debates about the
nature and loyalty of the country's multi-ethnic population and about government
policies in areas such as asylum seekers and immigration procedures as the country
seeks to protect itself in a changing world. Britain has thus become intimately
involved in the globalized debates of the early twenty-first century, from which
it cannot isolate itself as it might have tried to do at some periods in its earlier
history.

PLATE 1.5 Bomb attack on London bus, Tavistock Square, 7 July 2005.
Suicide bombers attack the London transport system (including the Underground) destroying a
double decker bus and killing 56 people (13 on the bus).
(*Rex Features*)

Structural change

Historically, structural change in Britain has been inevitably conditioned by social, economic, legal, religious and political developments. Some were abrupt and often violent, while others occurred in slower, more pragmatic fashion. The resulting structural features have taken different forms and sizes; operate on national and local levels; and condition cultural identities, values and attitudes, frequently by a mixing of both these levels.

Today, the major formal features, such as Parliament, law and government, are concerned with state or public business and initiate policies in 'top-down' form. This means that decisions are decided by centralized and multi-level bodies (whether elected or appointed) in the power hierarchy and then imposed on lower levels. Some of these processes are much criticized in Britain because they allegedly distance decision-makers from the general public, undercut accountability and result in a so-called 'democratic deficit'. Many British people frequently complain that they should be consulted more closely about institutional changes in their society and have a greater voice in local and national affairs, rather than being conditioned by isolated political and economic elites. This situation has arguably led to a disenchantment with and withdrawal from the political process.

But there are many other structures on both public and private levels of social activity, such as sports, families, leisure activities, neighbourhoods, youth culture, faith groups, local communities and habitual ways of life which have their own particular value-systems and organizations. They often have a 'bottom-up' form in which policies and behaviour are said to be linked closely to the concerns of society's grassroots. They may illustrate more localized, informal and democratic characteristics than the top-down model. But even local communities (such as local government, sports clubs and small interest groups) can be dominated by elites which may be in conflict with other individuals who object to being controlled by the leadership. This behaviour on both national and local levels emphasizes the strong individualistic streak in the British mentality, which views 'authority' with suspicion and has historically often led to schism and nonconformity in many areas of society.

The 'British way of life' and British identities are determined by how people function within and react, whether positively, negatively or apathetically, to social structures. These are not remote abstractions but directly and immediately affect individuals in their daily lives. For example, government policies impinge upon citizens and their families; commercial organizations influence choices in food, music, clothes and fashion; the media try to shape news values and agendas; sponsorship and advertising may determine the nature of sports, the media and other activities; devolved government bodies in Scotland, Wales and Northern Ireland initiate policies for their own areas; local government throughout the UK conditions local activities; and community life is subject to small-scale (and sometimes eccentric) influences.

These structural features necessarily reflect a range of practices on both high and popular cultural levels. High cultural forms continue in Britain, which may often appeal to a minority and be tied into class concerns, although the blurring of class barriers, expanded education and a decline in deference have now opened them up for more widespread participation. But there have always been popular cultural activities which have become more numerous and diverse since the 1960s because of greater affluence and more varied life opportunities. Such a mass popular culture (reflected in for example sport, television, music and fashion) is now a significant and, for some, trivializing element in British life. It influences social patterns, modes of behaviour, economic consumption and the development of very different lifestyles.

The number and variety of top-down and bottom-up structures mean that there are many different and often conflicting 'ways of life' in contemporary Britain, which all contribute to the pluralistic nature of the society. Some critics thus argue that the main defining features of British life are a healthy diversity and change at all levels. Others maintain that these phenomena, particularly from the 1960s, have led to social fragmentation and anti-social behaviour; a weakened sense of community and civic responsibility; a decline in nationally-accepted values and identities; uncertainty; and confusion. Yet others suggest that an emphasis upon 'pluralism' and 'diversity' is misleading and stress instead those normative and traditional behaviour patterns or beliefs which arguably still exist for most people in the country.

Organizational structures must adapt to new situations if they are to survive and their present roles may be very different from their original functions. Pressures are consequently placed on them to more adequately reflect and respond to current public worries and concerns. The performances of British national and local institutions are vigorously debated and many are found wanting. Questions are asked as to whether the existing structures can cope with and reflect the needs, complexity and demands of contemporary life, and whether (and how) they might be reformed in order to operate more efficiently and responsively. Such questioning is also linked to debates on 'modernization' (often employed by British politicians and 'opinion-formers' to indicate 'positive progress') and very opposed arguments about how the country should be organized socially, politically and economically. It is often debatable whether this soul-searching actually results in appropriate action or merely promotes divisive, fashionable and temporary programmes, which quickly fail.

Contemporary conditions

A leader in *The Times* (London, 2 November 2005) argued that:

> Britons have long prided themselves on pragmatism and common sense. The British way of life, an accretion of centuries of experience in these islands, has largely been based on what works: the social structures, economic relationships and the framework of justice. There was never a need for a formal constitution; the law, evolving in response to changing circumstances, was based on shared values, general tolerance and a common understanding of rights and duties.
>
> But in the last 30 years, this complacency has been shaken. A multicultural Britain can no longer rely for its cohesion on common background. Devolution, regional nationalism, ethnic division and religious extremism have so widened the divisions that the old certainties no longer prevail. What now passes for common sense? What is the glue holding this disparate society together? What is Britishness?
>
> Five years ago the question was academic. Now it is as acute as it is sensitive. Immigration has enhanced and enlivened the country, but has brought to Britain people with beliefs, values and backgrounds far removed and sometimes at odds, with the prevailing culture. A misunderstood multiculturalism has led to social and cultural fragmentation at the expense of a common core. And the shock of the 7/7 bombings has raised the question: what does it mean to be British?

Britain today is a complex society in which significant diversity and change have created problems as well as advantages. While the country may give an impression of homogeneous or uniform behaviour in certain respects, there are divisions, such as the influence of London in its relationship to the rest of the country; the cultural distinctiveness and separate identities of Wales, Scotland, Northern Ireland and England; demands for greater autonomy in local government and less centralized control from London; disparities between affluent and economically depressed areas throughout the country (including the crime, decay and social deprivation of many inner-city locations); alleged cultural and economic gaps between North and South; political variety (reflected in concentrated support for different political parties in different parts of Britain); continuing debates on the positions of women, small-interest groups and minority ethnic communities (the latter involving tensions between British national identity and ethnicity); campaigns or demands for a variety of individual and collective rights (with the conflict between rights and responsibilities); a gulf between rich and poor (with a growing underclass of disadvantaged, alienated or rootless people); tensions between the cities and the countryside; and generational differences between young and old in all ethnic groups (accompanied by the increasing longevity of the elderly and their growing numbers in the population statistics).

Such features illustrate some, if not all, of the present divisions in British society. They also suggest a decline in the allegedly traditional deference to authority, consensus views and support for national institutions (such as monarchy, the professions, churches and Parliament). The people are now more nonconformist, multi-ethnic, secular and individualistic than in the past. Opinion polls suggest that the British themselves feel that they have become more aggressive, more selfish, less tolerant, less kind, less moral, less honest and less polite. Their society is sometimes portrayed in research surveys as one riddled with mistrust, coarseness and cynicism in which materialism, egotism, relativistic values, celebrity worship, vulgarity, trivialization and sensationalism constitute the new modes of behaviour.

On some levels, such developments have led to a visible increase in anti-social behaviour, yobbishness, public scruffiness, vandalism, serious alcohol and drug abuse, disputes between neighbours, violent crime and assaults, public disorder, the growth of criminal gangs and increased gun and knife attacks, which disturb many British people. The tolerant civic image of individual liberty, social cohesion, identity and community, which foreigners and Britons often have of the country, has supposedly suffered. For some critics, this has been replaced by social fragmentation, instability, isolation and the disintegration of communities.

Critics, politicians (particularly in the Labour government) and a majority of respondents in public opinion polls want a return to civic responsibility, consensus or inclusive politics and a caring society in which individuals feel that they have a place. But these hopes may often conflict with the changes which have affected Britain over the past 60 years and which have produced a society with different experiences and expectations. The question remains whether negative images of contemporary Britain are widespread and representative of the whole society, or are the result of occasional 'moral panics' often generated by an intrusive media and some social commentators. Opinion polls indicate that many British people feel that the negatives have increased and are now more apparent in everyday life.

Nevertheless, despite major domestic social changes, international pressures and more internal ethnic diversity, there is still a conservatism in British life which regards change with suspicion. This may lead to tension between the often enforced need for reform and a nostalgia for an assumed ideal past, causing difficulties for progress, the evolution of social structures and solving the society's problems. Historical fact demonstrates that the past in Britain was not as idyllic as is sometimes imagined and there were periods when the levels of social violence, poverty and deprivation were much greater than they are now, both in the cities and the countryside. But the myth and older patterns of behaviour still hold considerable attraction for many people. There is consequently a tension between presumed tradition and attempts at modernization (however defined) or change.

Fundamental change does not come easily to old cultures such as Britain and social structures (or the human beings who operate them) are often resistant to major alteration. It is argued that Britain since the 1960s has been unwilling to face large-scale reassessment in its social, political, economic and institutional structures. A relative economic decline since the late nineteenth century was joined to a political system and national mentality which could not cope with the reality or needs of the post-industrial and culturally-diverse society that Britain had become. Much of this decline was supposedly due to long-term and global events which were not reversible. But it is argued that the country still suffers from structural defects, which need radical rethinking. Pragmatic evolution and a complacent attachment to past habits are, in this view, no longer sufficient.

Britain does have its problems, which some critics argue are made worse by an alleged lack of governmental competence and vision. But, despite the often lurid picture of social decay painted by many commentators, the essential fabric of British society is not falling apart. Biased ideological views and a British capacity for self-denigration and complaint can encourage unbalanced, sensational views and media reporting with the result that events may be exaggerated beyond their national importance or representative value.

Britain has changed over the past 60 years. Most British people now enjoy greater prosperity and opportunities than in the past, so that poverty today is a relative, rather than an absolute, concept. Many parts of the economy have experienced strong growth relative to other European countries since 2001, although economic forecasts in 2005 reported a slowdown in national performance before an upturn in 2006. But opinion polls suggest that greater prosperity has not brought greater happiness for many Britons. Consumerism, multi-ethnic growth, feminism and an expanded role for women (particularly in a mobile workforce), greater individual freedom and more (if not complete) tolerance for alternative lifestyles (such as the increased acceptance of gays), technological advances and new economic policies have helped to transform Britain, sometimes for the better, sometimes for the worse. But continuing structural and social problems, as well as very varying life-chances and opportunities for the people, warn against undue complacency.

Assumptions about British life have in fact been strongly questioned in recent decades. Conservative governments under Margaret Thatcher (1979–90) tried to reform social structures and promote new economic attitudes. They attempted to reduce the state's role in public affairs and replace it by 'market forces'. The focus was upon economic growth; competition; privatization (ownership of state concerns transferred to the private sector often by the sales of shares in new companies); the creation of choice and standards in public services like education and health; and the reform of bodies such as the trade unions, some professions and local government. People were encouraged to be more responsible for their own affairs without automatic reliance on the state for support (the 'dependency culture') and to adopt more individual competitiveness and efficiency (the 'enterprise culture').

Such policies were partly successful on some economic and political levels, but there was resistance to the alleged accompanying selfishness and social divisiveness. While some people applauded the freedoms of an enterprise culture, others strongly wished for more intervention and funding in public social services. This suggests that it is difficult to change Britons' attitudes and that many people still look to the state for support in areas such as health, education and social security. Nevertheless, free market or neo-liberal economic programmes continued under the Conservative Prime Minister John Major (1990–7).

Meanwhile, the Labour Party modernized its internal structures and policies and moved to the political centre in an attempt to change its public image. Since gaining power in 1997 (repeated in 2001 and 2005), the Labour government under Tony Blair has followed and even extended the Conservative economic approach, while initially pursuing cautious fiscal and monetary policies. It has also attempted (not without opposition) to modernize Britain by supposedly creating a 'new, young and inclusive' society. Some critics argue that it is expanding many of the earlier Conservative social and economic ideas, which had either proved unpopular or impossible to implement at the time. Labour claims that it is addressing social and economic realities, emphasizes personal initiative and responsibility and stresses that hard choices must be made. It has spent large amounts of public money on education, health, transport, social security and the police service in order to prevent their collapse, raising fears of personal income tax rises to pay for them. But a majority of respondents to opinion polls feel that they have not seen great improvements in public services under the Labour government and many have lost their trust in the Labour leadership. The difficulties involved in balancing the free market and social welfare models of society continue. It also seemed by 2005 that budget deficits and reduced growth indicated that the government was losing its grip on the economy.

Opposition to some government policies (such as the local government property tax, National Health Service reforms and privatization under Thatcher or fuel prices, rural programmes and Iraq under Blair) and acceptance of others demonstrate that social change can occur in various, often interconnected, ways. Some social structures wither away because they are no longer used. Others are reformed internally as new situations arise. Additional forces for change are opposition political parties with their alternative programmes; interest or pressure groups exerting influence upon decision-makers; grassroots movements protesting at some action or lack of action; rebellion by Members of Parliament (MPs) of all parties against proposed government legislation; campaigns by the media to promote reform or uncover scandals; and the weight of public opinion for or against official plans. However, central government initiatives in London (and increasingly those of devolved government in Scotland and Wales) are the single most important factor in determining structural change at national and local level as politicians implement policies or respond to events.

The British allow their governments a great deal of power in the running of the country. But there is a limit to their tolerance and their disquiet may be shown in public opinion polls (such as a declining trust in government ministers and policies), demonstrations (such as street protests against the Iraq war and banning of fox hunting) and general election results (such as 2005 when the Labour majority in the House of Commons was significantly cut by some 100 seats). Most politicians have been traditionally sensitive to the views of the people, since their hold upon political power is dependent upon the electorate. Governments usually govern with at least one eye on public opinion and generally attempt to gain acceptance for their policies. They have to move cautiously (even with majorities in the House of Commons like the Labour government) and may suffer setbacks in some of their programmes.

The British assume, rightly or wrongly, that they have an individual independence and liberty within the framework of social institutions and are quick to voice disapproval if their interests are threatened. Protest is a natural and traditional reaction, as well as being a safety valve against more serious social and political disruption. But dissension may be neutralized by the promise of reform, or simply ignored by government, politicians and bureaucrats. Adequate responses may not come from the authorities and there is always the danger of more serious conflict and public alienation. However, peaceful evolution still characterizes much of British life despite occasional civil disturbances and government attempts to effect radical (and sometimes unpopular) change in recent years.

The British today are confronting different cultural and economic realities than in the imperial past when they had a more defined world role. They do not enjoy the benefits of earlier industrial revolutions, such as cheap raw materials, cheap labour and an uncompetitive world market, but have moved to a post-industrial economy in which the service sector and job flexibility dominate. The society has seen a decline in traditional certainties and become more mobile, stressful and conflict-ridden. Critics argue that the old pragmatic methods of innovation, which illustrate the British tendency to muddle through difficulties without long-term planning or fundamental reform, are no longer sufficient for an era in which specialized education and training, high-technology competence and a need to respond to international competition are the main determinants.

British attitudes to Britain

British Social Attitudes: 1988–9 (pp. 121–2) suggested that

> The [British] public's trust in the pillars of the British establishment is at best highly qualified . . . [They] seem intuitively to have discovered that the surest protection against disillusionment with their public figures

and powerful institutions is to avoid developing illusions about them in the first place.

This observation is still valid and may have grown stronger in recent years as opinion polls indicate increasing dissatisfaction with politicians and authority figures; scepticism at the performance of institutions and their bureaucracies; disengagement from formal political engagement reflected in low election turnout and membership of political parties; but a trend towards political action represented by public protests, demonstrations, petitions, media campaigns and membership of single issue or interest groups. These attitudes partly reflect an individualistic, independent and dissenting British tradition that has been cynical, irreverent and critical about state structures and powerful individuals. Historically, institutions such as the monarchy, Parliament, law and the Church have often had to earn the approval and support of the British people, which could also be taken back.

Britons are concerned about the state of Britain and public issues. Opinion polls and research surveys report on central areas of British life which affect people on a personal everyday level. These reveal respondents' views about how the country is operating, but they do have to be approached with a certain caution. They may only deal with topical rather than long-term concerns and responses to particular questions may therefore change considerably within a short period. Questions may also be posed to influence the answers given, sometimes resulting in contradictory responses. Unprompted questions ask respondents to suggest concerns of their own choosing. Prompted questions ask them to choose from a list of issues shown or read to them. Nevertheless, polls can be significant and often accurate indications of how people are reacting to the state of British society. In spite of their denials, politicians take seriously the results of polls, surveys and focus groups.

Many Britons are worried about the quality and services of their society and where the country is heading. A collated unprompted MORI opinion poll in May 2005 prior to the general election (see Table 1.1) found that certain issues were important for them. Concerns about crime (law and order, violence and vandalism), the National Health Service (including hospitals), race relations (including immigration and asylum seekers), and education topped the list. This ranking continued the trend in which crime, health and education have been consistently very prominent in recent years. Immigration has varied in importance and was high in 2005 to some extent because Conservative parliamentary candidates for the House of Commons had concentrated on this issue during the election campaign.

Defence, foreign affairs and international terrorism had climbed up the list to 14 per cent after the 11 September 2001 terrorist attacks on New York, the wars in Afghanistan and Iraq and the threat of terrorism in Britain. The issues of pensions and social security (14 per cent) had also advanced because of the crisis facing pension provision in Britain and people's fears about their finances in old age. But previous primary concerns such as the economy, the European common currency (euro), the European Union, the European Constitutional Treaty, devolution, trade unions and Northern Ireland had lost their immediacy. However, any of these areas can easily rise in the lists should they become of topical concern, such as higher inflation and interest rates resulting from a downturn in the economy. Many worries are 'bread and butter' issues, such as housing at 8 per cent, while others reflect the inward state of the nation, such as morality and individual behaviour at 10 per cent, drug abuse at 7 per cent and environmental concerns and pollution at 6 per cent.

A series of different opinion polls in 2005 confirmed these findings and indicated that the 2005 election campaign showed significant changes in people's concerns compared to the 2001 general election. Many fewer regarded Europe (and the question of an EU Constitutional Treaty or membership of the European

---

TABLE 1.1 The most important issues facing British society today (%), 2005

Crime/law and order/violence/vandalism (40)
National Health Service/hospitals (36)
Race relations/immigration/immigrants (27)
Education (26)
Defence/foreign affairs/international terrorism (14)
Pensions/social security (14)
Economy/economic situation (11)
Morality/individual behaviour (10)
EU/Europe/euro (9)
Housing (8)
Taxation (8)
Unemployment/factory closure/lack of industry (7)
Drug abuse (7)
Pollution/environment (6)
Poverty/inequality (5)
Transport/public transport (4)
Public services in general (3)
Local government/council tax (3)
Inflation/prices (2)
Petrol prices/fuel (2)
Countryside/rural life (1)
Low pay/minimum wage/low wages (1)
Nuclear weapons/nuclear war/disarmament (1)

Source: MORI May, 2005
(*Note*: Some respondents have voted for more than one topic.)

common currency – the euro) as key issues, but questions of asylum seekers and immigration loomed larger. The biggest debate was over how important Iraq was likely to be as an electoral issue. Commentators argued that personal 'bread and butter' issues were more likely to influence how most people actually cast their vote, although it was possible that Iraq could affect Labour voters in marginal constituencies. In the event, the election resulted in a sharp decline in the Labour government's overall majority. This was attributed to a mixture of Iraq, a growing distrust of Labour and a feeling that the government had not delivered its promises on a range of public services. It seems that in an analysis of all types of polls, respondents felt that health was the most important issue facing the country, followed by immigration, education and crime, although the order between them did change somewhat in individual polls.

However, events do influence public opinion. Following completed and failed terrorist attacks on the London transport system on the 7 and 21 July 2005, MORI opinion polls placed defence/foreign affairs/international terrorism as the unprompted top concern for British people at 58 per cent. But, although very high, this figure has to be placed in context. It does not reach the even higher percentages reached in the 1980s and early 1990s about the economy and losing one's job. The leading issues (apart from defence and terrorism) continued to hold their positions in the public mind with race relations/immigration at 32 per cent, the National Health Service at 29 per cent, crime at 25 per cent, education at 20 per cent and the economy at 10 per cent.

This ranking does not imply that other issues are unimportant. The list in Table 1.1 shows a wide range of concerns from the economy to nuclear weapons and includes many structural features or institutions which are of immediate daily concern to the British public and condition their attitudes to British society. They collectively suggest a picture of contemporary Britain, which will be examined in closer detail in later chapters. They also allow commentators to range widely in their opinions of Britain from those indicating a country in terminal decline to those who suggest more positive outcomes despite the problems. The latter would suggest the traditional self-image of an evolutionary society which is coping with pressures.

Further reading

1 Abercrombie, N. and Warde, A. (2000) *Contemporary British Society* Oxford: Blackwell Publishers

2 *Annual Abstract of Statistics* London: Office for National Statistics and Palgrave Macmillan

3 Black, J. (2002) *A History of the British Isles* London: Palgrave Macmillan

4 Black, J. (2004) *Britain since the Seventies: Politics and Society in the Consumer Age* London: Reaktion Books Ltd

5 Blair, T. (1996) *New Britain: My Vision of a Young Country* London: Fourth Estate

6 English, R. and Kenny, M. (eds) (1999) *Rethinking British Decline* London: Macmillan

Exercises

Explain and examine the following terms:

insular	grassroots	pragmatic	sponsorship
deference	conservatism	inner-city	diversity
consensus	kilts	pluralism	ethnic
nostalgia	autonomy	post-industrial	modernization
myth	dependency	nonconformist	evolution
enterprise	Thatcher	yobbishness	community
hierarchies	homogeneous	inclusive	apathetic

Write short essays on the following topics:

1   Examine the view that Britain is a quaint, old-fashioned museum piece, backward-looking and conventional.

2   Examine the idea of structural and social change. Consider the forces which might condition or bring it about.

3   What do the list of concerns in Table 1.1 tell us about British people and their society?

7   Ferguson, N. (2004) *Empire: How Britain Made the Modern World* London: Penguin Books

8   Halsey, A.H. and Webb, J. (2000) *Twentieth-Century British Social Trends* London: Palgrave/Macmillan

9   Marwick, A. (2000) *A History of the Modern British Isles 1914–1999* Oxford: Blackwell Publishers

10 Sampson, A. (2004) *Who Runs This Place?: The Anatomy of Britain in the 21st Century* London: John Murray (Publishers)

11 Savage, S.P. and Atkinson, R. (2001) *Public Policy Under Blair* London: Palgrave/Macmillan

12 *UK: the Official Yearbook of the United Kingdom of Great Britain and Northern Ireland* London: Office for National Statistics and Palgrave Macmillan

Websites

Central Office of Information: www.coi.gov.uk
Prime Minister's Office: www.number-10.gov.uk
British Tourist Authority: www.visitbritain.com
British Council: http://www.mori.com/polls/1999/britcoun.shtml
The *MORI Organization*: www.mori.com
Office for National Statistics: www.statistics.gov.uk
The National Archives: www.nationalarchives.gov.uk

Chapter 2

The country

- ■ Geographical identities
- ■ Physical features and climate
- ■ Agriculture, fisheries and forestry
- ■ Energy resources
- ■ Transport and communications
- ■ Attitudes to the environment
- ■ *Exercises*
- ■ *Further reading*
- ■ *Websites*

Britain's physical geography is inevitably connected to concerns about how the country's natural resources and associated industries are organized. A MORI poll in June 2001 (before the 11 September terrorist attacks on the USA) reported that Britons' greatest international concern (ahead of poverty, famine, population growth and war) was the world environment. But a later MORI poll in July 2005 (addressed to domestic issues after terrorist bombs in London) found that concerns about defence, terrorism, race relations, crime, education and the National Health Service had become more important to respondents than the environment, which rated 7 per cent and worries about the countryside and rural life were at 1 per cent. Furthermore, the MORI Social Research Institute in May 2004 reported that respondents felt that environmental matters such as global warming and weather change can only be tackled through international agreement rather than by individual national policies.

While many British people may say they are aware of and worried about their environment, they differ in their knowledge of the issues and how personally active and consistent they should be in combating pollution. In practice, individuals, companies, public authorities and government departments continue to harm the natural environment in Britain, despite manifesting their concerns about it.

The UK government Department for the Environment, Food and Rural Affairs (Defra) has formal responsibility for much of the physical geography of Britain and how it is used, although there are frequent complaints about the adequacy of its performance. Other government and European Union policies also condition the rural and urban landscape, but these can sometimes conflict with each other. A knowledge of Britain's geography therefore serves to contextualize environmental issues, as well as indicating the role that the land plays in forming British identities.

Geographical identities

The country's title for constitutional and political purposes is the United Kingdom of Great Britain and Northern Ireland, with the short forms 'UK' and 'Britain' being used for convenience. Most British people identify themselves at one level with this larger national unit and respond to a sense of Britishness, however variously it may be defined. Britain comprises those areas lying off the north-west coast of continental Europe which are politically united as the UK and are often known geographically as the British Isles. The mainland of England, Scotland and Wales forms the largest island with the political title of Great Britain. Northern Ireland shares the second-largest island with the Republic of Ireland, which has been governed independently since 1921. Smaller islands, like Anglesey, the Isle of Wight, the Orkneys, Shetlands, Hebrides and Scillies, are also part of the British political union.

But the Isle of Man in the Irish Sea and the Channel Islands off the north coast of France are not part of the United Kingdom. They each have their own identities, legal systems, legislatures and administrative structures and are self-governing Crown Dependencies which have a historical relationship with the British Crown. However, the British government is responsible for their defence and foreign relations and can intervene if good administration is not maintained.

On a smaller level of geographical and national identification, Britain is divided into Scotland, Wales, England and Northern Ireland. The people of these countries have always had a sense of distinctiveness and been conscious of their individual geographies. These feelings appear to have increased in Scotland, Wales and (arguably) Northern Ireland since the devolution of some political power from the London Parliament (1998–9) by the establishment of a Parliament in Edinburgh and Assemblies in Cardiff and Belfast. England was not included in this devolution process, but the reform seems to have provoked a greater awareness among the English of their own separate identity.

Britain is also often divided up into 'regions'. These may sometimes reflect a specific identity, although opinions differ on how strong this actually is. Regions are not the same as local government structures (see Chapter 4) and are physically larger. They can be politico-economic structures for British and EU purposes; assistance and development areas; service locations for supplies of gas, water and electricity; or based, as in Figure 2.3, on former economic planning regions. Following devolution, Scotland, Wales and Northern Ireland tend to be regarded as national units rather than 'regions' and there are nine regions in England, which take the form of Government Offices (GOs) or Regional Development Agencies (RDAs). These unelected bodies are appointed by government to organize regional development. It was intended that they would develop into elected regional government assemblies (or councils) in England analogous to the devolved structures in Wales, Scotland and Northern Ireland. This has not happened and English people have little identity with the RDAs, which are often regarded (rightly or wrongly) as remote, government-controlled, artificial and unaccountable to their regional constituents.

On a smaller level, localism (rather than regionalism) is more significant in British life as a cultural, identifying factor. It illustrates a sense of belonging, which becomes more evident with increasing distance from London and the UK government. It reflects a determination by local populations to assert their individual identities and is often based primarily on ancient county structures, but also on cities, towns and villages and, to a lesser extent on local government areas.

Identification with smaller local areas was more significant when the British were a rural people living in villages and were less mobile. Today, such identity may also be focussed on cities (such as Manchester, Liverpool, Newcastle, Birmingham, Glasgow, Edinburgh, Belfast, London, Swansea and Cardiff) or on English counties, such as Yorkshire and Kent rather than the larger artificially-constructed RDAs. New local government authorities in Wales, Scotland and Northern Ireland have replaced some of the old county labels, but the former geographical identities often persist for people living in these areas.

Physical features and climate

Historically, Britain's physical features have influenced human settlement, population movements, military conquest and political union. They have also conditioned the location and exploitation of industry, transport systems, agriculture, fisheries, woodlands and energy supplies. Today they continue to influence such activities and are tied to public concerns about pollution, temperature change, the state of the natural environment and the quality of food products. Some have been affected by government policies (such as privatization) and European Union directives on agriculture, fisheries and global warming. Many Britons live in densely populated areas. They are directly affected by these issues and by the actions of public authorities and private bodies upon the environment.

In recent years, the countryside in particular has become a fierce political issue. Rural inhabitants, groups such as the Countryside Alliance, conservationists and farmers feel neglected by the UK central government and politicians. They object to the alleged destruction and pollution of the physical environment and the supposed ignorance of country life shown by metropolitan planners. There has historically been a tension between urban and rural cultures, but many people (even in the cities) feel a traditional (if romanticized) nostalgia and identity for the countryside.

Britain's geographical position is marked by latitude 50°N in southern England and by latitude 60°N across the Shetlands. It thus lies within only 10° of latitude and has a small and compact size when compared with some European countries. Yet it also possesses a great diversity of physical features, which surprises those visitors who expect a mainly urban and industrialized country. The many beauty spots and recreation areas, such as National Parks in England, Scotland and Wales and areas of natural beauty throughout the country, may be easily reached without much expenditure of time or effort.

Britain's physical area covers some 93,025 square miles (242,842 square kilometres). Most is land and the rest comprises inland water such as lakes and rivers. England has 50,052 square miles (129,634 sq km), Wales has 7,968 (20,637), Scotland has 29,799 (77,179) and Northern Ireland has 5,206 (13,438). England is significantly larger than the other countries and also has the biggest population (49,856,000 or 84 per cent) in a UK total of 59,600,000 in 2003. These factors partly explain the English dominance in British history and the mixed (often hostile) attitudes of Scotland, Ireland and Wales towards their neighbour.

FIGURE 2.1 The British Isles and the Republic of Ireland

The distance from the south coast of England to the most northerly tip of the Scottish mainland is 600 miles (955 km), and the English east coast and the Welsh west coast are 300 miles (483 km) apart. These relatively small distances have aided the development of political union and communications and contributed to largely standardized social, economic and institutional norms throughout Britain. But, prior to the eighteenth century, there were considerable obstacles to this progress, such as difficult terrain and inadequate transportation.

Britain's varied physical characteristics are a source of identification for many people, such as the Giant's Causeway in Northern Ireland, the cliffs of Dover in southern England, the Highlands of Scotland and the Welsh mountains. These result from a long geological and climatic history. Earth movements forced mountains to rise from the sea-bed to form the oldest parts of Britain. Warmer, sub-tropical periods then created large swamp forests covering lowland zones. These, in turn, were buried by sand, soil and mud, and the forests' fossil remains became coal deposits. Later, the climate alternated between warmth and Arctic temperatures. During the latter Ice Age periods, glaciers moved southwards over the islands, with only southern England free from their effects.

Highland areas were slowly worn away by weathering agents such as wind, ice and water. This process rounded off the mountain peaks and moved waste materials into lowland zones, where they were pressed into new rocks and where the scenery became softer and less folded. The geological and weathering changes shaped valleys and plains and dictated the siting of Britain's major rivers, such as the Clyde in Scotland; the Tyne, Trent, Severn and Thames in England and Wales; and the Bann and Lagan in Northern Ireland.

Natural forces have also affected the coastlines as the seas have moved backwards and forwards over time. Parts of the coastal area have either sunk under the sea or risen above it. These processes continue today, particularly on the English coasts. Geological tilting from north to south, rising sea levels and sea erosion have resulted in the loss of land, houses and farms, while the sea's retreat in some places has created either chalk and limestone uplands or sand beaches along the coasts.

Britain was originally part of the European mainland. But the melting of the glaciers in the last Ice Age caused the sea level to rise. The country was separated from the continent by the North Sea at its widest, and by the English Channel at its narrowest, points. The shortest stretch of water between the two land masses is now the Strait of Dover between Dover in southern England and Calais in France (24 miles, 38 km).

There are many bays, inlets, peninsulas and estuaries along the coasts and most places in Britain are less than 75 miles (120 km) from some kind of tidal water. Tides on the coasts and in inland rivers (in addition to heavy rainfall) can cause flooding in many parts of the country. Local and national authorities must choose between deliberately losing land to the sea through managed retreat plans or providing substantial finance to construct defences against this threat. For example, a London flood barrier was completed in 1984 across the river Thames and there are proposals for more protection of the capital. Flooding, which is now tied to climate and weather change, continues to seriously affect many low-lying inland areas throughout the country, with people suffering property and financial loss.

The coastal seas are not deep and are often less than 300 feet (90 metres) because they lie on the Continental Shelf, or raised sea-bed adjacent to the mainland. The warm North Atlantic Current (Gulf Stream) heats the sea and air as it travels from the Atlantic Ocean across the Shelf. This gives the country a more temperate climate than would otherwise be the case, given its northerly position, although there are fears that a melting of the Arctic ice packs may upset this balance and result in much colder weather conditions. The Gulf Stream also influences the coastal fish breeding grounds, on which the national fishing industry is considerably dependent.

Britain's physical relief can be divided into highland and lowland Britain (see Figure 2.2). The highest ground is mainly in the north and west. Most of the lowland zones, except for the Scottish Lowlands and central areas of Northern Ireland, are in the south and east of the country, where only a few points reach 1,000 feet (305 metres) above sea level.

The north and west consist of older, harder rocks created by ancient earth movements, which are generally unsuitable for cultivation. The south and east comprise younger, softer materials formed by weathering processes, which have produced fertile soils and good agricultural conditions. Much of the lowland area, except for urban and industrial regions, is cultivated and farmed. It largely comprises fields, which are divided by fences or hedges. Animal grazing land in upland zones is separated either by moorland or stone walls.

England

England (population 49,856,000 in 2003) covers two-thirds of the island of Great Britain and consists mainly of undulating or flat lowland countryside, with highland areas in the north and south-west. Eastern England has the low-lying flat lands of the Norfolk Broads, the Cambridgeshire and Lincolnshire Fens and the Suffolk Marshes. Low hill ranges stretch over much of the country, such as the North Yorkshire Moors, the Cotswolds, the Kent and Sussex Downs and the Chiltern Hills.

Highland zones are marked by the Cheviot Hills (between England and Scotland); the north-western mountain region of the Lake District and the Cumbrian Mountains; the northern plateau belt of the Pennines forming a backbone across north-west England; the Peak District at the southern reaches of the Pennines; and the south-western plateau of Devon and Cornwall.

The heaviest population concentrations centre on the largest towns and cities, such as London and in south-east England generally; the West Midlands region around Birmingham; the Yorkshire cities of Leeds, Bradford and Sheffield; the

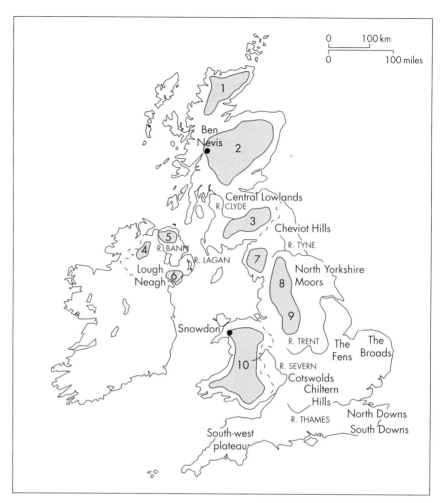

1 North-West Highlands	4 Sperrin Mountains	8 Pennines
2 Central Highlands	5 Antrim Mountains	9 Peak District
(Grampians)	6 Mourne Mountains	10 Welsh Massif (Cambrians)
3 Southern Uplands	7 Cumbrian Mountains	

FIGURE 2.2 Highland and lowland Britain

north-western area around Liverpool and Manchester; and the north-east region comprising Newcastle and Sunderland.

Wales

Wales (population 2,938,000 in 2003) is a highland country, with moorland plateau, hills and mountains, which are often broken by deep river valleys. This upland mass contains the Cambrian Mountains and descends eastwards into

PLATE 2.1 Welsh countryside, Powys.
Valleys and fields in Powys, a county in central Wales.
(*Andy Drysdale/Rex Features*)

England. The highest mountains are in Snowdonia in the north-west, where the dominant peak is that of Snowdon (3,560 feet, 1,085 metres).

The lowland zones are restricted to the narrow coastal belts and to the lower parts of the river valleys in south Wales, where two-thirds of the Welsh population live. The chief urban concentrations of people and industry are around the bigger southern cities, such as the capital Cardiff, Swansea and Newport. In the past, the highland nature of Wales hindered conquest, agriculture and the settlement of people.

Scotland

Scotland (population 5,100,000 in 2003) may be divided into three main areas. The first is the North-West and Central Highlands (Grampians), together with a number of islands off the west and north-east coasts. These areas are thinly populated, but comprise half the country's land mass. The second is the Central Lowlands, which contain one-fifth of the land area but three-quarters of the Scottish population, most of the industrial and commercial centres and much of the cultivated land. The third is the Southern Uplands, which cover a number of hill ranges stretching towards the border with England.

The Highlands, with their lochs and fiord coastlines, and the Southern Uplands are now smooth, rounded areas since the original jagged mountains have

PLATE 2.2 Ben Nevis and Loch Linnhe, Scotland.
Ben Nevis (the highest mountain in the UK) and Loch Linnhe in the Scottish Highlands.
(*The Travel Library/Rex Features*)

been worn down. The highest point in the Central Highlands is Ben Nevis (4,406 feet, 1,343 metres), which is also the highest place in Britain.

The main population concentrations are around the administrative centre and capital of Edinburgh; the commercial and formerly heavy-industry area of Glasgow; and the regional centres of Aberdeen (an oil industry city) and Dundee. The climate, isolation and harsh physical conditions in much of Scotland have made conquest, settlement and agriculture difficult.

Northern Ireland

Northern Ireland (population 1,700,000 in 2003) has a north-east tip which is only 13 miles (21 km) from the Scottish coast, a fact that has encouraged both Irish and Scottish migration. Since 1921–2, Northern Ireland has had a 303-mile (488-km) border in the south and west with the Republic of Ireland. It has a rocky northern coastline, a south-central fertile plain and mountainous areas in the west, north-east and south-east. The south-eastern Mourne Mountains include the highest peak, Slieve Donard, which is 2,796 feet high (853 metres). Lough Neagh (153 square miles, 396 sq km) is Britain's largest freshwater lake and lies at the centre of the country.

PLATE 2.3 The Giant's Causeway, Antrim, Northern Ireland.
The Giant's Causeway was created 60 million years ago when a field of lava cooled and formed hexagonal blocks of basalt.
(*Alisdair MacDonald/Rex Features*)

Most of the large towns, like the capital Belfast, are situated in valleys which lead from the lough. Belfast lies at the mouth of the river Lagan and has the biggest population concentration. But Northern Ireland generally has a sparse and scattered population and is a largely rural country.

Climate

The relative smallness of the country and the influences of a warm sea and westerly winds mean that there are no extreme contrasts in temperature throughout Britain. The climate is mainly temperate, but with variations between coolness and mildness. Altitude modifies temperatures, so that much of Scotland and highland areas of Wales and England are cool in summer and cold in winter compared with most of England. Temperatures are lower in the north than the south and national average temperatures rarely reach 32°C (90°F) in the summer or fall below −10°C (14°F) in the winter. But the ten warmest years since 1861 occurred from the early 1990s, with 1998, 2002 and 2003 being the hottest, indicating for some critics the effects of man-made global warming from carbon emissions rather than natural change.

The main factors affecting rainfall in Britain are depressions (low pressure areas) which travel eastwards across the Atlantic Ocean; prevailing south-westerly winds throughout much of the year; exposure of western coasts to the Atlantic Ocean; and the fact that most high ground lies in the west.

The heaviest annual rainfalls are in the west and north (a 60 inches, 1,600 millimetres average covering all heights), with an autumn or winter maximum. The high ground in the west protects the lowlands of the south and east, so that annual rainfall here is moderate (30 inches, 800mm). March to June tend to be the driest months; September to January the wettest; and drought conditions are infrequent, although they have occurred more frequently in recent years and can cause problems for farmers, water companies and consumers.

Low pressure systems normally pass over northern areas and can produce windy, wet and unstable conditions. In recent years, Britain has had more frequent storms, heavier rainfall and flooding, with suggestions that such weather changes are linked to global warming. But high-pressure systems, which occur throughout the year, are stable and slow-moving, resulting in light winds and settled weather. They can give fine and dry effects, both in the winter and summer.

Sunshine in Britain decreases from south to north; inland from the coastal belts; and with altitude. In summer, average daily sunshine varies from five hours in northern Scotland to eight hours on the Isle of Wight. In winter, it averages one hour in northern Scotland and two hours on the English south coast.

These statistics show that Britain is not a particularly sunny country, although there are periods of relief from the general greyness. The frequent cloud-cover over the islands means that even on a hot summer's day there may be little sunshine breaking through the clouds, giving humid, sticky conditions. Sunshine can frequently mix with pollutants to give poor air quality both in the cities and rural areas.

Such climatic features give the British weather its changeability and what some regard as its stimulating variety. Discrepancies between weather forecasts and actual results often occur and words such as 'changeable' and 'unsettled' are generously employed. The weather is virtually a national institution, a topic of daily conversation and for some a conditioning factor in the national character. Britons tend to think that they live in a more temperate climate than is the case. However, it is argued that in future Britain can expect wetter autumns and winters with more frequent storms; warmer springs and summers; and periods of unpredictable weather and temperatures. These developments are said to be due to global warming, whether created naturally or from human sources.

Agriculture, fisheries and forestry

Agriculture

Soils vary in quality from the thin, poor ones of highland Britain to the rich, fertile land of low-lying areas in eastern and southern England. The climate usually allows a long, productive growing season without extremes. But farmers can sometimes have problems because of droughts, too much rain and too little sunshine at ripening time or unseasonal weather due to climate change.

Britain's long agricultural history includes a series of farming revolutions from Neolithic times. Today, there are 304,000 farm units, ranging from small farms to huge business concerns and two-thirds are owner-occupied. They use 77 per cent of the land area, although there is concern that farmland is being increasingly used for building and recreational purposes. Only some 533,000 people (1.4 per cent of the workforce) are engaged in farming. But agriculture provides 64 per cent of all Britain's food needs and its exports are important although its share of the Gross Domestic Product (GDP) declined to 0.8 per cent (or £7.9 billion) in 2003. Many farms in Scotland, Northern Ireland, Wales and northern and south-western England specialize in dairy farming, beef cattle and flocks of sheep. Some farms in eastern and northern England and Northern Ireland concentrate on pig production. Poultry meat and egg industries are widespread with intensive 'factory farming'. Most of the other farms in southern and eastern England and in eastern Scotland grow arable crops like wheat, barley, oats, potatoes, oilseed rape, and sugar beet. Horticultural products such as apples, berries and flowers are also widely grown.

Agriculture is still a significant industry and organized interest group. It is productive, intensive, mechanized and specialized. But, after a profitable period in the early 1990s, farming experienced a difficult period due to the high value of the pound, a fall in farm prices and a series of disasters such as BSE (Bovine

Spongiform Encephalopathy) in cows (1996), its link to CJD (Creutzfeldt-Jakob disease) in humans, swine fever and foot and mouth disease (2001). Animals were lost, farming income was reduced, especially for small farmers and many left the industry or turned their land to non-farming activities. But agriculture saw a 28 per cent increase in total income (including subsidies) in 2003 despite its decrease in GDP.

The Common Agricultural Policy (CAP) of the European Union (EU), which accounts for 48 per cent of the EU's budget, has also affected British farmers. Its original protectionist aims were to increase productivity and efficiency; stabilize the market; ensure regular supplies of food; give farmers reasonable rewards by providing them with subsidies; set minimum guaranteed prices for food products through price support; and standardize the quality and size of produce.

British governments have argued that the CAP is unwieldy, costly for consumers, bureaucratic, restrictive for producers, open to fraud and leads to surplus food. They maintain that British farming should reflect the needs of the market; meet consumers' demands; reduce subsidies; and emphasize better land management. Countries in the Third World have also objected to EU subsidies undercutting their farmers and home markets. They and the USA react to restrictions on foreign foodstuffs entering the EU, which have now been somewhat liberalized.

EU reform and simplification of the CAP from 2004–5 coincided with the entry of Eastern European nations into the EU and continuing negotiations with the World Trade Organization (WTO) over tariff barriers. Farm subsidies are being reduced and are now more dependent upon environmental protection, competition, a market-orientation, cuts in over-production, food safety and animal health. But there continues to be conflict within the EU (especially between Britain and France) over the extent of cuts in subsidies.

Fisheries

Britain is one of Europe's leading fishing nations and operates in the North Sea, the Irish Sea and the Atlantic. The fishing industry is important to the national economy and is centred on ports around the coasts. The most important fish catches are cod, haddock, whiting, herring, mackerel, plaice and sole, which are caught by the 7,271 registered vessels of the fishing fleet. The fish-farming industry (salmon, trout and shellfish) is a large and expanding business, particularly in Scotland.

But employment in and income from fishing have declined substantially in recent years from its previous levels. This is partly due to changes in fish breeding patterns and a reduction in fish stocks because of overfishing. Many fishermen have become unemployed and fishing towns on the English and Scottish coasts have suffered. But the industry still accounts for 73 per cent of Britain's fish consumption. Fishermen number 11,774, with some two jobs in associated occupations (such as fish processing) for every one fisherman. The British government believes that the industry can be profitable and sustainable if it modernizes to cope with the pressure of global competition.

The industry has also been affected by the EU's Common Fisheries Policy (CFP) and British government policies, which have affected the fishermen's old freedom of operation. The need to conserve fish resources and prevent overfishing is stressed. Zones have been created in which fishermen may operate and quota systems operate inside and beyond the zones to restrict fish catches. Measures to limit the time fishing vessels spend at sea and to decommission (take out of operation) fishing boats have further restricted employment and the fishing fleet. Fishermen are angry with British government and EU policies and their loss of livelihood. But without fish conservation, there will be reduced supplies in future.

Forestry

Woodlands cover 6.6 million acres (2.7 million hectares) of Britain and comprise 9 per cent of England, 17 per cent of Scotland, 14 per cent of Wales and 6 per cent of Northern Ireland. These figures amount to some 12 per cent of total UK land area, which represents a doubling of trees since 1947. Some 35 per cent of productive national forests are managed by the state Forestry Commission or government departments and the rest by private owners. About 35,000 people are employed in the state and private forestry industries and 10,000 are engaged in timber processing.

However, these activities contribute only 15 per cent to the national consumption of wood and associated timber products, which means that the country is heavily dependent upon wood imports. The government has encouraged tree planting programmes in Scotland, Wales and the English Midlands, and allowed the sale of state woodlands to private owners in order to reduce public expenditure and to increase productivity. New plantings, controlled felling, expansion of timber industries and a profitable private sector may reduce Britain's present dependence upon imports and benefit the environment.

Forestry policy is supposed to take conservation factors into account in the development of timber facilities. But such aims are not always achieved and there is disquiet about some government programmes. Environmentalists campaign against the destruction of woodlands for road building and airport expansion, advocate increased tree planting to combat global warming and pollution and try to preserve the quality of the existing woodlands. These in recent years have been badly affected by disease, unreasonable felling and substantial storm damage in 1987 and 1990.

Energy resources

Primary energy sources are oil, gas, nuclear power, hydro-power and coal. The most important secondary source generated from these is electricity. Some 200,000 people work in energy production; three of Britain's largest companies (Shell, BP and British Gas) are in this sector; and the energy industries accounted for 3.3 per cent of GDP in 2003. But there are problems with energy sources and concerns about pollution and environmental damage. Most energy industries have now been privatized, but there is still criticism about their services and regulation.

Since 1980, Britain has produced an increased amount of its own energy needs. This is due to the growth in offshore oil and gas supplies, which make a crucial contribution to the economy and to the balance of payments through the export of crude oil and oil products. Multinational companies operate under government licence and extract these fuels from the North Sea and Atlantic fields.

But, because governments have encouraged high extraction rates, large supplies of oil and gas will continue only into the early twenty-first century. There is already some dependence on imported foreign gas and oil as British supplies diminish. Development of existing resources and the search for alternative forms of energy are crucial for Britain and its economy. The positions of coal and nuclear power need to be more adequately debated and further research is required into renewable energy such as biomass, solar, wind, wave and tidal power.

Coal is an important natural energy resource, but there are objections to its use on pollution and cost grounds. After a reduction in the workforce and the closure of uneconomic pits in the 1980s, the coal industry was privatized. But coal is expensive and there is a lack of demand from big consumers, such as electricity power stations, which use gas, oil and cheap coal imports. There have been more pit closures and the future of the industry is uncertain.

Electricity is mainly provided by coal-, gas- and oil-fired power stations, a small amount from hydro-electric power and 22 per cent by 12 nuclear power stations. The expansion of nuclear power (partially privatized in 1996) to satisfy energy needs has been uncertain. But the Labour government in 2005 indicated in a change of policy that it wanted to replace ageing reactors and possibly build more nuclear stations to cope with the problems of global warming, a decrease in oil and gas supplies and obligations to reduce carbon emissions . However, a MORI Social Research Institute poll in February 2003 found that 43 per cent of British people were opposed to nuclear power as a source of energy and 32 per cent were in favour. A University of East Anglia/MORI poll in 2003 found that 65 per cent of the public are concerned about radioactive waste and 55 per cent believe the risks outweigh the benefits. But a poll by the Nuclear Industry Association in January 2005 suggested that public opposition to nuclear power has declined slightly.

Alternative forms of renewable energy are becoming more important. Electricity generation by wind power is already operative on land and at sea,

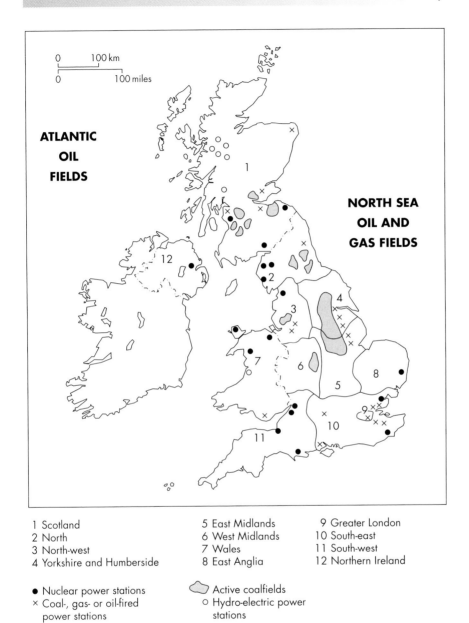

FIGURE 2.3 The British regions and energy sources

1 Scotland	5 East Midlands	9 Greater London
2 North	6 West Midlands	10 South-east
3 North-west	7 Wales	11 South-west
4 Yorkshire and Humberside	8 East Anglia	12 Northern Ireland

● Nuclear power stations   ◌ Active coalfields
× Coal-, gas- or oil-fired   ○ Hydro-electric power
   power stations   stations

although there is opposition to wind farms in the countryside and their fossil links to power stations, as well as doubts about their economic viability. The use of tidal and wave power is being implemented on some coasts and estuaries and solar energy is already provided, with plans for more research. These, and other, forms of renewable energy such as biomass and excavating heat from rocks and the earth's core are important for Britain's future energy needs, particularly as environmental concerns grow. But their capacity is limited at present to 3 per cent of all energy and electricity production, although the Labour government wishes to increase this amount to 10 per cent by 2010, 15 per cent by 2015 and 20 per cent by 2020. If nuclear power is phased out in Britain and replaced by potential wind power alone, this would still leave some three-quarters of electricity to be generated by fossil fuels. But renewable sources of energy such as wind and solar power are supported by 88 per cent of the British people according to a MORI Social Research Institute poll in February 2003, although such plans may be opposed if sited in unacceptable areas.

Critics argue that insufficient research and funds are being devoted to alternative supplies; that the advantages of nuclear power have not been sufficiently investigated; that oil and gas have been wasted rather than extracted more slowly; that not enough consideration has been given to a cleaner coal industry; and that industry has been reluctant to use more environmentally-friendly technology which would cut harmful emissions. Britain's domestic and industrial energy users are still extravagant when compared to other European countries, although its power consumption is lower than emerging industrial nations such as India and China. The provision of cheap and environmentally suitable energy for both domestic and industrial use is already a problem for Britain and energy prices have risen steeply in recent years. But the Labour government's plans to generate more electricity from carbonless and low-carbon sources such as wind, wave, tidal, hydro, solar and biomass has already resulted in the British environmental technology industry being the world's fifth-largest with more than 7,000 companies. Forecasters at the Department of Trade and Industry believe that Britain's renewable energy market, at present worth £280 million, will grow to over £19 billion by 2020 and become increasingly attractive to investors as the industry sells its expertise on both the British and world markets.

Transport and communications

Transport and communications are divided between the public and private sectors of the economy, although many state businesses have now been privatized. Roads, railways, shipping and civil aviation provide the country's transport system. British Telecom, competing telecommunications companies and the Post Office supply most communications needs.

Transport

Central and local government agencies are responsible for different types of road in the *road network*. Motorways and trunk roads are the largest elements and carry most of the passenger traffic and heavy goods vehicles. But some roads are in bad condition and unable to handle the number of vehicles on them, leading to Britain having the heaviest road traffic congestion in Europe. Expansion, modernization and repair of roads are environmentally damaging and may also be inadequate to meet the estimated future number of vehicles. While the Labour government has cancelled some controversial road-building programmes in an attempt to cut the demand for road space and to persuade drivers to adopt alternative methods of transport, new road building is still planned (particularly in connection with new house building).

There are 31 million licensed vehicles, which include 25 million private cars, 426,000 goods vehicles, one million motorcycles and 96,000 buses. Car transport is most popular and accounts for 80 per cent of passenger mileage, while buses and coaches take 2 per cent. Britain has one of the highest densities of road traffic in the world, but also a relatively good safety record in which road accidents and casualties have continued to decrease as an average over time. But the introduction of more speed cameras to control drivers is highly controversial and opposed by motorists.

Private road haulage has a dominant position in the movement of inland freight. Lorries have become larger and account for 80 per cent of this market. Critics campaign to transfer road haulage to the railways and the publicly-owned inland waterways (canals). But the waterways are used for only a small amount of freight transportation because of expense, although they are popular for recreational purposes and holidays. Rail freight, however, is increasing for bulk commodities.

Public bus services have declined (particularly in rural areas) because of the increased cost of providing the services, which has led to increased private car usage. Conservative governments deregulated bus operations and most local bus companies have now been privatized, although some services are still operated by local government authorities. There has been a considerable expansion in private long-distance express coach services, which are cheaper than the railways. But bus services generally in Britain are underfunded and inadequate for potential demand.

The world's first public passenger steam *railway* opened in 1825 between Stockton and Darlington in north-east England. After 100 years of private operation, the railways became state-owned in 1947. But they were privatized in 1997. A company (Railtrack) owned the railway lines and infrastructure while the trains and stations were leased to and operated by 25 private regional companies. But after poor performance, the government took control of Railtrack in 2001 and it was renamed Network Rail. This, however, does not amount to a renationalization of the railway system, which ostensibly continues in private hands with government subsidies.

Rail passenger services account for 5 per cent of all passenger mileage and consist of a fast inter-city network, linking all the main British centres; local trains which supply regional needs; and commuter services in and around the large areas

of population, particularly London and south-east England. Increased electri-
fication of lines and the introduction of diesel trains such as the Inter-City 125s
travelling at a maximum speed of 125 mph (201 km/h), have improved rail
journeys considerably. But such speeds and facilities are still inferior to those in
other countries and current railway systems do not permit the greater speeds
available to newer trains.

Many railway lines and trains are old and need replacing. Privatization has not
solved the problems of financing and lack of adequate services. A number of fatal
crashes in recent years and the resulting repair of large sections of track caused
chaos in the railway network and drew attention to the shortcomings of the
railway system. The situation is slowly returning to normal; passenger totals are
increasing rapidly; newer trains are being introduced on West and East Coast
services; and railways are being updated. But there is still much criticism about
the performances of the privatized rail companies, fare increases, overcrowding,
cancellations, delays, unpunctuality, late arrivals, staffing and poor services.
Similar complaints are also made about the London Underground system (the
Tube), which covers 254 miles (408 km) of railway line in the capital, and which
has been partly privatized. It is argued that the inadequate state of Britain's
railways is due largely to underfunding, at a time of increasing demand, with
expenditure and state subsidies being below European averages, despite profits
for the railway companies.

The *Channel Tunnel*, privately run by a French/British company (Eurotunnel),
opened for commercial use in 1994 under the English Channel with the two
terminals, Folkstone and Coquelles, being 31 miles (50 km) apart. It was meant
to improve passenger and freight rail travel between Britain and mainland Europe
and has succeeded in taking business from sea/ferry services. It provides a drive-
on, drive-off shuttle service for cars, coaches and freight vehicles, as well as
passenger trains (Eurostar) from Waterloo Station in London. But a high-speed
rail connection between Folkestone and London is still uncompleted, although
it will eventually run into a new European terminus at St Pancras station, which
will replace Waterloo.

Although there are over 300 *ports* in Britain, most are small concerns. The
bigger ports, like Clyde, Dover, Hull, Grimsby, Southampton, Felixstowe and
Cardiff, service most of the trade and travel requirements. But work, labour and
the shipping fleet have declined since the peak year of 1975. The cargo market is
now dominated by a small number of large private sector groups. But 75 per cent
of Britain's overseas trade (by value) is still carried by sea, although passenger
mileage has been reduced. Both may decline further because of competition with
the Channel Tunnel.

Britain's *civil aviation* system accounts for 1 per cent of passenger mileage and
is in the private sector following the privatization of the former state-owned
airline, British Airways, in 1987. There are other carriers, such as British Midland
International, Britannia Airways and Virgin Atlantic, which run scheduled and

charter passenger services on domestic and international routes, as well as air freight services. There has also been a recent increase in cheap-price airlines, such as Easy-Jet. All are controlled by the Civil Aviation Authority (CAA), an independent, partially privatized body which regulates the industry and air traffic control.

There are 142 licensed civil aerodromes in Britain, varying considerably in size. Heathrow and Gatwick Airports outside London are the largest. These airports, together with Stansted in south-east England and Glasgow, Edinburgh and Aberdeen in Scotland, are owned by the private sector BAA. They handle 73 per cent of air passengers and 84 per cent of air cargo. Most of the regional airports, such as Luton, Manchester, Birmingham, Belfast, Newcastle and East Midlands, are controlled by local authorities and cater for the country's remaining passenger and cargo needs.

Expansion of existing airports (particularly regional facilities) and the provision of new ones will be necessary if Britain is to cope with increased consumer demand and competition from Europe. But such projects are very expensive and controversial because of environmental problems, such as construction work, noise, pollution and traffic. There is also disquiet about plane congestion in the skies over Britain and the amount of pollution caused by aircraft. A MORI Social Research Institute poll in February 2003 found that 42 per cent of respondents were opposed to building more airports in the UK and 31 per cent supported the idea.

The inadequacy of British transport systems stems from the lack of an integrated infrastructure of roads, railways and airports catering for passengers and freight. This could arguably ease road congestion, satisfy demand and improve the environment. But such developments involve considerable expense and Britain invests less in transport than any other European country. Governments are reluctant to spend more public money, although the Labour government has partnerships with the private sector to allow the latter to invest in the state transport infrastructure.

Communications

Communications systems in Britain are also divided between the public and private sectors. The main suppliers are private telecommunications companies and the public Post Office.

Telecommunications is one of the most competitive and rapidly expanding sectors of the economy. *British Telecom (BT)* was privatized in 1984, has some 71 per cent of market share and provides domestic and international telephone and telecommunications systems, with 20 million domestic and 8.5 million business subscribers. There was much criticism of BT's performance after privatization. Although some service problems were solved, and it became an influential world force, it has again experienced problems with its funding and expansion programmes.

The private companies, Vodafone and Cable and Wireless, compete fiercely with British Telecom. Other competitors, such as cable networks NTL and Telewest, (which have now merged) are growing rapidly and have been licensed to provide telecommunications facilities and the development of broadband services.

The strongest and most competitive growth in recent years has been in mobile telephones and services provided over the Internet. By 2004, the number of mobile phone users had risen to over 54.7 million (with network suppliers such as Orange, O_2, Vodaphone, T-Mobile and 3) and access to the Internet and e-mail covered 53 per cent of households. However, Internet access and usage is much greater in companies, libraries and schools.

The *Post Office*, established in 1635, is a crown-owned body and is responsible for collecting, handling and delivering some 80 million letters and parcels every day. It has sorting offices throughout the country with sophisticated handling equipment, based on the postcodes which every address in Britain has. Local post offices throughout the country (although controversially reduced in rural and some urban areas) provide postal and other services and the large Parcelforce Worldwide operates domestically and overseas. The Post Office's international connections and customers are expanding and the growth of electronic communications has had only a limited effect on its markets. The Post Office does not have a monopoly on the collection and delivery of letters. But licensed competition by private sector couriers and express operators, although limited at present, is likely to increase, and there are proposals to split the service into two or partly privatize it.

Attitudes to the environment

There is public concern in Britain about pollution, traffic congestion, the lack of an adequate public transport system, the quality and exploitation of the natural habitat, the use of energy sources, the safety of agricultural products, the effects of global warming and the damage caused to personal health by environmental problems. Although many individuals are directly affected by these factors, it is often difficult to detect how widespread their concern is and whether people understand the issues and are prepared to act on them, often at the expense of their own lifestyles.

Opinion polls show that respondents believe that environmental protection should rate higher than economic growth; environmental problems should be tackled; and they are prepared to make sacrifices to clean up the environment and conserve wildlife. But such views do not always lead to sensitive behaviour and there is widespread vandalism and dirtiness in both rural and urban areas. An example of such mixed signals was a MORI Social Research Institute poll in February 2003 which found that while 63 per cent of respondents supported a

10 pence charge on plastic bags (27 per cent opposed) to encourage people to re-use bags and reduce plastic waste, only 48 per cent supported (41 per cent opposed) variable charging for waste (depending on how much people throw away rather than recycle).

Awareness of environmental issues coincided with the rise and political attraction of the Green movement in the 1980s and all mainstream political parties eventually adopted 'green' policies. An Environment Agency was created; Acts of Parliament are supposed to safeguard the environment, reduce pollution and penalize polluters; and EU legislation makes very stringent demands in these areas.

But such action is often insufficient and ineffective. Environmental controls and planning rules may lack force; polluters evade regulations and taxes or suffer only minor fines; insufficient pressure is put on companies to modernise their facilities, adopt cleaner technology and file environmental reports on their activities; and there are disputes over protection costs between local and central government. A MORI poll in March 2002 found that between 87–92 per cent of respondents believed that the government should protect the environment, employment conditions and health, even when regulations conflict with the economic interests of multinational companies. Polls in *The Ecologist* magazine in 2001 found that 65 per cent of respondents thought that the Labour government had not improved the environment since coming to power in 1997 and was spending too little on it. Critics claim that government environmental policies are in fact contradictory and often conflict with European Union programmes.

It is argued that traffic congestion, an increase in cars, industrial usage, more aircraft and energy consumption cause pollution and climate change. In this view, carbon emissions are the man-made contribution to global warming, a claim which gained greater scientific support in 2005 from a study of rising temperatures in the world's oceans. The need to shift from a fossil fuel to a low carbon economy, in order to protect the world's climate and future generations has to be reinforced, according to MORI research in 2004 where 63 per cent of the British public would like to see urgent action taken by their leaders. Britain, the European Union and the signatories to the 1997 Kyoto Agreement see global warming as one of the greatest dangers facing the world community and its environment. Yet United Nations research in 2005 indicated that even concerted international effort to control global warming will not appreciably reduce projected temperature rises by 2100.

The debate about the effects of global warming is still confused. MORI opinion polls in 2002–3 suggested that the British public, in spite of good intentions, was uncertain about the seriousness of global warming, ignorant of its consequences and unwilling to embrace costly and inconvenient action. Nevertheless, there is an apparent willingness among some sections of the public to take specific measures, such as buying unleaded petrol, using energy saving light bulbs and recycling household rubbish to reduce domestic energy use. But the polls suggested that there still remained a strong need to raise further public understanding of global warming and Britain's role in tackling it.

Critics maintain that the British government is at odds with European Union environmental policy on carbon emissions trading, which can allow British industry to avoid the heaviest penalties for its pollution. The government seems to argue that the development of cleaner technology, cars, factories and power stations is the answer, since reductions in industrial production will harm the economy.

Britain has in fact reduced carbon emissions and the Labour government is concerned to improve its record to a 20 per cent reduction by 2010. But pollution will worsen as the deterioration in public transport encourages more people to use private vehicles. Britons are overly dependent on the car (with families owning more and bigger vehicles) and alternatives have been neglected. The car is now seen as the greatest transport problem and the government has made attempts to curb its unnecessary use, ration road space in favour of buses, increase taxes or charges on car usage in cities and give funding to local schemes which improve public transport.

A congestion charge has been introduced in London by the Mayor of London, whereby owners are charged for driving into central areas. This has reduced traffic by some 25 per cent. But, according to a MORI Social Research Institute poll in February 2003, while 50 per cent of Londoners now support the charge (34 per

PLATE 2.4 Bendy bus, London.
This single decker bus is replacing the traditional double decker red bus (Routemaster) on most routes in London.
(*Rex Features*)

cent opposed) the British people nationally are divided on using congestion charging in other cities to reduce traffic (42 per cent for and 41 per cent against). Opposition to congestion charges grew in 2005 when local government outside London (following referendums) decided against the proposal.

These findings suggest that people refuse to give up their cars, are unwilling to give up their 'right' to drive into towns and cities and believe that improved buses and park-and-ride schemes are better alternatives. While polls consistently show that a majority of respondents wish for better public transport, cuts in traffic pollution, reduction of congestion and removal of freight from the roads, they are less keen on keeping cars out of towns/cities or banning cars completely. They seem to accept car taxes, charges or tolls as an inevitable part of their dependence upon the car.

Critics, on the other hand, argue that the government is blocking public transport schemes to reduce congestion and emissions by stopping drivers using their cars because it is reluctant to lose income (£42 billion a year) from road and fuel taxes. Instead, they feel that the government is relying on the faster intro- duction of greener and technologically-improved cars rather than attempting to cut car numbers.

British governments have broached the idea of an integrated transport system (roads, rail and air), but have not provided a model which would deliver it and relieve environmental pressures. The problem arises because of the varied geography of Britain's cities and the devolution of control to local authorities. It is thus difficult to implement one overall plan and to agree on who will pay the costs. A 2001 poll in *The Ecologist* showed that 61 per cent of respondents did not want more roads to relieve traffic congestion, pollution, noise and damage to roads and property. They preferred money to be spent on alternatives and a large majority in a 2001 *MORI* poll wanted to see more goods carried by rail. But this solution requires an upgraded and more efficient railway network. Although there is growing demand for passenger rail travel the railway system suffers from underfunding.

Land usage and property building are also contentious issues in contemporary Britain. Agricultural, woodland and greenfield land is being used for building and recreational purposes to a greater extent than in the past; there has been an increase in suburban sprawl as house building encroaches on rural areas; there is an estimated need for some one million new homes nationwide to counter house shortages and demographic change; the Labour government is pressing for 640,000 houses to be built in south-east England and the south Midlands (even on land subject to flooding); and giant supermarkets or shopping centres are being located in the countryside.

Research surveys and opinion polls regularly report that people are worried about the future of the countryside and want to stop housing development, building work and road/airport schemes which damage the environment. Government policies are supposed to force local planning authorities to build homes on available brownfield land within towns before granting permission to develop greenfield sites. But the latter is increasingly being allowed and brownfield house building leads to much smaller and crowded housing plots, as well as building speculation.

Air pollution in Britain is caused by factories, power stations, cars, buses, lorries and domestic homes discharging carbon emissions into the air. It seriously affects both urban and rural areas, is a threat to people's health (particularly the elderly, asthmatics and those with respiratory problems) and was linked for the first time in 1997 to heart attacks. Although pollution was reduced by Clean Air Acts in the 1950s and 1960s, it still reaches harmful levels, particularly in summer when pollutants mix with sunshine and still humid conditions to produce high ozone levels.

Other forms of environmental damage, such as sea and beach pollution, are partly caused when untreated sewage and toxic industrial waste are pumped into the sea by commercial companies. Britain has reduced discharge levels but, although 90 per cent of beaches meet EU quality standards, pollution levels on some beaches still exceed safety levels. Rivers are also polluted by industrial waste, toxic fertilizers, pesticides and farm silage. This has caused public concern about the safety of drinking water from reservoirs and the water companies (the worst business polluters in 2001) have been pressurized into raising the quality of their services. Many rivers, lakes and estuaries have now been cleaned up and more stringent controls of the oil and shipping industries in the North Sea have reduced pollution levels.

Problems have been experienced with the exploitation of energy resources, such as expense, capacity and availability, and there are environmental concerns about the burning of fossil fuels (coal, oil and gas), global warming and the damage to the countryside caused by new developments. Nuclear expansion had been halted because of government uncertainty about nuclear energy and also because of public opposition to nuclear facilities, the danger of radioactive leaks, the reprocessing of nuclear waste at the Thorp and Sellafield plants in north-west England and the dumping of radioactive waste at sea. But it now appears that the Labour government will embrace a new generation of nuclear power stations for civil use.

Public concern surrounds the agricultural industry because of its widespread use of fertilizers and pesticides, its methods of animal feeding and the effects of intensive farming on the environment. Much hedgerow, which is important for animal and vegetable life, has been lost as fields have become bigger and farming more mechanized. The quality and standards of food products, particularly those devoted to intensive farming, are of concern. Cases of food poisoning have risen sharply and there are worries about standards of hygiene in the food and farming businesses. The BSE scare seriously affected the consumption of beef and other meats and led to a drop in demand for traditional foods. The foot and mouth outbreak in 2000–1 also raised questions about the quality of British food and intensive methods of farming.

PLATE 2.5 Windscale (now Sellafield) nuclear power plant, Cumbria, England, where nuclear fuel is reprocessed so that it can be used again.
(*Malcolm Gilson/Rex Features*)

Yet there is public disquiet about the use of genetically-modified (GM) crops. The MORI Social Research Institute in February 2003 found that 56 per cent of respondents were opposed and only 14 per cent supported it, although the Labour government has decided to expand the experiment. The success of organic farming in Britain has been small, largely because of the cost of such goods and confusion about their actual benefit, although the MORI Social Research Institute in February 2003 found that 69 per cent of respondents supported it and 8 per cent were opposed. An NOP poll in 2001 reported that 82 per cent of respondents favoured a return to traditional farming methods, even if this meant paying more for food. A *Good Housekeeping* magazine poll in August 2001 found that only 1 in 6 people trust the supermarkets to sell safe food; 3 in 4 were more concerned than ever before about the safety of the food they buy; and although 97 per cent of respondents buy most of their food from supermarkets, their faith in them has suffered. For example, serious flaws in the regulation of Britain's complicated food industry in 2005 allowed millions of contaminated products containing a cancer-causing dye to reach supermarket shelves without proper safety checks.

Exercises

Explain and examine the following terms:

Britain	Heathrow	Intercity 125	Post Office
weathering	Highland Britain	Lough Neagh	Ben Nevis
arable	Channel Islands	horticulture	BT
CAP	earth movements	the Tube	drought
The Shetlands	British Telecom	postcodes	GM crops
BSE	global warming	CFP	tidal
CAP	organic food	'regionalism'	RDAs

Write short essays on the following topics:

1 Does Britain have an energy crisis? If so, why?

2 Examine the impact of Britain's membership of the European Union upon its agricultural and fisheries industries.

3 What are the reasons for environmental concerns in Britain?

4 Should cars be restricted on Britain's roads and banned from city centres? Give your reasons, for and against.

Further reading

1 Barnett, A. and Scruton, R. (1999) *Town and Country* London: Vintage

2 Champion, A.G. and Townsend, A.R. (1990) *Contemporary Britain: A Geographical Perspective* London: Edward Arnold

3 Clapp, B.W. (1994) *An Environmental History of Britain since the Industrial Revolution* London: Longman

4 Connelly, J. and Smith, G (1999) *Politics and the Environment: From Theory to Practice* London: Routledge

5 Gray, T. (1995) *UK Environmental Policy in the 1990s* London: Macmillan

6 Harvey, G. (1998) *The Killing of the Countryside* London: Vintage

7 *Regional Trends*, Office for National Statistics, London: The Stationery Office

8 *Your Region, Your Choice: Revitalizing the English Regions* (2002), London: The Stationery Office

Websites

Office for National Statistics: www.statistics.gov.uk
Environment, Food and Rural Affairs: www.defra.gov.uk
Department for Transport: www.dft.gov.uk
Transport for London: www.tfl.gov.uk
Office of the Rail Regulator: www.rail-reg.gov.uk
Strategic Rail Authority: www.sta.gov.uk
Office of Telecommunications: www.oftel.gov.uk
Office of Water Services: www.open.gov.uk/ofwat
Office of Gas and Electricity Markets: www.ofgem.gov.uk
Scottish Executive: www.scotland.gov.uk
Northern Ireland Executive: www.nio.gov.uk
Northern Ireland Department for Regional Development: www.drdni.gov.uk
Welsh Assembly Government: www.wales.gov.uk
Countryside Commission: www.countryside.gov.uk
The Green Party: http://www.greenparty.org.uk
British Geological Survey: www.bgs.ac.uk
The Met Office: www.metoffice.com
The National Archives: www.national archives.gov.uk
MORI Social Research Institute: www.mori.com/environment

The people

The British Isles have attracted settlers, invaders and immigrants throughout their history. The contemporary British are consequently composed of people from worldwide origins and are divided into what eventually became known as the English, Scots, Welsh and Northern Irish. These populations themselves have mixed roots derived from diverse settlement and immigration patterns over time in the individual nations. There has also been considerable internal migration throughout the British Isles (particularly in the nineteenth century) as individuals have moved between the four nations. In a similar blending process, the English language, which binds most of these people together linguistically, is a mixture of Germanic, Romance and other world languages.

Descent patterns are important elements in considering the varied ethnicities of the British peoples today. An individual may have a mixed ethnic family background resulting at one level from intermarriage at various times between English, Irish, Scottish or Welsh people. For example, opinion polls show that one in four adult Britons (English, Scottish or Welsh) claim to have Irish roots or bloodlines in their ancestry, although experts argue that the true figure is probably one in ten. At another level, there are immigrant minorities with their own ethnic identities who have come to Britain. They may have sometimes intermarried with the indigenous population, or maintained their own separate ethnic culture or eventually acquired a formal British identity through naturalization. Their second-generation children have often been born in Britain and may reflect several allegiances in addition to British nationality.

These historical developments have created a contemporary society with multinational and multi-ethnic characteristics. But, since assimilation or integration processes are not always successful, controversial questions continue to be asked about the meaning of 'Britishness', the nature of identities and loyalties in the population and the validity of government immigration and asylum policies.

Early settlement to AD 1066

There is no accurate picture of what the very early settlement of the present British Isles was actually like and there were long periods when the islands were apparently uninhabited. Historians and archaeologists constantly revise traditional theories about the gradual growth of the country as new evidence comes to light.

The earliest human bones found (1993) in Britain (West Sussex) are 500,000 years old (Boxgrove Man). But butchered animal bones and stone artefacts discovered in East Anglia in 2002 show evidence of earlier hominid activity 700,000 years ago. The first people were probably Palaeolithic (Old Stone Age) nomads from mainland Europe, who used rudimentary stone implements. It is likely that they travelled to Britain mainly by land at those times when the country was joined to the European land mass. *Homo sapiens* appeared during this Palaeolithic period.

Mesolithic (Middle Stone Age) settlers from about 8300 BC arrived in the transition period between the Palaeolithic and the Neolithic eras and between the end of the last glacial period and the beginnings of agriculture. Neolithic (New Stone Age) arrivals from about 4000 BC had more advanced skills in stone carving, began to form settled agricultural communities and to tame wild animals, leading to the growth of the human population. Some probably came from central Europe and settled in eastern Britain. Others arrived by sea from Iberian (Spanish-Portugese) areas and populated Cornwall, Ireland, Wales, the Isle of Man and western Scotland. Their descendants live today in the same western parts. Neolithic groups built large wood, soil and stone monuments, like Stonehenge and Avebury, and later arrivals (the Beaker Folk) introduced a Bronze Age culture.

From about 600 BC there was a movement of Celtic tribes into the islands from mainland Europe, bringing an Iron Age civilization with them. The Celts were not a unified group, had at least two main languages and were divided into different tribes with conflicts between them. Celtic civilizations dominated the islands until they were overcome by warring Belgic tribes (also of Celtic origin) around 200 BC.

The Belgic tribes were subjected to a series of Roman expeditions from 55 BC. The eventual Roman military occupation of the islands (except for Ireland and most of Scotland) lasted from AD 43 until AD 409. The term 'Britain' probably derives from the Greek and Latin names given to England and Wales by the Romans, although it may stem from Celtic originals. It is argued that the Romans did not mix well with the existing population and that their lasting influence was slight. But some Christian practices spread throughout the islands, political and legal institutions were introduced, new agricultural methods and produce were imported and there is still physical evidence of the Roman presence throughout much of England.

After Roman withdrawal, Germanic tribes such as Angles (from which 'England' is derived), Saxons and Jutes from north-western Europe invaded the country. They either mixed with the existing population or pushed it westwards, although the degree of this displacement has been disputed recently. The country was effectively divided into seven separate and often warring Anglo-Saxon kingdoms in England, with largely Celtic areas in Wales, Scotland and Ireland.

Many of these regions suffered from Scandinavian (Viking) military invasions in the eighth and ninth centuries AD, until the Scandinavians were defeated in England, Scotland and Ireland in the tenth to eleventh centuries. The Scandinavian presence, after initial fleeting raids, was reflected in some permanent settlement, assimilation, farming, political institutions and the adaptation of Scandinavian words.

Early English history was completed when the Anglo-Saxons were defeated by French-Norman invaders at the Battle of Hastings in AD 1066 and England was subjected to their rule. The Norman Conquest was a watershed in English history and marked the last successful external military invasion of the country. It influenced the English people and their language (since French was the language of the nobility for the next 300 years) and initiated many of the social, legal and institutional frameworks, like a feudal system, which were to characterize future British society.

But Celtic civilizations continued in what are now Wales, Scotland and Ireland, which were divided into separate (and often warring) kingdoms, princedoms, tribes and clans. Roman rule had not extended to Ireland and Scotland. Anglo-Norman rule of Ireland was initially patchy and was not successfully imposed upon Scotland. The latter was inhabited (except for Angles in the south) by the original Picts and later Scots from Ireland who colonized western Scotland (AD 200–400), giving their name to present-day Scotland.

Different peoples had thus entered the British Isles from the south-west, the east and the north by 1066. But settlement was often hindered by climatic and geographical obstacles, particularly in the north and west. Many newcomers tended to concentrate initially in southern England and settlement patterns were not uniform over all of Britain at the same time. Despite some intermixture between the various settlers, there were ethnic differences between the English and the people of Ireland, Wales and Scotland, as well as varying identities between groups in all the countries. It is this mixture, increased by later immigration and internal migration, which has produced the present ethnic and national diversity in Britain.

The early settlement and invasion movements substantially affected the developing fabric of British life and formed the first tentative foundations of the future modern state. The newcomers often imposed their cultures on the existing society, as well as adopting some of the native characteristics. Today there are few British towns which lack any physical evidence of the successive changes. They also influenced social, legal, economic, political, agricultural and administrative institutions and contributed to the evolving language.

There are no realistic population figures for the early British Isles. The nomadic lifestyle of groups of up to 20 people gradually ceased and was replaced by more permanent settlements of a few hundred inhabitants. It is estimated, for example, that the English population during the Roman occupation was one million. By the Norman period, the eleventh-century Domesday Book showed an increase to 2 million. The Domesday Book was the first systematic attempt to evaluate England's wealth and population, mainly for taxation purposes.

TABLE 3.1 Early settlement to AD 1066

2,500,000–c. 8300 BC	Palaeolithic (Old Stone Age)
c.8300 BC	Mesolithic (Middle Stone Age)
c.4000 BC	Neolithic (New Stone Age)
c.2000 BC	Beaker folk (Bronze Age)
c.600 BC	Celts (Iron Age)
c.200 BC	Belgic tribes
AD 43	The Romans
AD 410	Germanic tribes (Anglo-Saxons)
Eighth to eleventh centuries	The Scandinavians
AD 1066	The Norman conquest

Growth and immigration up to the twentieth century

England, Scotland, Wales and Ireland had more clearly defined identities and geographical areas by the twelfth century, although 'tribal' and royalist conflict continued in the four nations for centuries. Political and military attempts were then made by England over succeeding centuries to unite Wales, Scotland and Ireland under the English Crown. English monarchs tried to conquer or ally themselves with these other countries as a protection against threats from within the islands and from continental Europe, as well as for increased power and possessions. Internal colonization and political unification of the islands gradually created what became the British state. This process was accompanied by fierce and bloody struggles between and within the nations, often resulting in lasting tensions and bitterness.

Ireland was invaded by Henry II in 1169. Parts of the country were occupied by Anglo-Norman nobles but little direct authority was initially exercised from England. More extensive later colonization of Ireland by the English and the Scots became a source of conflict between the countries. But it also led to Irish settlements in Scotland, London and west coast ports like Liverpool. Ireland became part of the United Kingdom in 1801 but, after periods of violence and political unrest, was divided in 1921 into the Irish Free State eventually to become the Republic of Ireland and Northern Ireland (which remains in the UK).

Wales, after Roman control, remained a Celtic country, although influenced by Anglo-Norman and Angevin-Plantagenet England. Between 1282 and 1285 Edward I's military campaign brought Wales under English rule, and he built castles and deployed garrisons there. Apart from a period of freedom in 1402–7, Wales was integrated legally and administratively with England by Acts of Union 1536–42.

The English also tried to conquer Scotland by military force, but were ultimately repulsed at the Battle of Bannockburn in 1314. Scotland remained

PLATE 3.1 Scottish piper in traditional dress playing bagpipes. (*J. Valkonen/IBL/Rex Features*)

PLATE 3.2 Girls in Welsh national costume, Cardiff, 1991.
On the occasion in 1991 of Prince William's first official engagement in Wales.
(*Rex Features*)

independent until the political union between the two countries in 1707, when the creation of Great Britain (England/Wales and Scotland) took place. But Scotland and England had shared a common monarch since 1603 when James VI of Scotland became James I of England (Union of the Two Crowns).

England, Wales and Scotland had meanwhile become predominantly Protestant in religion as a result of the European Reformation and Henry VIII's break with Rome. But Ireland remained Catholic and tried to distance itself from England, thus adding religion to colonialism as a foundation for future problems.

Britain therefore is not a single, ethnically-homogeneous country, but rather a recent and potentially unstable union of four old nations. Great Britain (1707) is only slightly older than the USA, which is often regarded as a young country, and the United Kingdom (1801) is younger. Nor did the political unions appreciably alter the relationships between the four nations. The English often treated their Celtic neighbours as colonial subjects rather than equal partners and Englishness became a powerful strand in developing concepts of Britishness, because of the dominant role that the English have played in the formation of Britain.

However, despite the tensions and bitterness between the four nations, there was a steady internal migration between them. This mainly involved movements of Irish, Welsh and Scottish people into England. Relatively few English emigrated to Wales and Scotland, although there was English and Scottish settlement in Ireland over the centuries.

Immigration from abroad into the British Isles also continued due to factors such as religious and political persecution, trade, business and employment. Immigrants have had a significant impact on British society. They have contributed to financial institutions, commerce, industry and agriculture, and influenced artistic, cultural and political developments. But immigrant activity and success have also resulted in jealousy, discrimination and violence from the indigenous populations.

In addition to political integration, Britain's growth and the mixing of its people were also conditioned first by a series of agricultural changes and second by a number of later industrial revolutions. Agriculture started with Neolithic settlers and continued with the Saxons in England who cleared the forests, cultivated crops and introduced inventions and equipment which remained in use for centuries. Their open-field system of farming (with strips of land being worked by local people) was later replaced by widespread sheep-herding and wool production.

Britain expanded agriculturally and commercially from the eleventh century, and also developed manufacturing industries. Immigration was often characterized by financial and agricultural skills. Jewish money-lenders entered England with the Norman Conquest, to be followed later by Lombard bankers from northern Italy. This commercial expertise created greater wealth which was influenced by the merchants of the German Hansa League, who set up their trading posts in London and on the east coast of England. Around 1330, Dutch and Flemish weavers arrived, who by the end of the fifteenth century had helped to transform England into a major nation of sheep farmers, cloth producers and textile exporters. Fourteenth-century immigration also introduced specialized knowledge in a variety of manufacturing trades.

Some immigrants stayed only for short periods. Others remained and adapted themselves to British society, while sometimes preserving their own cultural and ethnic identities. Newcomers were often encouraged to settle in Britain and the policy of using immigrant expertise continued in later centuries. But foreign workers had no legal rights and early immigrants, such as Jews and the Hansa merchants, could be summarily expelled.

Agricultural and commercial developments were reflected in changing population concentrations. From Saxon times to around 1800, Britain had an agriculturally-based economy and some 80 per cent of the people lived in villages in the countryside. Settlement was mainly concentrated in the south and east of England, where the rich agricultural regions of East Anglia and Lincolnshire had the greatest population densities. During the fourteenth century, however, the steady increase of people was halted by a series of plagues and numbers did not start to increase again for another 100 years.

As agricultural production moved into sheep farming and clothing manufactures, larger numbers of people settled around woollen ports, such as Bristol in the west and coastal towns in East Anglia. Others moved to cloth-producing areas in the West Country and the Cotswolds and initiated the growth of market towns. The south midland and eastern English counties had the greatest densities of people and the population at the end of the seventeenth century is estimated at 5.5 million for England and Wales and 1 million for Scotland.

Other newcomers continued to arrive from overseas, including gypsies, blacks (associated with the slave trade) and a further wave of Jews, who in 1655 created the first permanent Jewish community. In the sixteenth and seventeenth centuries, the country attracted a large number of refugees, such as Dutch Protestants and French Huguenots, who were driven from Europe by warfare, political and religious persecution and employment needs. This talented and urbanized immigration contributed considerably to the national economy and added a new dimension to a largely agricultural population. But, from around 1700, immigration into the country decreased over the next 200 years. Britain was exporting more people than it received, mainly to North America and the expanding colonies worldwide.

A second central development in British history was a number of industrial revolutions in the eighteenth and nineteenth centuries. These transformed Britain from an agricultural economy into an industrial and manufacturing country. Processes based on coal-generated steam power were discovered and exploited. Factories and factory towns were needed to mass-produce new manufactured goods. Villages in the coalfields and industrial areas grew rapidly into manufacturing centres. A drift of population away from the countryside began in the late eighteenth century, as people sought work in urban factories to escape rural poverty and unemployment. They moved, for example, to textile mills in Lancashire and Yorkshire and to heavy industries and pottery factories in the West Midlands.

The earlier agricultural population changed radically in the nineteenth century into an industrialized workforce. The 1801 census (the first modern measurement of population) gave figures of over 8 million for England, Wales half a million, 1.5 million for Scotland and over 5 million for Ireland. But, between 1801 and 1901, the population of England and Wales trebled to 30 million. The numbers in Scotland increased less rapidly, due to emigration, but in Ireland the population was reduced from some 8 to 4 million because of famine, deaths and emigration. The greatest concentrations of people were now in London and industrial areas of the Midlands, south Lancashire, Merseyside, Clydeside, Tyneside, Yorkshire and South Wales.

The industrial revolution reached its height during the early nineteenth century. It did not require foreign labour because there were enough skilled and professional trades among all British workers and a ready supply of unskilled labourers from Wales, Scotland, Ireland and the English countryside. Welshmen from North Wales went to the Lancashire textile mills; Highland Scots travelled to the Lowland Clydeside industries; and Irishmen flocked to England and Scotland to work in the manual trades of the industrial infrastructure constructing roads, railways and canals. These migratory movements created ethnic conflicts (which sometimes grew into violent confrontations), but also degrees of assimilation.

Industrialization expanded commercial markets, which attracted new immigrants who had the business and financial skills to exploit the industrial wealth. Some newcomers joined City of London financial institutions and the import/export trades, to which they contributed their international connections. Other settlers were involved in a range of occupations and trades. Immigration to Britain might have been greater in the nineteenth century had it not been for the attraction of North America, which received large numbers of newcomers from around the world, including Britain.

By the end of the nineteenth century, Britain was the world's leading industrial nation and one of the richest. But it gradually lost its world lead in manufacturing industry, most of which was in native British hands, as foreign competition grew. However, its position in international finance, some of which was under immigrant control, was retained.

Immigration from 1900

Although immigrants historically had relatively free access to Britain, they could be easily expelled; had no legal rights to protect them; and entry restrictions were increasingly imposed. But the 1871 census showed that only 157,000 people in Britain out of a population of 31.5 million were born outside the British Empire.

Despite these low figures, economic immigrants and asylum seekers fleeing oppression caused public and political concern, which continued throughout the twentieth century. In the early years of the century, Jews and Poles escaped persecution in Eastern Europe and settled in the East End of London, which has always attracted immigrant groups. Demands for immigration control grew and an anti-foreigner feeling spread, fuelled by the nationalism and spy mania caused by the First World War (1914–18). But laws (like the Aliens Act of 1905), which were designed to curtail foreign entry, proved ineffective. By 1911 the number of people in Britain born outside the empire was 428,000 (1 per cent of the population).

Despite legal controls, and partly as a result of the 1930s world recession and the Second World War, refugees first from Nazi-occupied Europe and later from Soviet bloc countries as well as economic immigrants entered Britain. After the war, refugees such as Poles, Latvians, Ukrainians among other nationalities chose to stay in Britain. Later in the twentieth century, other political refugees arrived, such as Hungarians, Czechs, Chileans, Libyans, East African Asians, Iranians, Vietnamese and other Eastern Europeans. Italian, French, German, Irish, Turkish, Cypriot, Chinese, Spanish and Commonwealth economic immigrants increasingly entered the country. These groups (and their descendants) today form sizeable ethnic minorities and are found throughout Britain. Such newcomers have often suffered from discrimination at various times, some more than others.

But public and political concern in the immediate post-war period turned to the issues of race and colour, which were to dominate the immigration debate for the rest of the twentieth century and focussed on non-white Commonwealth immigration. Before the Second World War, most Commonwealth immigrants to Britain came from the largely white Old Commonwealth countries of Canada, Australia and New Zealand, and from South Africa. But all Commonwealth citizens (white and non-white) continued to have relatively free access and were not treated as aliens.

From the late 1940s, increasing numbers of people from the non-white New Commonwealth nations of India, Pakistan and the West Indies came to Britain (sometimes at the invitation of government agencies) to fill the vacant manual and lower-paid jobs of an expanding economy. West Indians worked in public transport, catering, the National Health Service and manual trades in London, Birmingham and other large cities. Indians and Pakistanis later arrived to work in the textile and iron industries of Leeds, Bradford and Leicester (which may soon become the first British city to have a non-white majority population). By the

1970s, non-white people became a familiar sight in other British towns such as Glasgow, Sheffield, Bristol, Huddersfield, Manchester, Liverpool, Coventry and Nottingham. There was a considerable dispersal of such immigrants throughout Britain, although many tended to settle in the central areas of industrial cities. This concentrated settlement pattern has grown in recent years and raises concern about the isolation of some ethnic groups from the majority white population and its institutions.

Non-white communities have now increased and work in a broad range of occupations. Some, particularly Indian Asians and the Chinese, have been successful in economic and professional terms. Others (such as Bangladeshis and some West Indians and Pakistanis) have experienced problems with low-paid jobs, unemployment, educational disadvantage, decaying housing in the inner cities, isolation, alienation and discrimination. It is argued that Britain possesses a deep-rooted (or institutional) racism based on the legacy of empire and notions of racial superiority, which continues to manifest itself and has hindered the integration of the non-white population into the larger society. Some young non-whites who have been born in Britain feel bitter at their experiences and at their relative lack of educational and employment possibilities and advancement.

PLATE 3.3 Notting Hill Carnival, 2004.
Costume parade, August 2004, London. Originally a West Indian street carnival with steel bands, it now includes other ethnic groups.
(*Stephanie Paschal/Rex Features*)

An opposing argument (frequently employed after the 7 July 2005 London bombings) is that ethnic communities should themselves confront their own internal problems (such as generational differences) and integrate more with the majority population and its institutions. There are also increasing tensions between non-white ethnic groups.

So many New Commonwealth immigrants were coming to Britain that from 1962 governments treated most Commonwealth newcomers as aliens and followed a two-strand policy on immigration. This consisted, first, of Immigration Acts to restrict the number of all immigrants entering the country and, second, of Race Relations Acts to protect the rights of those immigrants already settled in Britain.

Race Relations Acts make it unlawful to discriminate against individuals on grounds of racial, ethnic or national origin in areas such as education, housing, employment, services and advertising. Those who suffer alleged discrimination can appeal to Race Relations Tribunals and anti-discrimination bodies have also been established, culminating with the Commission for Racial Equality in 1976. This body, which is not without its critics, applies the Race Relations Acts, works for the elimination of discrimination and promotes equality of opportunity.

There is still criticism of the immigration laws and race-relations organizations. Some people argue that one cannot legislate satisfactorily against discrimination and others would like stricter controls on immigrant entry. The concerns of some white people are made worse by racialist speeches; the growth of nationalist parties like the National Front and the British National Party; and racially-inspired violence. Non-white citizens, on the other hand, often feel that they too easily and unfairly become scapegoats for any problems that arise. Some become alienated from British society and reject institutions such as the police, legal system and political structures. Government policies since the 1940s have not always helped to lessen either white or non-white anxieties.

Immigration and race remain problematic. They are complex matters, are exploited for political purposes from both the right and the left, and can be over-dramatized. Many (if by no means all) non-white immigrants and their British-born children have slowly adapted to the larger society, whilst sometimes retaining their ethnic identities. Britain does have a relatively stable diversity of cultures and the highest rate of intermarriage and mixed race relationships in Europe, with one in eight children under five having parents from different ethnic backgrounds. But outbreaks of racial tension, violence and harassment do occur and there are accusations that the police and the courts ignore or underplay race crimes. On the other hand, a concern for some critics is that race and immigration problems are not being openly and fairly debated in the present climate of alleged 'political correctness' and 'inclusiveness'.

The non-white population was earlier composed of immigrant families or single people. This structure has changed as more dependants join settled immigrants, as British-born non-whites develop their own family organizations and as more people intermarry. The emphasis had gradually switched to debates about what constitutes a 'multi-ethnic society' and what such a society should provide for its people. But the term 'immigrant' has become prominent again as debates about immigration and asylum seekers have become a focus for public concern and debate.

Apart from a few categories of people who have a right of abode in Britain and are not subject to immigration control, all others require either entry clearance or permission to enter and remain. Generally speaking, such newcomers (apart from short-term visitors) need a work permit and a guaranteed job if they hope to stay in the country for longer periods of time. But dependants of immigrants already settled in Britain may be granted the right of entry and permanent settlement.

There are legal distinctions between immigration into Britain (a controlled entry system often based on economic and dependency factors), political asylum (fleeing from fear of persecution) and a category of migrant workers (based on Britain's economic needs). In 2004, net migration into Britain amounted to 223,000 immigrants who were accepted for permanent settlement (more than in previous years). People from India, Pakistan and Africa made up the largest proportions, with many being dependants of settled immigrants. This suggests that a significant primary immigration continues, despite restrictive legislation since the 1960s.

After the enlargement of the European Union in May 2004 to 25 members (including East European states), the government established a scheme of work permits. These are issued to legal migrants seeking work in Britain, initially for at least a year. In 2004, a record 340,000 legal migrants came to fill vacancies in the job market, covering the hospitality and catering industry, transport, the health sector and teachers. Some 130,000 people from East European EU countries registered for work, with Poland, Lithuania and Slovakia providing the largest numbers. A further 181,400 work permits were issued to people from outside the EU.

These statistics mean that the estimated number of people arriving to live in Britain from all categories rose to a record 582,000 in 2004. Government projections suggest that such figures (even allowing for people emigrating from the country) indicate that immigration will fuel an estimated 7.2 million growth in the population over the next 25 years. The Labour government argues that it must compete in the international market place and attract those immigrants and migrant workers that the economy needs to compensate for a declining labour force, an ageing population and a shortage of both skilled and unskilled workers. Opponents of this policy maintain that the indigenous unemployed in Britain itself should undertake education and training to fill the job vacancies.

In recent years, there has been controversy about the increased numbers of asylum seekers entering Britain and suspicions that many are economic migrants rather than being genuinely in humanitarian need. In 2003, the top five countries from which registered asylum seekers came to Britain were Iraq, Somalia, China,

Zimbabwe and Iran. The Labour government has tried to tighten (ineffectually for some critics) the rules for the admission of asylum seekers and to increase the number of deportations of those who fail in their applications. However, it is estimated that there may be at least 600,000 illegal asylum seekers, migrant workers and immigrants in Britain. The government does not know the exact figure and its drive to remove failed asylum-seekers faltered in 2004, although asylum applications fell by one-third from 2003 to 2004.

Opinion polls in the 1990s had suggested that race relations, immigration and asylum were of less concern to Britons than they were from the 1940s to the 1980s. A 1995 MORI poll found that 78 per cent of respondents did not consider themselves to be prejudiced against people of other races. But a 2001 *Guardian* newspaper poll reported that 70 per cent of readers thought that race relations were not getting better. A MORI poll in January 2005 found that race relations and immigration had climbed to third place (26 per cent) in a list of the most important issues facing British society. Some critics and politicians maintain that immigration and asylum regulations need to be reformed and that concerns about ethnic relations have to be honestly faced.

New conditions for naturalization and redefinitions of British citizenship were contained in the Nationality Act of 1981. It was criticized as providing further restrictions on immigration, particularly from the New Commonwealth. Acceptance for settlement does not mean automatic British citizenship. Naturalization only occurs when certain requirements have been fulfilled, together with a period of residence.

In 2002 the Labour government introduced more specific requirements for the attainment of British citizenship through naturalization. Applicants must now demonstrate knowledge about life in Britain, reach an acceptable level of English proficiency, attend a citizenship ceremony and swear a citizenship oath and pledge to the Queen and the UK. This move has been seen as an attempt to emphasize for immigrants the centrality of Britishness and British values.

However, it is important that emigration from Britain is also considered if the immigration/race debate is to be kept in perspective. Historically, there has usually been a balance of migration, with emigration cancelling out immigration in real terms. But there have been periods of high emigration. Groups left England and Scotland in the sixteenth and seventeenth centuries to become settlers in Ireland and North America. Millions in the nineteenth and twentieth centuries emigrated to Australia, New Zealand, South Africa, Canada, other colonies and the USA. Emigration meant that Britain had a net loss of people during the 1970s and 1980s. This trend has been reversed since the late 1990s and more immigrants have entered Britain than emigrants have left. For example, there was a net migration in 2004 of 223,000, a significant increase over previous years despite 360,000 people leaving Britain. In addition to New Commonwealth and African immigrants, more entrants have come from the Old Commonwealth and the EU than in previous years.

Ethnic minorities

The historical immigration picture has to be seen in the context of contemporary society and the ways in which the British population is described or describes itself. The 2001 census classified 92.1 per cent (54,154,000) of the British population as white and 7.9 per cent (4,635,000) as belonging to minority ethnic groups. 'Minority ethnic', in British statistics, excludes people from white minorities and therefore refers only to non-white groups. The census shows that this category has increased by 53 per cent since the previous census in 1991 and is shown in Table 3.2.

The non-white minority ethnic groups, some 50 per cent of whom were born in Britain, constitute a relatively small proportion of the total British population. Some 50 per cent of them live in London (as opposed to 10 per cent of the total white population) where they make up 29 per cent of all residents. By contrast, less than 4 per cent of non-white groups live in the north-east and south-west of England, where minority ethnic groups make up only 2 per cent of the population. Prior to the 2001 census, statistics for this category were estimates and the results were under-estimated. Respondents to the 2001 census were for the first time able to reply more accurately in reporting their ethnic identity. This resulted in the large percentage of those (15 per cent of all ethnic minorities) who described themselves as 'mixed'.

TABLE 3.2 Ethnic minorities in Britain 2001 (thousands)

	Minority ethnic population	Percentage of total national population	Percentage of ethnic population
Mixed	677	1.2	14.6
Asian or Asian British			
Indian	1,053	1.8	22.7
Pakistani	747	1.3	16.1
Bangladeshi	283	0.5	6.1
Other Asian	248	0.4	5.3
Black or Black British			
Black Caribbean	566	1.0	12.2
Black African	485	0.8	10.5
Black other	98	0.2	2.1
Chinese	247	0.4	5.3
Other	231	0.4	5.0
Total ethnic minorities	4,635	7.9	100

Source: adapted from Census, Office for National Statistics, 2001

However, there are also many other ethnic minority communities in Britain, which are usually classified as white. Immigration from the Republic of Ireland continues; the Irish have historically been a large immigrant group and at the 2001 census 691,000 people in Great Britain identified themselves as White Irish. Movement from Old Commonwealth countries (such as Australia, Canada and South Africa) has increased. There has been an increase in immigrants from European Union countries (such as Germany, Spain, Italy and France), who have the right to seek work and reside in Britain, together with newcomers from the USA and Middle East. At the 2001 census, 1.4 million people identified themselves as 'Other White'.

Population movements from 1900

Industrial areas with heavy population densities developed in the nineteenth century in Britain. But considerable internal population shifts occurred in the twentieth century, which were mainly due to economic and employment changes.

There was a drift of people away from industrial Tyneside and South Wales during the 1920s and 1930s trade depressions as coal production, steel manufacture and other heavy industries were badly affected. This movement increased during the second half of the twentieth century and since the 1950s there has been little population increase in industrial areas of the Central Lowlands of Scotland, Tyneside, Merseyside, West Yorkshire, South Wales and Northern Ireland, which have seen a rundown in traditional industries and rises in unemployment. Instead, people moved away from these regions to the English Midlands with their diversified industries and to London and south-east England where employment opportunities (despite fluctuations) and affluence were greater. Over the same period, there was also considerable immigration into Britain, followed at the end of the twentieth century by increases in the number of asylum seekers. Such groups have tended to settle in urban and inner-city areas throughout the country, although the heaviest concentration has been in London.

The reduction of the rural population and the expansion of urban centres continued into the twentieth century. But, by the middle of the century, there was a reverse movement of people away from the centres of big cities such as London, Manchester, Liverpool, Birmingham and Leeds. This was due to bomb damage during the Second World War, slum clearance and the need to use inner-city land for shops, offices, warehouses and transport utilities. So-called New Towns in rural areas and council housing estates outside the inner-cities were specifically created to accommodate the displaced population. Road systems were built with motorways and bypasses to avoid congested areas and rural locations around some cities were designated as Green Belts, in which no building was permitted. However, Green Belts are now being encroached upon for house construction and other purposes.

Many people choose to live some distance from their workplaces, often in a city's suburbs, neighbouring towns (commuter towns) or rural areas. This has contributed to the decline of inner-city populations and one British person in five now lives in the countryside with the rest in towns and cities. Densities are highest in Greater London and south-east England and lowest in rural regions of northern Scotland, the Lake District, Wales and Northern Ireland. The latest figures (2002) suggest an increasing movement of people to rural areas and population gains in Wales and Scotland, with losses in Northern Ireland and England (such as London).

In 2003 the population of the United Kingdom was 59,600,000, which consisted of England with 49,856,000, Wales with 2,938,000, Scotland with 5,100,000 and Northern Ireland with 1,700,000. These figures give a population density for the United Kingdom of some 600 persons per square mile (242 per sqkm), well above the European Union average. England has an average density of some 940 persons per square mile (381 per sqkm) and this average does not reveal the higher densities in areas of the country, such as London, the West Midlands, West Yorkshire, Greater Manchester, Merseyside, Tyne and Wear, Edinburgh and Cardiff. Within Europe, only the Netherlands has a higher population density than England.

The British population grew by only 0.3 per cent between 1971 and 1978, which gave it one of the lowest increases in Western Europe, and continued to decline in the 1980s. But numbers started to increase slightly from the late 1990s partly due to a greater number of births than deaths and partly to increasing immigration. The population is expected to be over 66 million by 2050, after which it will begin to fall again. The non-white ethnic minorities are growing 15 times faster than the white population and are also much younger. It is estimated that the counties of southern and central England will have the highest population growth up to 2011 and that the heaviest population losses will occur on Tyneside and Merseyside.

TABLE 3.3 Populations of major British cities (est. 2005)

Greater London	7,074,265	Liverpool	467,995
Birmingham	1,020,589	Edinburgh	448,850
Leeds	726,939	Manchester	430,818
Glasgow	616,430	Bristol	399,633
Sheffield	530,375	Cardiff	315,040
Bradford	483,422	Belfast	297,300

Source: City Mayors European Cities, 2005

REGINA LIBRARY
RIVIER COLLEGE
NASHUA, NH 03060

Attitudes to national, ethnic and local identities

Immigration to Britain has often been seen as a threat to a presumed British national identity with its presumed moral and social values. Yet the peoples of the British Isles have always been culturally and ethnically diverse and it is difficult to determine objectively what their general values might be. There are many differences between England, Wales, Scotland and Northern Ireland and distinctive ways of life and identities within each nation at national and local levels. The meaning of 'Britishness' as an umbrella term to describe all the people of the contemporary UK is consequently problematic. The latest approach (which in some ways echoes older concepts of a British national identity) is to see it in civic and cultural terms, which everyone in Britain can share, rather than with ethnic or racial characteristics. But despite the Labour government's plans to address Britishness in school citizenship classes and citizenship ceremonies, the term still lacks precise definition and can mean many things to many people.

The history of the British Isles before the eighteenth century is in fact not about a single British identity or political entity. It is about four different nations and their peoples, who have often been hostile towards one another. 'Britishness' since the 1707 union between England/Wales and Scotland had been largely identified with the representative and centralized values of state and civic institutions, such as monarchy, Parliament, law and Protestant churches, as well as the expanding empire and military successes. Concepts of Britishness became more widely used and accepted in the nineteenth century following the 1801 UK union and were tied to the Victorian monarchy, the empire and Britain's industrial and military position in the world. These elements have since weakened as Britain has declined as a global power; religious faith has decreased and respect for Parliament, the monarchy and the law has lessened.

Terms such as 'British' and 'Britain' can seem artificial to many people in the contemporary UK population, who have retained their own different ethnic and cultural identities. Additionally, foreigners often call all British people 'English' and have difficulties in appreciating the distinctions, or the irritation of the non-English population at such labelling. The Scots, Welsh and Northern Irish are regarded largely as Celtic peoples (with many admixtures over the centuries), while the English are simplistically considered to be Anglo-Saxon in origin. It has been recently argued that the 'British' today do not have a strong sense of a 'British' identity. In this view, there needs to be a rethinking of what it means to be British in the contexts of a multinational, multi-ethnic UK, a changing Europe and a globalized world.

There has obviously been ethnic and cultural assimilation in Britain over the centuries, which resulted from adaptation by immigrant groups to the host society and an internal migration between the four nations. Social, political and institutional standardization and a British awareness were established. However, the British identification was often equated with English norms because of England's historical role. Political unification occurred under the English Crown and UK state power was mainly concentrated in London and the English dominated numerically.

For these reasons, English nationalism has historically been the most potent of the four nationalisms and the English had no real problem with the dual national role. But some of them now seem unsure about their British identity in a devolved Britain and have emphasized their sense of Englishness. The Scots and Welsh have historically tended to be more aware of the difference between their nationalism and Britishness; resent the English dominance; see themselves as different from the English; and regard their cultural feelings as crucial. Their sense of identity is conditioned by the tension between their distinctive histories and a centralized London government.

National identity was historically largely cultural in Wales and more politicized in Scotland. Nevertheless, the British political union was generally accepted, except for nationalists in Ireland. This resulted in the partition of the island in 1921. Today, the union is not acceptable to some people in the minority Catholic population of Northern Ireland. Political nationalism increased in the 1960s and 1970s in Scotland and to some extent in Wales. Following the achievement of a degree of devolved self-government in 1998–99, calls for full independence in these two nations are not strong, except from the Scottish National Party (SNP) and (arguably) the Welsh National Party (Plaid Cymru). It also seems that Scottish, Welsh and Northern Irish devolution has sparked a resurgence in English nationalism.

The Welsh, English and Scots seemed increasingly to be defining themselves more in terms of their individual nationalities, rather than as British. A *Sunday Times* poll in 2000 found that schoolchildren saw themselves as English (66 per cent), Scottish (82) or Welsh (79). Some 84 per cent of English children regarded England as their home (rather than Britain) and 75 per cent felt that their nationality was important to them. But, at the same time, there was little interest in the creation of regional English assemblies and little desire for a break-up of the United Kingdom.

There are also differences at regional and local levels within the four nations themselves. Since the English, for example, are historically an ethnically mixed people, their customs, accents and behaviour vary considerably and some local identifications may be strong. Regions like the north-east have reacted against London influences and want some form of decentralized political autonomy (although the north-east actually voted against regional government in a 2004 referendum). The Cornish see themselves as a distinctive cultural element in English society and have an affinity with Celtic and similar ethnic groups in Britain and Europe. The northern English regard themselves as superior to the southern English, and vice versa. On a smaller level, English county and city loyalties are still maintained and are shown in sports, politics, food habits, competitions, cultural activities or a specific way of life.

In Wales, there are cultural and political differences between the industrial south (which tends to support the Labour Party) and the rest of the mainly rural country: between Welsh-speaking Wales in the north-west and centre (which supports Plaid Cymru) and English-influenced Wales in the east and south-west (where the Conservative Party has some support); between some of the ancient Welsh counties; and between the cities of Cardiff and Swansea.

Yet Welsh people generally are very conscious of their differences from the English, despite the fact that many Welsh people have mixed English-Welsh ancestry. Their national and cultural identity is grounded in their history; literature; the Welsh language (actively spoken by 19 per cent of the population); sport (such as rugby football); and festivals like the National Eisteddfod (with its Welsh poetry competitions, dancing and music). It is also echoed in close-knit industrial and agricultural communities and in a tradition of social, political and religious dissent from English norms. Today, many Welsh people still feel that they are struggling for their national identity against political power in London and the erosion of their culture and language by English institutions and the English language. A limited form of devolution has helped to alleviate these feelings and increase Welsh identity.

Similarly, Scots generally unite in defence of their national identity and distinctiveness because of historical reactions to the English. They are conscious of their traditions, which are reflected in cultural festivals and different legal, religious and educational systems. There has been resentment against the centralization of political power in London and alleged economic neglect of Scotland (although the UK government provides greater economic subsidies per head of population to Scotland, Wales and Northern Ireland than England). Devolved government in Edinburgh has removed some of these objections and focussed on Scottish identity.

But Scots are divided by three languages (Gaelic, Scots and English with the former being spoken by 1.5 per cent of the Scottish population or 70,000 people), different religions, prejudices and regionalisms. Cultural differences separate Lowlanders and Highlanders; allegiance to ancient Scottish counties is still relatively strong: and rivalries exist between the two major cities of Edinburgh and Glasgow.

In Northern Ireland, the social, cultural and political differences between Roman Catholics and Protestants have long been evident and today are often reflected in geographical ghettos. Groups in both communities feel frustration with the English and hostility towards the British government in London. But the Protestant Unionists are loyal to the Crown; regard themselves as British; and wish to continue the union with Britain. Many Catholic Nationalists feel Irish and would prefer to be united with the Republic of Ireland. The attempt at devolution in Northern Ireland has not succeeded in eradicating deep-seated differences between the two communities.

These features suggest that the contemporary British are a very diverse people with varying identities. To complicate the picture even further, there are ethnic minorities (both white and non-white) within Britain who may use dual or multiple identities and embrace different loyalties. Many call themselves British or more specifically English, Welsh, Irish or Scottish, while still identifying with their countries of origin or descent. Sometimes they employ their ethnic ties to define themselves as Afro-Caribbean, Black British or British Indians. They may also embrace religious identities, such as British Muslims, British Hindus or British Jews.

There is disagreement about whether multiple identity among ethnic minorities (with individuals differing on how they label themselves) is achievable or desirable. Some critics query whether it is possible in fact for an ethnic minority person (whether by birth abroad or by descent in Britain) to feel British. Others argue that British and ethnic minority allegiances can be unproblematically and tolerantly combined, so that for example one can be both British and Pakistani. But a *Sunday Times* survey in November 2001 suggested that 68 per cent of Muslims considered that being Muslim was more essential than being British (14 per cent). Yet a YouGov poll for *The Daily Telegraph* on 23 July 2005 following bomb attacks in London reported that 77 per cent of Muslim respondents replied that the bombings were not justified, 48 per cent felt very loyal to Britain and 33 per cent felt fairly loyal, while 10 per cent had no opinion.

These findings should be seen in the context of statistics from the Office of National Statistics in 2004 which suggested that a majority of people from non-white ethnic minorities are in fact asserting their Britishness. Feelings about a British identity are increasingly influenced by cultural factors (and civic values) rather than simply ethnic origins and are strongest (87 per cent) among people of mixed race. Some 81 per cent of 'black other', 80 per cent of black Caribbeans and 75 per cent of Indian, Pakistani and Bangladeshi groups have the same response. Such feelings of Britishness are particularly strong among the young and among groups in which the majority of people were born in Britain.

An interesting further result from these statistics is that almost 98 per cent of white British people (which includes English, Scottish, Welsh and Northern Irish) feel British. This high percentage could indicate that while they may have a primary allegiance to their Englishness or Scottishness for example they, like the non-white minorities, are responding to Britishness in cultural or civic terms rather than simply ethnic origins. Britishness, in this view, can be acquired irrespective of where one is born or one's descent patterns. The problem lies in defining more precisely what these cultural or civic terms actually are. They might exist in a blending of multi-ethnic realities and a shared British cultural framework arising out of both what are assumed to be traditional British values and new conditionings.

Foreigners often have either specific notions of what they think the British are like or, in desperation, seek a unified picture of national character, often based upon stereotypes, quaint traditions or tourist views of Britain. The emphasis in Britain today, however, seems to be a movement away from such images and a focus on positive cultural signs rooted in a multi-ethnic society. A British Council/MORI poll in 1999 found that overseas respondents felt that Britain is a 'multicultural' society though opinion was divided as to whether or not it is also racially tolerant. The poll found that the countries that are least willing to believe that UK society is racially tolerant are those that are least aware of its 'multicultural' composition.

But 'multiculturalism' is a strongly debated issue in Britain. Most would agree that as an adjective it accurately and factually describes the country's multi-ethnic population. However, some critics and politicians from the 1970s onwards adopted it as a political agenda and favoured the separate development of cultural groups and the preservation of their ethnic identities. Others, including non-white groups, deny the value of such a position, seeing it as 'ethnic tribalism', and argue for assimilation or integration under a British identity. The latter implies an acceptance of basic common values, including those represented by civic, social and political structures, which have primacy over individual cultural identities.

These concerns are central to attempts to define 'Britishness'. Surveys (like the Springpoint *I? UK – Voices of Our Times*, 1999) had suggested that there is a popular movement away from the allegedly negative, imperial and English-dominated historical implications of Britishness to a more positive, value-based, inclusive image with which the four nations and their populations can feel comfortable. A Britishness which encompasses opportunity, respect, tolerance, supportiveness, progress and decency is supposedly attractive to the Celtic nations and ethnic minorities.

But these values have to be realized within defining institutional (or even state) structures. Since there has never been a homogeneous British population, British nationhood has been progressively created by settlers, invaders and immigrants who have brought their individual contributions to a British identity. Critics argue that this experience and a common citizenship allows the British to define Britishness in civic, rather than racial, terms. It does not describe an ethnic identity, exists irrespective of birthplace and is dependent on one's position as a citizen of Britain.

In this view, the success of any country depends on full integration, not multiculturalism. The term 'British' has evolved into one embracing many different types of people and cultures. Britishness becomes a contemporary set of shared values, beliefs, opinions and identities which encompass a way of life and state legislation intended to promote inclusiveness. Rather than being divisive, critics maintain that it is the most inclusive and non-discriminatory term to describe the peoples who comprise the United Kingdom.

Exercises

Explain and examine the following terms:

nomads	bypass	Anglo-Saxon	industrialization
Neolithic	East End	Hansa	National Front
density	Celtic	devolution	Hastings
Merseyside	Domesday Book	immigrant	naturalization
racism	multiculturalism	Iberian	discrimination
census	emigration	Huguenots	Green Belt

Write short essays on the following topics:

1 Describe in outline the history of settlement and immigration in Britain.

2 Examine the changing patterns of population distribution in Britain.

3 Is it correct to describe contemporary Britain as a 'multi-ethnic' and 'multinational' society? If so, why?

4 Critically examine the attempts to define 'Britishness'.

Further reading

1 Alibhai-Brown, Y. (2001) *Who Do We Think We Are? Imagining the New Britain* London: Allen Lane

2 Bryant, C.G.A. (2006) *The Nations of Britain* Oxford: Oxford University Press

3 Colley, L. (1996) *Britons: Forging the Nation 1707–1837* London: Vintage

4 Colls, R. (2002) *Identity of England* Oxford: Oxford University Press

5 Davies, N. (2000) *The Isles: A History* London: Macmillan

6 Donnell A. (2001) *Companion to Contemporary Black British Culture* London: Routledge

7 Grant, A. and Stringer, K.J. (eds) (1995) *Uniting the Kingdom? – The Making of British History* London: Routledge

8 Harvie, C. (1998) *Scotland and Nationalism: Scottish Society and Politics, 1707 to the Present* London: Routledge

9 McKay, S. (2000) *Northern Protestants: An Unsettled People* Belfast: Blackstaff Press

10 Nairn, T. (2000) *After Britain* London: Granta Books

11 O'Connor, F. (1993) *In Search of a State: Catholics in Northern Ireland* Belfast: Blackstaff Press

12 Owusa, K. (1999) *Black British Culture and Society* London: Routledge

13 Paxman, J. (2000) *The English: A Portrait of a People* London: Penguin Books

14 Phillips, M. and Phillips, T. (1999) *Windrush: The Irresistible Rise of Multi-racial Britain* London: HarperCollins

15 Solomos, J. (2003) *Race and Racism in Britain* London: Palgrave Macmillan

16 Storry, M. and Childs, P. (eds) (2002) *British Cultural Identities* London: Routledge
17 Ward, P. (2004) *Britishness since 1870* London: Routledge
18 Winder, R. (2005) *Bloody Foreigners: The Story of Immigration to Britain* London: Abacus

Websites

Campaign for the English Regions: http://www.cfer.org.uk
Devolution: http://www.britishcouncil.org/devolution/index.htm
Looking into England: www.britishcouncil.org/studies/english
British Studies Now: www.britishcouncil.org/studies/bsn.htm
Scotland Office: www.scottishsecretary.gov.uk
Wales Office: www.walesoffice.gov.uk
Northern Ireland Office: www.nio.gov.uk

Chapter 4

Politics and government

- Political history
- The British governmental and political framework
- Constitution and monarchy
- UK Parliament: role, legislation and elections
- The party political system
- The UK government
- UK parliamentary control of government
- Attitudes to politics
- *Exercises*
- *Further reading*
- *Websites*

Political history in Britain and Ireland over the past 800 years illustrates the growth of what is now the United Kingdom (UK) state and evolutionary changes in its composition. The weakening of non-democratic monarchical and aristocratic power in England, Scotland, Wales and Ireland led eventually to political and legislative authority being centralized in London in a UK parliament, a UK government and a powerful UK Prime Minister. Changing social conditions resulted in a growth of political parties, the extension of the vote to all adults, the development of local government and a twentieth century devolution (transfer) of some political power to Wales, Scotland and Northern Ireland. These historical processes were accompanied by political, social and religious conflicts as well as by constitutional compromise.

The political structures are still vigorously debated and there is considerable public disillusionment with the political process and politicians. The UK government in London is accused of being too secretive, too centralized, too isolated, too media-reactive, too controlling and insufficiently responsive to the needs of the diverse peoples of the United Kingdom. It is argued that the UK Parliament has lost control over the UK government; that political power has bypassed Parliament and shifted to a presidential Prime Minister with a prime ministerial office in Downing Street; that unelected appointed bodies (such as quangos or quasi-autonomous non-governmental organizations) and political advisers have become too influential; that the Civil Service has been politicized and lost its independence; that there are serious weaknesses at devolved and local governmental levels; and that the British political system must be reformed in order to make it more efficient, accountable and adaptable to modern requirements.

The Labour government from 1997 embarked on a process of so-called 'modernization' in constitutional and political areas, such as devolution, reform of the House of Lords (including the proposed creation of a Supreme Court separate from the Lords) and the introduction of human rights and freedom of information legislation. But these developments have been criticized for creating more problems than they have solved. It is felt that the traditional strengths and structures of British democracy must be retained, where valid, rather than being replaced by inadequate alternatives. In this view, the British constitution and separation of powers must be revitalized. Otherwise they could be vulnerable to the arrogance of executive power.

Political history

Early political history in the islands is the story of four geographical areas (now England, Wales, Scotland and Northern Ireland) and their turbulent struggles for independent nationhood. But an English political and military expansionism over the centuries conditioned the development of the other three nations. Ireland was invaded by England in the twelfth century; England and Wales were united by the 1536–42 Acts of Union; the thrones of England and Scotland were dynastically amalgamated in 1603; England/Wales and Scotland were united as Great Britain by the 1707 Acts of Union; the 1801 Act of Union joined Great Britain and Ireland as the United Kingdom; and southern Ireland (later known as the Republic of Ireland) became independent in 1921, leaving Northern Ireland in the UK. In this process, English governmental systems were generally adopted in the modern period for all of the UK until Scotland, Wales and Northern Ireland regained some of their former political identities under devolution in 1998–9.

Decline of the monarchy and the rise of Parliament

Early monarchs or political leaders in the four nations had considerable power, but generally accepted advice and feudal limitations on their authority. However, later English kings, such as King John (1199–1216), ignored these restraints and powerful French-Norman barons opposed John's dictatorial rule by forcing him to sign Magna Carta in 1215. This document protected the aristocracy rather than the ordinary citizen. It was later regarded as a cornerstone of British (not merely English) liberties: restricted the monarch's powers; forced him or her to take advice; increased aristocratic influence; and stipulated that citizens should not be imprisoned without trial.

Such inroads into royal power encouraged embryonic parliamentary structures. An English Council was formed in 1258 by disaffected nobles under Simon de Montfort, who in 1264 summoned a broader Parliament. These aristocratic and part-time initiatives were followed in 1275 by the Model Parliament of Edward I (1272–1307), which was the first representative English Parliament. Its two Houses (as now) consisted of the Lords/Bishops and the Commons (male commoners). An independent Scottish Parliament was first created in 1326 and Ireland had a similarly old Parliament, dating from medieval times.

However, the English Parliament was too large to rule the country effectively. A small Privy Council (royal government outside Parliament) comprising the monarch and court advisers, developed. It continued as a powerful influence until it lost authority to increasingly strong parliamentary structures in the late eighteenth and early nineteenth centuries.

But, although the English Parliament had limited powers against the monarch, there was a return to royal dominance in Tudor England (1485–1603). The nobility had been weakened by wars and internal conflicts (like the Wars of the Roses between Yorkists and Lancastrians). Monarchs controlled Parliament and summoned it only when they needed to raise money. Tudor monarchs (of Welsh ancestry) united England and Wales administratively, politically and legally in the sixteenth century. They also intervened in Ireland, with frequent campaigns against Irish insurgents.

Following the Tudors, James VI of Scotland became James I of England in 1603, formed a Stuart dynasty and considered himself to be king of Great Britain. But the two countries were not closely joined politically or culturally. However, the English Parliament now showed more resistance to royal rule by using its weapon of financial control. It refused royal requests for money and later forced the Stuart Charles I to sign the Petition of Rights in 1628, which prevented him from raising taxes without Parliament's consent. Charles ignored these political developments and then failed in his attempt to arrest parliamentary leaders in the House of Commons. The monarch was in future banned from the Commons.

Charles's rejection of parliamentary ideals and belief in his right to rule without opposition provoked anger against the Crown and a Civil War broke out in 1642. The Protestant Parliamentarians under Oliver Cromwell won the military struggle against the Catholic Royalists. Charles was beheaded in 1649; the monarchy was abolished; Britain was ruled as a Protectorate by Cromwell and his son Richard (1653–60); and Parliament comprised only the House of Commons. Cromwell also asserted the Protestant and parliamentary cause in Scotland and Ireland, which provoked lasting hatred in these countries.

Cromwell's Protectorate became unpopular and most people wanted the restoration of the monarchy. The two Houses of Parliament were re-established and in 1660 they restored the Stuart Charles II to the throne. Initially Charles cooperated with Parliament, but his financial needs, belief in royal authority and support of Catholicism lost him popular and parliamentary backing. Parliament ended his expensive wars and imposed further reforms.

The growth of political parties and constitutional structures

The growing power of the English Parliament against the monarch in the seventeenth century saw the development of more organized political parties in Parliament. These derived partly from the religious and ideological conflicts of the Civil War. Two groups (Whigs and Tories) became dominant. This is a characteristic feature of British two-party politics, in which political power generally shifts between two main parties. The Whigs were mainly Cromwellian Protestants and gentry, who did not accept the Catholic James II as successor to Charles II and wanted religious freedom for all Protestants. The Tories generally supported royalist beliefs, and helped Charles II to secure James's right to succeed him.

But James's attempt to rule without Parliament and his ignoring of its laws caused a further reduction in royal influence. His manipulations forced the Tories to join the Whigs in inviting the Dutch Protestant William of Orange to intervene. William arrived in England in 1688. James fled to France and William succeeded to the throne as England's first constitutional monarch. Since no force was involved, this event is called the Bloodless or Glorious Revolution. Royal powers were further restricted under the Declaration of Rights (1689), which strengthened Parliament. Future monarchs could not reign or act without Parliament's consent and the Act of Settlement (1701) specified that monarchs must be Protestant.

The Glorious Revolution affected the constitution and politics. It effectively created a division of powers between an executive branch (the monarch and Privy Council); a parliamentary legislative branch (the House of Commons, the House of Lords and the monarch); and the judiciary (judges independent of monarch and Parliament). Acts of Union joining England/Wales and Scotland followed in 1707. Scotland lost its Parliament and power was centralized in the London Parliament.

Parliamentary influence grew in the early eighteenth century, because the Hanoverian George I lacked interest in British politics. He distrusted the Tories with their Catholic sympathies and appointed Whigs like Robert Walpole to his

PLATE 4.1 Sir Robert Walpole (1676–1745), first Lord of the Treasury and Chancellor of the Exchequer by Michael Dahl (1656–1743).
Whig politician who strengthened parliamentary authority and has been called Britain's first prime minister.
(*©Wakefield Museums and Galleries, West Yorkshire/Bridgeman*)

Privy Council. Walpole became Chief Minister in 1721 and led the Whig majority in the House of Commons, which comprised land and property owners. Walpole increased the parliamentary role and he has been called Britain's first Prime Minister.

But parliamentary authority was not absolute and later monarchs tried to restore royal power. However, George III lost much of his standing after the loss of the American colonies (1775–83). He was obliged to appoint William Pitt the Younger as his Tory Chief Minister and it was under Pitt that the office of Prime Minister really developed. Meanwhile, Ireland's Parliament achieved legislative independence in 1782. But it represented only the privileged Anglo-Irish minority and the Roman Catholic majority was excluded. In 1801, Ireland was united with Great Britain by the Act of Union to form the UK. The Irish Parliament was abolished and Irish members sat in both Houses of the London Parliament.

PLATE 4.2 George III (1738–1820) by Allan Ramsay (1713–84).
King of Great Britain and Ireland 1760–1820. Remembered for his bouts of insanity, attempts to govern personally, and in whose reign the American colonies were lost. His reign also coincided with a great expansion of empire and trade, the beginnings of the industrial revolution and a strengthening creative and artistic period.
(©*Wallace Collection, London UK/Bridgeman*)

The expansion of voting rights

Although parliamentary control continued to grow in the late eighteenth and early nineteenth centuries, there was still no widespread democracy in Britain. Political authority was in the hands of landowners, merchants and aristocrats in Parliament and most people did not possess the vote. Bribery and corruption were common, with the buying of those votes which did exist and the giving away or sale of public offices.

The Tories were against electoral reform, as were the Whigs initially. But the country was rapidly increasing its population and developing industrially and economically. Pressures for political reform became irresistible. The Whigs reformed the parliamentary system and extended voting rights to the growing middle class in the First Reform Act of 1832 so that some 50 per cent of the population had the vote. Later Reform Acts in 1867 and 1884 gave the vote to men with property and a certain income. Working-class males were only gradually given the vote in the late-nineteenth century and gained some limited representation in Parliament. All males over twenty-one and certain limited categories of women over thirty received the vote in 1918. Eventually in 1928 all males and females aged twenty-one possessed the vote (with some exceptions) and the age limit was further reduced to eighteen in 1969.

Prior to 1928, most wives and their property had been the legal possessions of their husbands. The traditional role of women of all classes had been confined to that of mother in the home, although some (married and single) found employment in home industries and factories or as domestic servants, teachers and governesses.

Women's social and political position became marginally better towards the end of the nineteenth century. Elementary education was established and a few institutions of higher education began to admit women in restricted numbers. Some women's organizations had been founded in the mid-nineteenth century to press for greater political, employment and social rights. But the most famous suffrage movement was that of the Pankhursts in 1903. Their Women's Social and Political Union campaigned for votes for women and an increased female role in society. However, it is argued that a substantial change in women's status in the mid-twentieth century occurred because of a recognition of the essential work that they performed during two World Wars.

The growth of governmental structures

The elements of modern British government developed somewhat haphazardly in the eighteenth and nineteenth centuries. Government ministers were generally members of the House of Commons and gradually became responsible to the Commons rather than the monarch. They shared a collective responsibility for the policies and acts of government, and had an individual responsibility to Parliament for their own ministries. The prime ministership developed from the monarch's Chief Minister to 'first among equals' and finally the leadership of all ministers. The central force of government became the parliamentary Cabinet of senior ministers, which grew out of the Privy Council. The government was formed from the majority party in the House of Commons. The largest minority party became the Official Opposition, which attempted through its policies to become the next government chosen by the people.

Historically, the elected House of Commons gained political power from the unelected monarch and House of Lords and became the main element in Parliament. Subsequent reforms of the Lords (the Parliament Acts of 1911 and 1949) restricted their political authority. Later Acts created non-hereditary titles (life peers), in addition to the existing hereditary peerages. The House lost most of its hereditary members in 2000 (92), and now has only delaying and amending power over parliamentary legislation and cannot interfere with financial bills.

The nineteenth century also saw the growth of more organized political parties. These were conditioned by changing social and economic factors and reflected the modern struggle between opposing ideologies. The Tories became known as the Conservatives in the early 1830s. They believed in established values and the preservation of traditions; supported business and commerce; had strong links with the Church of England and the professions; and were opposed to radical ideas.

The Whigs, however, were becoming a progressive force and wanted social reform and economic freedom without government restrictions. They developed into the Liberal Party, which promoted enlightened policies in the late nineteenth and early twentieth centuries. But the party declined from 1918 after the emergence of the new Labour Party. Following an alliance with the now-defunct Social Democratic Party in the 1980s, it merged and became the Liberal Democrats. It is the third-largest party in UK politics but lacks substantial representation in the House of Commons.

The Labour Party, created in its present form in 1906, became the main opposition party to the Conservatives after the Liberals' decline and continued the traditional two-party system in British politics. It was supported by the trade unions, the working class and some middle-class voters. The first Labour government was formed in 1924 under Ramsey MacDonald. But it only achieved majority power in 1945 under Clement Attlee, when it embarked on radical programmes of social and economic reform, which laid the foundations for a welfare and nationalized state.

The British governmental and political framework

Contemporary politics in Britain operate on UK, devolved, local government and European Union (EU) levels (see Figure 4.1). The UK Parliament and government

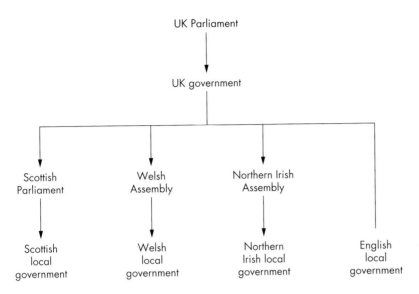

FIGURE 4.1 The British governmental and political framework

in London govern the UK as a whole in many areas. A Parliament in Scotland, Assemblies in Wales and Northern Ireland and a London Authority have varying degrees of devolved self-government (from the UK Parliament) and handle their own devolved powers. Local government throughout Britain organizes society at local levels. A further tier of government is the European Union (EU) which increasingly affects British life and political policies. These structures mean that Britain today has a 'multi-level governance' model with the various tiers influencing each other.

Local government

Britain has had a local government system in one form or another for centuries. It began with the Anglo-Saxon division of England into large counties and small parishes, which were organized by the monarch's local representatives.

Local government has grown through the centuries, particularly in the nineteenth century. It now provides local services throughout the UK, such as education, health, fire services, transport, social services, sanitation and housing, through elected councils. In England, it is administered through professional staff and an elected non-professional two-tier system of county and district councils, with some single-tier (unitary) authorities. Scotland and Wales have 32 and 22 unitary authorities respectively, while Northern Ireland has 26 district councils.

Although people count on the services of local government, the system at present is languishing, is subjected to centralized control and funding from the London government and no longer itself provides the full range of traditional local services. Interest in local government is low and opinion polls suggest that dissatisfaction with local councils has increased. Critics argue for a more rigorous and independently financed localism accountable to local interests and free from central government interference and control.

Devolution

Devolution (self-government or transfer of some powers from the Westminster Parliament) was first adopted in Ireland. Growing nationalist feelings in the nineteenth century led to calls for Home Rule for Ireland with its own Parliament in Dublin. But early attempts failed. Hostilities continued in the twentieth century until Ireland was partitioned in 1921–2 into the Irish Free State (later the Republic of Ireland) with its own Parliament and Northern Ireland. The latter had a devolved Parliament (1921–72), but remained part of the UK.

Political and cultural nationalism also grew in Wales and Scotland from the 1960s. After failed attempts to give them devolved political power, the Labour government created in 1999 (after referendums) an elected Parliament with legislative and tax-varying powers in Scotland and a non-legislative, non-tax-raising elected Assembly in Wales. Northern Ireland achieved an elected Assembly in 1998, which has some legislative and executive authority, except for reserved UK powers over policing, security matters, prisons and criminal justice.

Devolution is a tier of decentralized government. It allows these countries (with their Executives and First Ministers) to decide more of their own affairs, in devolved matters such as education, health, transport, environment, home affairs and local government. The Westminster Parliament still has reserved powers over UK matters such as defence, foreign affairs, social security, taxation, broad economic policy and immigration. Roles and procedures (except for elections) in local and devolved structures are generally similar to those at the UK level.

The devolution experiment had a shaky start. The Welsh Assembly in practice lacks extensive powers, the London Parliament provides its primary legislation and it had initial political problems. The Northern Irish Assembly was suspended in 2000, 2001 and 2004 largely because of the failure of the IRA to disarm until 2005, and the province is still under direct rule from London. The Scottish Parliament initially attracted criticism, being seen as parochial, ineffective and controlled by London, although it is now becoming more independent. Devolution still needs to settle down and justify its existence. Critics argue that the devolved structures are inadequate and that the Labour government has not thought through the implications of its policies, particularly in terms of the anomalous position of England.

England has no intermediate devolved tier. It has a network of unelected, appointed Regional Development Agencies (RDAs), now sometimes known as Regional Assemblies or Councils, which implement UK government politico-economic programmes in the regions. But these areas do not provide elected devolved government. It was intended that they could form the basis for a future regional devolution of power from Westminster, analogous to the devolved structures in Scotland, Wales and Northern Ireland. But a referendum of the people in north-east England in 2004 failed to produce support for the policy.

Devolution does not mean independence or separation for Scotland, Wales and Northern Ireland nor a British federal system, although it is argued that a form of 'quasi-federalism' has been created. The Labour government says that devolution will strengthen the UK and that legal sovereignty still rests with the UK Parliament at Westminster. In this sense, Britain has a unitary political system and remains a union of England, Scotland, Wales and Northern Ireland (the United Kingdom).

There was an initial fear that devolution would lead to independence for Scotland and Wales and the breakup of the UK. But *British Social Attitudes* (2000–1) reported that while some English thought of themselves as strongly British, many have become more aware of being English in response to devolution. They do not view devolution as a threat to the union and have adapted to the new situation.

Since July 2000 London has been run by an elected Greater London Authority with its elected mayor and assembly. But the London mayor does not have the same executive and financial authority of American city mayors, on which the reform was supposed to be based. It was hoped that similar mayors

PLATE 4.3 Ken Livingstone, Mayor of London at an anti-terror briefing, 8 July 2005. First elected Mayor of the new devolved Greater London Authority 2000, reelected 2004.

(*Rukhsana Hamid/Rex Features*)

would be elected in other British cities, in an attempt to increase devolved powers, but the experiment has not proved to be attractive in most areas.

Constitution and monarchy

The constitution

The constitutional system has experienced relatively few major upheavals since 1688 and existing principles have been pragmatically adapted to new conditions. However, some significant changes have occurred over the years such as entry to the EU in 1973 and devolution in 1998–9, which have had constitutional implications.

The powers of the state in many countries are defined and laid down in a written document (or constitution) and are often classified as executive, legislative and judicial. These powers relate to distinctive institutions and are kept separate. In Britain there is no clear separation of powers, particularly between the executive and the legislature and even the definition of the executive is problematic.

Britain is sometimes described as a constitutional monarchy, where the monarch reigns as head of state without executive powers under constitutional limitations. Britain is also referred to, more commonly, as a parliamentary system, where the Westminster Parliament (consisting of the House of Commons, the House of Lords and formally the monarch) in London is the legislature and possesses supreme power to make laws in UK matters.

The executive UK government (sitting mainly in the House of Commons) governs by passing its policies (many of which are applicable to most of Britain) through Parliament as Acts of Parliament and operates through ministries or departments headed by Ministers or Secretaries of State.

The judicial branch is independent of the legislative and executive branches of government. The judges (judiciary) of the higher courts determine the law and interpret Acts of Parliament.

These branches, although distinguishable from each other, are not entirely separate. For example, the monarch is formally head of the executive, the legislature and the judiciary. A Member of Parliament (MP) in the House of Commons and a peer of the House of Lords may both be in the government of the day. A Law Lord in the House of Lords also serves that House as the highest appeal court.

All the branches are supposed to operate according to the British constitution. But Britain has no written constitution contained in one document. Instead, the constitution consists of distinctive elements, most of which are in written form. These are statute law (Acts of Parliament); common law or judge-made law; conventions (principles and practices of government which are not legally binding but have the force of law); some ancient documents like Magna Carta; and EU law.

The constitutional elements are said to be flexible enough to respond quickly to new conditions. UK law and institutions can be created or changed by the Westminster Parliament through Acts of Parliament. The common or judge-made law can be extended by the judiciary and conventions can be altered, formed or abolished by general agreement.

In constitutional theory, the British people, although historically subjects of the Crown, have political sovereignty to choose the UK government, while Parliament, consisting partly of elected representatives in the Commons, has legal supremacy to make laws and is the focus of UK sovereignty. But challenges to traditional notions of parliamentary sovereignty have arisen and the Westminster Parliament is no longer the sole legislative body in Britain. British membership of the European Union means that EU law is now superior to British national law in many areas and British courts must give it precedence in cases of conflict between the two systems. EU law is directly applicable in Britain and coexists with Acts of Parliament as part of the British constitution. The EU's Council of Ministers consists of heads of government and ministers from the member states and is the EU's supreme law-making or law-initiating body. Some 60 per cent of all Britain's laws are now EU law.

Since devolution, Parliament can still legislate for the UK as a whole and for any parts of it separately. But it has undertaken not to legislate on devolved matters without the agreement of the devolved Parliament and Assemblies. The Scottish Parliament can thus legislate on devolved matters in Scotland in which Westminster has no say. Conflicts between the two Parliaments will be resolved by the Judicial Committee of the Privy Council. The Welsh Assembly has no

PLATE 4.4 The Scottish Parliament, Edinburgh, July 2005.
Scotland gained its own Parliament after devolution in 1999. The Parliament building is a new construction completed in 2005.
(*David Cairns/Rex Features*)

PLATE 4.5 The Welsh Assembly, Cardiff, 1999.
After devolution in 1999, Wales gained its own Assembly.
(*Peter Lawson/Rex Features*)

primary legislative powers, although the Northern Irish Assembly can legislate in devolved matters. Ultimately, however, the UK Parliament still has the legal right to abolish the Scottish Parliament, the Welsh and Northern Irish Assemblies and to withdraw from the EU.

Criticisms of the constitutional system

The British system was admired in the past. It combined stability and adaptability with a balance of authority and toleration. But it has often been criticized. UK governments are able to pass their policies through Parliament because of big majorities in the Commons. This means that there are few effective parliamentary restraints upon a strong government. There has also been concern at the absence of constitutional safeguards for citizens against state power, since historically there have been few legal definitions of civil liberties or human rights in Britain.

These features are seen as potentially dangerous, particularly when UK governments and administrative bodies are arguably too centralized and secretive. It is maintained that Britain is controlled by small groups or bodies which may be unelected and are appointed by government. There have been campaigns for more open government and more effective protection of individual liberties in the forms of a written constitution (to define and limit the powers of Parliament and government); greater judicial scrutiny of parliamentary legislation; a Freedom of

PLATE 4.6 Prime Minister Tony Blair meets with 'political cabinet' in the Cabinet Room, 10 Downing Street, 31 March 2005.
A special meeting (chaired by Tony Blair – third left) to agree the 2005 election date and party manifesto.
(*Reuters/TV Grab*)

Information Act (to allow the public to examine official documents held for example by Whitehall departments, local councils, the NHS, schools and universities); the creation of a Supreme Court to preserve the independence of the judiciary from Parliament; and incorporation of the European Convention on Human Rights into domestic law (enabling British citizens to pursue cases in Britain instead of going to the European Court of Human Rights).

In response to these concerns, the Labour government created a Freedom of Information Act in 2000 and incorporated the European Convention into British law by the creation of a Human Rights Act, 1998. Both developments could potentially improve the civil and constitutional rights of British people.

However, the Freedom of Information Act is criticized as lacking teeth and it can be manipulated by the authorities concerned. The Human Rights Act is having a controversial effect on many levels. It allows the courts to rule in cases of alleged breaches of fundamental human rights which are brought to them. While they cannot directly overrule an Act of Parliament they can declare that such an Act is in breach of the Human Rights legislation. In effect, this could force a government to change its legislation and is seen as an encroachment upon parliamentary sovereignty. The courts and the judges have also arguably achieved greater influence by their rulings under the Human Rights Act. The implications of the Act have yet to be fully worked out, but it is argued that abuse of the process and frivolous claims do occur.

Critics feel that the British parliamentary system is out of date, consider that a written constitution is needed to control executive and administrative bodies and claim that the UK political system no longer works satisfactorily. They maintain that its traditional bases are inadequate for the organization of a complex society. It is felt that political policies have become too conditioned by party politics at the expense of consensus; that government is too removed from popular and regional concerns and does not reflect contemporary diversity; that it operates on too many unaccountable levels; that national policies lack a democratic and representative basis; and that the constitution can be abused by the executive. However, changes have been made to the apparatus, indicating that evolutionary principles may be successfully adapted to new demands and conditions.

The monarchy

The correct constitutional title of the UK Parliament is the 'Queen-in-Parliament'. This means that state and government business is carried out in the name of the monarch by the politicians and officials of the system. But the Crown is only sovereign by the will of Parliament and acceptance by the people.

The monarchy is the oldest secular institution in Britain and there is hereditary succession to the throne, but only for Protestants. The eldest son of a monarch currently has priority over older daughters. The monarchy's continuity has been interrupted only by Cromwellian rule (1653–60), although there have been different dynasties such as the Tudors, Stuarts and Hanoverians.

Royal executive power has disappeared. But the monarch still has formal constitutional roles and is head of state, head of the executive, judiciary and legislature, 'supreme governor' of the Church of England and commander-in-chief of the armed forces. Government ministers and officials are the monarch's servants and many public office-holders swear allegiance to the Crown. The monarchy is thus a permanent fixture in the British system, unlike temporary politicians. It still has a practical and constitutional role to play in the operation of government.

The monarch is expected to be politically neutral; is supposed to reign but not rule; and cannot make laws, impose taxes, spend public money or act unilaterally. The monarch acts only on the advice of political ministers, which cannot be ignored, and contemporary Britain is therefore governed by Her Majesty's Government in the name of the Queen. She has a similar role in the devolved governments.

The monarch performs important duties such as the opening and dissolving of the UK Parliament; giving the Royal Assent (or signature) to bills which have been passed by both Houses of Parliament; appointing government ministers and public figures; granting honours; leading proceedings of the Privy Council; and fulfilling international duties as head of state.

A central power still possessed by the monarch is the choice and appointment of the UK Prime Minister. By convention, this person is normally the leader of the political party which has a majority in the Commons. However, if there is no clear majority or if the political situation is unclear, the monarch could in theory make a free choice. In practice, advice is given by royal advisers and leading politicians in order to present an acceptable candidate.

The monarch has a right to be informed of all aspects of national life by receiving government documents and meeting regularly with the Prime Minister. The monarch also has the constitutional right to encourage, warn and advise ministers. The impact of royal advice on formal and informal levels could be significant and raises questions about whether such influence should be held by an unelected figure who could potentially either support or undermine political leaders.

Much of the cost of the royal family's official duties is met from the Civil List (public funds which are approved by Parliament). Following concern over expense, the Civil List has now been reduced to a few members of the immediate royal family. Other costs incurred by the monarch as a private individual or as sovereign come either from the Privy Purse (finance received from the revenues of some royal estates) or from the Crown's own investments, which are very considerable and on which the monarch now pays income tax.

Critics of the monarchy argue that it lacks adaptability, is out-of-date, non-democratic, expensive, associated with aristocratic privilege and establishment thinking and reflects an English rather than a British identity. It is argued that the monarchy's distance from ordinary life sustains class divisions and hierarchy in society. It is also suggested that, if the monarch's functions today are merely ceremonial and lack power, it would be more rational to abolish the office and replace it with a cheaper non-executive presidency.

Critics who favour the monarchy argue that it is popular, has adapted to modern requirements and is a symbol of national unity. It is a personification of the state; shows stability and continuity; has more prestige than politicians; is not subject to political manipulations; plays a worthwhile role in national institutions; is neutral; performs ambassadorial functions; and promotes the interests of Britain abroad.

The monarchy in recent years has attracted criticism, although it appears to have coped and kept its appeal despite the difficulties. A MORI poll in April 2004 echoed positive findings over the past few years and found that 71 per cent of respondents wanted to retain the monarchy, while 20 per cent wished for an elected Head of State. After the present Queen, 47 per cent wished to keep the monarchy as it is while 35 per cent wanted it to have a smaller role and fewer members.

Polls also suggest that the monarchy should be modernized to reflect changes in British life. But traditionalists fear that a modernized monarchy would lose that aura of detachment which is described as its main strength. It would then be associated with change rather than the preservation of existing values. At present, it balances somewhat uncomfortably between tradition and modernizing trends.

The Privy Council

The ancient Privy Council is still constitutionally tied to the monarchy. Historically, it developed from a small group of royal advisers into the executive branch of the monarch's government. But its powerful position declined in the eighteenth and nineteenth centuries as its functions were transferred to a parliamentary Cabinet and new ministries. Today, its members (such as cabinet ministers) advise the monarch on the approval of government business which does not need to pass through Parliament and may serve on influential committees.

There are 400 Privy Councillors, but the body works mostly through small groups. A full council is only summoned on the death of a monarch and the accession of a new one or when constitutional issues are at stake. Should the monarch be indisposed, counsellors of state or a regent would work through the Privy Council.

Apart from its practical duties and its role as a constitutional forum, the most important tasks of the Privy Council today are performed by its Judicial Committee. It is the final court of appeal from some Commonwealth countries and dependencies. It may be used by some bodies in Britain and overseas; and also rules on any conflicts between Westminster and the Scottish Parliament.

UK Parliament: role, legislation and elections

Role

The UK Parliament is housed in the Palace of Westminster in London. It comprises the non-elected House of Lords, the elected House of Commons and the monarch. The two Houses contain members from England, Wales, Scotland and Northern Ireland and represent people with varied backgrounds and traditions. Parliament gathers as a unified body only on ceremonial occasions, such as the State Opening of Parliament by the monarch in the House of Lords. Here it listens to the monarch's speech from the throne, which outlines the UK government's forthcoming legislative programme.

In constitutional theory, Parliament has legal sovereignty in all matters and can create, abolish or amend laws and institutions for all or any part(s) of Britain. In practice, this means the implementation of the sitting government's policies.

PLATE 4.7 State Opening of Parliament, 17 May 2005.
The Queen delivers her speech from the throne (outlining the government's programme) in the House of Lords to the assembled members of the House of Lords and House of Commons.
(*Tim Rooke/Rex Features*)

All three parts of Parliament must normally pass a bill before it can become an Act of Parliament and law. Parliament also votes money to government; examines government policies and administration; scrutinizes European Union legislation; and debates political issues.

Parliament is supposed to legislate according to the rule of law, precedent and tradition. Politicians are generally sensitive to these conventions and to public opinion. Formal and informal checks and balances, such as party discipline, the Official Opposition, public reaction and pressure groups, normally ensure that Parliament legislates according to its legal responsibility. While critics argue that Parliament no longer operates satisfactorily and its programmes may not reflect the will of the people, a MORI poll in 2000 showed that satisfaction with the way Parliament works had (perhaps surprisingly) increased to 43 per cent with dissatisfaction at 29 per cent.

A Parliament has a maximum duration of five years, except in emergency situations. But it is often dissolved earlier and a general election called. A dissolution of Parliament and the issue of writs for the election are ordered by the monarch on the advice of the Prime Minister. If an MP dies, resigns or is given a peerage, a by-election is called only for that member's seat, and Parliament as a whole is not dissolved.

The *House of Lords* consists of Lords Temporal and Lords Spiritual. Lords Spiritual are the Archbishops of York and Canterbury and 24 senior bishops of the Church of England. Lords Temporal comprise some 92 peers and peeresses with hereditary titles elected by their fellows and about 577 life peers and peeresses, who have been appointed by political parties and an independent Appointments Commission; and finally the Lords of Appeal (Law Lords). The latter serve the House of Lords as the ultimate court of appeal for many purposes from most parts of Britain. This court does not consist of the whole House, but only 12 Law Lords who have held senior judicial office under the chairmanship of the Lord Chancellor. The Labour government has proposed the abolition of the office of Lord Chancellor and the creation of a Supreme Court separate from the House of Lords.

Daily attendance varies from a handful to a few hundred. Peers receive no salary for parliamentary work, but may claim attendance and travelling expenses. The House collectively controls its own procedure, but is often guided by the Lord Chancellor, who is a political appointee of the government and who sits on the Woolsack (a stuffed woollen sofa).

There have long been demands that the unrepresentative, unelected House of Lords should be replaced. The problem lies in deciding on an alternative model. A wholly elected second chamber could threaten the powers of the House of Commons and result in conflict between the two. An appointed House could consist of unelected members chosen by political parties or an independent Appointments Commission. As a first step, the Labour government abolished the sitting and voting rights of hereditary peers, except for 92 of them. Some life peers continue to be recommended by political parties while others are appointed by an independent Appointments Commission. It is possible that a future House of 750 members will be mainly appointed together with a small number (120) of elected members, no hereditary peers and a reduction (to 16) of Lords Spiritual. But there has been no definitive movement on this next step.

In this unsatisfactory and uncertain situation, the House of Lords nevertheless does its job well as an experienced and less partisan forum than the House of Commons and also takes on a legislative and administrative burden. It has an amending function, which may be used to delay government legislation for up to one year (possibly three months in future) or to persuade governments to have a second look at bills. It is a safeguard against over-hasty legislation by the Commons, is an antidote to powerful governments and has increasingly voted against Commons legislation. This is possible because the Lords are more independently minded than MPs in the Commons and do not suffer rigid party discipline. The House is now more evenly divided in terms of party affiliation. But it has a number of crossbenchers (or independents sitting across the back of the chamber) who do not belong to any political party. At present, Labour has 221 peers, the Conservatives have 216 and the Liberal Democrats have 79. But the presence of 192 cross-benchers means that no party has a majority. A MORI poll in 2000 showed that opinions about the Lords have hardly changed over the years with 32 per cent of respondents being satisfied and 29 per cent dissatisfied.

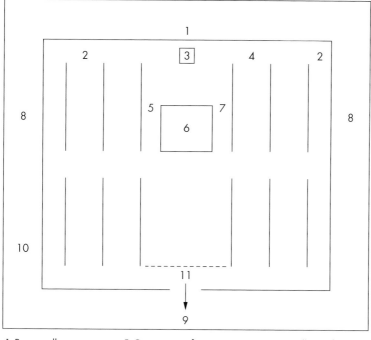

1 Press gallery	5 Government front	8 Galleries for MPs
2 Voting lobbies	bench	9 Public gallery
3 Speaker's chair	6 Dispatch box	10 VIP gallery
4 Civil servants	7 Opposition front bench	11 House of Lords

FIGURE 4.2 The House of Commons

The *House of Commons* comprises 646 Members of Parliament (MPs) who are chosen from all parts of the UK. They are elected by voters (from age 18) and represent citizens in Parliament. In 2005, 127 of them were women. But women face problems in being selected as parliamentary candidates and winning seats in the Commons. MPs are paid expenses and a salary, which is relatively low in comparison with similar jobs outside politics.

Legislation and procedure

Parliamentary procedure in both Houses of Parliament is based on custom, convention, precedent and detailed rules (standing orders). The House of Commons meets every weekday afternoon, although business can continue beyond midnight. Many MPs then spend the weekend in their constituencies attending to business. They may also follow their professions (such as lawyers) on a part-time basis. The organization and procedures of the Commons have been criticized. It is felt that the number of hours spent in the House should be reduced and that pay and resources should be improved. Women MPs feel that it should become a more women-friendly place instead of the traditional male club. But, after some changes in sitting hours, the Commons has reverted to evening sessions.

The Speaker is the chief officer of the House of Commons; is chosen by MPs; interprets the rules of the House; and is assisted by three deputy speakers. The Speaker is an elected MP who, on election to the Speaker's chair, ceases to be a political representative and becomes a neutral official (as do the Deputy Speakers).

The Speaker protects the House against any abuse of procedure by controlling debates and votes. Where there is a tied result, the Speaker has the casting vote, but must exercise this choice so that it reflects established conventions. The Speaker is important for the orderly running of the House. MPs can be very combative and often unruly, so that the Speaker is sometimes forced to dismiss or suspend a member from the House.

Debates in both Houses of Parliament usually begin with a motion (or proposal) which is then debated. The matter is decided by a simple majority vote at the end of discussion. In the Commons, MPs enter either the 'Yes' or 'No' lobbies (corridors running alongside the Commons chamber) to record their vote, but they may also abstain from voting.

The proceedings of both Houses are open to the public and may be viewed from the public and visitors' galleries. The transactions are published daily in *Hansard* (the parliamentary 'newspaper'); debates are televised; and radio broadcasts may be in live or recorded form. This exposure to public scrutiny has increased interest in the parliamentary process, although negative comments are made about low attendance in both Houses and the behaviour of MPs in the Commons.

Before the creation of new UK law (which may take a few days or many months) and changes to existing law a government will usually issue certain documents before the parliamentary law-making process commences. A Green Paper is a consultative document which allows interested parties to state their case before a bill is introduced into Parliament. A White Paper is not normally consultative, but is a preliminary document which details prospective legislation.

A draft law takes the form of a bill. Most bills are 'public' because they involve state business and are introduced in either House of Parliament by the government. Other bills may be 'private' because they relate to matters such as local government, while some are 'private members' bills' introduced by MPs in their personal capacity. These latter bills are on a topic of interest to MPs, but are normally defeated for lack of parliamentary time or support. However, some important private members' bills concerning homosexuality, abortion and sexual offences have survived the obstacles and become law.

Bills must pass through both Houses and receive the Royal Assent before they become law. The Commons is normally the first step in this process. The Lords, in its turn, can delay a non-financial bill. It can propose amendments, and if amended the bill goes back to the Commons for further consideration. This amending function is an important power and has been frequently used in recent

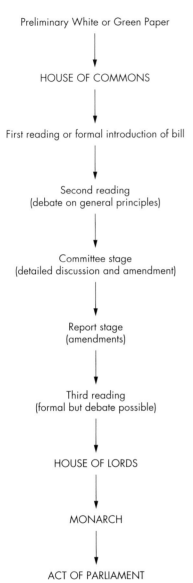

Preliminary White or Green Paper

HOUSE OF COMMONS

First reading or formal introduction of bill

Second reading
(debate on general principles)

Committee stage
(detailed discussion and amendment)

Report stage
(amendments)

Third reading
(formal but debate possible)

HOUSE OF LORDS

MONARCH

ACT OF PARLIAMENT

FIGURE 4.3 From bill to UK Act of Parliament

years. But the Lords' role today is to act as a forum for revision, rather than as a rival to the elected Commons. In practice, the Lords' amendments can sometimes lead to the acceptance of changes by the government, or even a withdrawal of the bill.

When the bill has eventually passed through the Lords, it is sent to the monarch for the Royal Assent, which has not been refused since the eighteenth century. After this, the bill becomes an Act of Parliament and enters the statute-book as representing the law of the land at that time.

UK Parliament elections

The UK is divided for Westminster parliamentary elections to the House of Commons into 646 constituencies (geographical areas of the country containing about 66,000 voters – although some may have many more or fewer). Each returns one MP to the House of Commons at a general election. Constituency boundaries are adjusted to ensure fair representation and to reflect population movements.

General elections are by secret ballot, but voting is not compulsory. British, Commonwealth and Irish Republic citizens may vote if they are resident in Britain, included on a constituency register of voters, are aged 18 or over and not subject to any disqualification. People not entitled to vote include mentally ill patients who are detained in hospital or prison, and persons who have been convicted of corrupt or illegal election practices.

Each elector casts one vote at a polling station set up on election day in a constituency by making a cross on a ballot paper against the name of the candidate for whom the vote is cast. Those who are unable to vote in person in their local constituency can register postal or proxy votes.

The turnout of voters has often been about 70 per cent at general elections out of an electorate of 43 million. The candidate who wins the most votes in a constituency is elected MP for that area. This system is known as the simple majority or the 'first past the post' system. There is no voting by the various forms of proportional representation (PR), except for EU Parliament and devolved government elections, which have a mixture of first-past-the-post and party-list voting.

Some see the Westminster electoral system as undemocratic and unfair to smaller parties. The Liberal Democrats campaign for PR voting, which would create a wider selection of parties in the House of Commons and cater for minority political interests. The two big parties (Labour and Conservative) have preferred the existing system since it gives them a greater chance of achieving power. The Labour government, after offering to examine the PR systems in Scotland and Wales to see whether they can be applied to Westminster elections, has not proposed any change to the present first-past-the-post system.

It is argued that the British people prefer stronger government which can result from the first-past-the-post system. PR systems are alleged to have weaknesses, such as party control of lists, coalition or minority government, frequent breakdown, a lack of firm policies, power-bargaining between different parties in order to achieve government status and tension afterwards. But weak and small-majority government can also result from first-past-the-post.

The party political system

British elections at parliamentary, devolved and local levels depend upon the party political system, which has existed since the seventeenth century. For UK parliamentary general elections, the parties present their policies in the form of manifestos to the electorate for consideration during the few weeks of campaigning prior to election day. A party candidate (chosen by a specific party) in a constituency is elected to the Westminster Parliament on a combination of party manifesto and the personality of the candidate. But party activity continues outside the election period itself, as the politicians battle for power and the ears of the electorate at all levels.

Since 1945 there have been nine Labour and eight Conservative UK governments in Britain. Some have had large majorities in the House of Commons, while others have had small ones. Some, such as the Labour government in the late 1970s and the Conservatives in the 1990s, had to rely on the support of

TABLE 4.1 British governments and Prime Ministers since 1945

Date	Government	Prime Minister
1945–51	Labour	Clement Attlee
1951–5	Conservative	Winston Churchill
1955–9	Conservative	Anthony Eden (1955–7)
		Harold Macmillan (1957–9)
1959–64	Conservative	Harold Macmillan (1959–63)
		Alec Douglas-Home (1963–4)
1964–6	Labour	Harold Wilson
1966–70	Labour	Harold Wilson
1970–4	Conservative	Edward Heath
1974–(Feb.)	Labour	Harold Wilson
1974–(Oct.)	Labour	Harold Wilson
1974–9	Labour	Harold Wilson (1974–6)
		James Callaghan (1976–9)
1979–83	Conservative	Margaret Thatcher
1983–7	Conservative	Margaret Thatcher
1987–92	Conservative	Margaret Thatcher (1987–90)
		John Major (1990–2)
1992–7	Conservative	John Major
1997–2001	Labour	Tony Blair
2001–5	Labour	Tony Blair
2005–	Labour	Tony Blair

smaller parties, such as the Liberals and Ulster Unionists, to remain in power. Most of the MPs in the House of Commons belong to either the Conservative or the Labour Party. This continues the traditional two-party system in British politics, in which power alternates between two major parties.

The Labour Party has historically been a left-of-centre party with its own right and left wings (now sometimes referred to as New and Old Labour). It emphasized social justice, equality of opportunity, economic planning and the state ownership of industries and services. It was supported by the trade unions (who had been influential in the party's development), the working class and some of the middle class. Its electoral strongholds are historically in Scotland, South Wales and the Midland and northern English industrial cities.

But traditional class-based and left-ideological support has changed with more social and job mobility. In the 1990s, the Labour Party tried to appeal to middle-class voters in southern England and to take account of changing economic and social conditions. Its leader (and current Prime Minister), Tony Blair, modernized the party as New Labour by moving to the centre, captured voters from the Conservatives and distanced himself from the trade unions, state ownership and the party's doctrinaire past. As a result, the party had landslide victories in the 1997 and 2001 general elections and gained a significant majority in the 2005 election. But there is a still substantial support for Old Labour positions in the party and this can lead to tension.

The Conservative Party is a right-of-centre party, which also has right and left wing sections. It regards itself as a national party and appeals to people across class barriers. It emphasizes personal, social and economic freedom, individual ownership of property and shares and law and order. The Conservatives became more socially and economically radical in their 18 years of government (1979–97). But policy splits in the party (particularly on Europe) have created tensions.

The party's support comes mainly from business interests and the middle and upper classes, but a sizeable number of skilled workers and women vote Conservative. The party's strongholds are in southern England, with scattered support elsewhere in the country. However, at the 1997 and 2001 general elections, it suffered a heavy defeat, gained no seats in Wales, only one in Scotland and did not greatly increase its support in England. Although improving its performance at the 2005 election, it is still far from being in a position to return to government. It is argued that the party (now led by David Cameron) needs to reorganize, strive for unity, cultivate an image which is more attractive to voters and develop policies which are more in tune with the changing face of British society.

The Liberal Democrats were formed in 1988 when the old Liberal Party and the Social Democratic Party merged into one party. Under their present leader Menzies Campbell, they see themselves as an alternative political force to the Conservative and Labour Parties, based on the centre-left of British politics. Their strengths are in local government, constitutional reform and civil liberties.

They are relatively strong in south-west England, Wales and Scotland and increased their MPs at the 2001 and 2005 general elections to become the biggest third party in Parliament since 1929. But they lack a clearly defined identity and policies which are recognized by the electorate. The Liberal Democrats have won some dramatic by-elections and have had considerable success in local government elections. But they have not made a large breakthrough into the Commons or the EU Parliament. Electoral reform to a form of PR might increase the number of their MPs.

Smaller parties are also represented in the House of Commons, such as the Scottish National Party; Plaid Cymru (the Welsh National Party); the Ulster Unionists and the Democratic Unionists (Protestant Northern Irish parties); the Social Democratic and Labour Party (moderate Roman Catholic Northern Irish party); and Sinn Fein (Republican Northern Irish party). Other small parties, like the Greens and fringe groups, may also contest a general election. A party which falls below a certain number of votes in the election loses its deposit (the sum paid when parties register for elections).

Social class and class loyalty used to be important factors in British voting behaviour. But these have now been replaced by property- and share-owning, job status and other considerations. A more volatile political situation exists as voters switch between Labour, Conservatives and Liberal Democrats and may employ 'tactical voting' in some constituencies to prevent specific party candidates from being elected. General elections are often won by a party which succeeds in 'marginal constituencies' where a slight vote swing can effect a change in party representation. In this situation, 'floating voters' who are not committed to a specific party can influence the result. The changing character of the electorate has moved political parties to the centre ground and forced them to adopt policies which are more representative of people's wishes and needs. But this means that the old ideological divides are no longer so obvious, important or relevant.

The party which wins most seats in the House of Commons at a general election usually forms the new government, even if it has not obtained a majority of the popular vote (the votes actually cast at an election). A party will have to gather more than 33 per cent of the popular vote before winning a large number of seats, and approach 40 per cent in order to expand that representation and form a government with an overall majority (a majority over all the other parties counted together). This majority enables it to carry out its election manifesto policies (the mandate theory).

But election success often depends on whether support is concentrated in geographical areas, for a party gains seats by its local strength. Smaller parties, which do not reach the percentages above and whose support is scattered, do not gain many seats in the Commons. It is this system of representation that PR supporters wish to change, in order to reflect the popular vote and the appeal of minority parties.

TABLE 4.2 General election results 2005

Party	Percentage of popular vote	Members elected
Labour (including Speaker)	35.3	356
Conservative	32.3	198
Liberal Democrat	22.1	62
Scottish National Party	1.5	6
Plaid Cymru	0.6	3
Ulster Unionists	0.5	1
Social Democratic and Labour Party	0.5	3
Sinn Fein	0.6	5
Democratic Unionists	0.9	9
Respect	0.3	1
Health Concern	0.1	1
Independent	0.1	1
Total seats		646
Turnout of voters	61.3%	
Overall Labour majority	66	
Non-Labour popular vote	64.7%	
All other parties' popular vote (except Labour, Conservatives and Liberal Democrats)	10.3%	

The situation is illustrated by the 2005 general election results (see Table 4.2). On a relatively low turnout of voters of 61.3 per cent Labour became the government with 35.3 per cent of the popular vote, while the opposition parties together obtained 64.7 per cent. Labour gained 356 seats with its share of the popular vote, the Conservatives received 198 seats with 32.3 per cent, while the Liberal Democrats with 22.1 per cent received 62 seats. Labour had a 66 seat overall majority in the House of Commons, down 101 seats from 2001 but still substantial in British terms. But only some 25 per cent of the total potential electorate actually supported Labour. The main reasons for this result were the relatively low turnout; the possible reactions to the Iraq war in some constituencies; disillusionment with the serving Labour government; the 'first past the post' system; the Liberal Democrats' popular support is spread widely (and thinly) over the country resulting in them coming second in many constituencies; the Labour and Conservative Parties traditionally having specific geographical areas in which most of their votes are concentrated; the Conservatives were unable to improve their position from the 1997 and 2001 elections; and some 'tactical voting' to defeat Conservative candidates.

The result of a general election may be a 'hung Parliament', where no one party has an overall majority. A minority or coalition government would have to be formed, in which the largest party would be able to govern only by relying on the support of smaller parties in the Commons. Critics are already suggesting that this may happen at the next general election, possibly in 2009.

The largest minority party becomes the Official Opposition with its own leader and 'shadow government'. It plays an important role in the parliamentary system, which is based on adversarial politics and the two-party tradition of government. Seating arrangements in the House of Commons reflect this system. Leaders of the government and opposition parties sit on facing 'front benches', with their supporting MPs, or 'backbenchers', sitting behind them. Some parties, such as the Liberal Democrats, dislike this confrontational style and advocate more consensus politics. Traditionally, the effectiveness of parliamentary democracy is supposed to rest on the relationship between the government and opposition parties and the observance of procedural conventions.

The opposition parties may try to overthrow the government by defeating it in a vote. But this is usually unsuccessful if the government has a majority and can count on the support of its MPs. The opposition parties consequently attempt to influence the formation of national policies by their criticism of pending legislation; by trying to obtain concessions on bills by proposing amendments to them; and by increasing support for their policies outside the Commons. They take advantage of any opportunity which might improve their chances at the next general election.

Inside Parliament, party discipline rests with the Whips, who are chosen from party MPs by the party leaders and who are under the direction of a Chief Whip. Their duties include informing members of forthcoming parliamentary business and maintaining the party's voting strength in the Commons by seeing that their members attend all important debates. MPs receive notice from the Whips' office of how important a particular vote is and the information will be underlined up to three times. A 'three-line whip' signifies a crucial vote and failure to attend or comply with party instructions is regarded as a revolt against the party's policy.

The Whips also convey backbench opinion to the party leadership. This is important if rebellion and disquiet are to be avoided. Party discipline is very strong in the Commons and less so in the Lords. A government with a large majority should not become complacent, nor antagonize its backbenchers. If it does so, a successful rebellion against the government or abstention from voting by its own side may destroy the majority and the party's policy.

Outside Parliament, control rests with the national and local party organizations, which can be influential. They promote the party at every opportunity, but especially at election time, when constituencies select the party candidates and are in charge of electioneering on behalf of their party.

The UK government

The UK government serves the whole of Britain and normally comprises individuals who are members of the successful majority party at a general election. It is centred on Whitehall in London where its ministries and the Prime Minister's official residence (10 Downing Street) are located. It consists of some 100 ministers who can be chosen from both Houses of Parliament and who are appointed by the monarch on the advice of the Prime Minister. They derive their authority from belonging to the majority party in the Commons and are collectively responsible to Parliament for the administration of national affairs.

The *Prime Minister* is appointed by the monarch and is usually the leader of the majority party in the Commons. His or her power stems from majority support in Parliament; the authority (or patronage) to choose and dismiss ministers; the leadership of the party in the country; and control over policy-making. The Prime Minister sits in the Commons, as do most ministers, where they may be questioned and held accountable for government actions. The Prime Minister was historically the connection between the monarch and Parliament. This convention continues in the weekly audience with the monarch, at which the policies and business of the government are discussed.

The Prime Minister has great power within the British system of government and it is suggested that the office has become like an all-powerful executive presidency, which bypasses Parliament and government departments. It is argued that government policy is decided upon by the Downing Street political machine with its array of bureaucrats and 'spin doctors'. But there are checks on this power, inside and outside the party and Parliament, which can on occasions bring down a Prime Minister. However, there is a greater emphasis upon prime ministerial government today, rather than the traditional constitutional notions of Cabinet government.

The *Cabinet* is a small executive body in the government and usually comprises twenty-one senior ministers, who are chosen and presided over by the Prime Minister. Examples are the Chancellor of the Exchequer (Finance Minister), the Foreign Secretary, the Home Secretary and the Secretary of State for Education and Skills. The Cabinet originated in meetings that the monarch had with ministers in a royal Cabinet. As the monarch withdrew from active politics with the growth of party politics and Parliament, this developed into a parliamentary body.

Constitutional theory has traditionally argued that government rule is Cabinet rule because the Cabinet collectively initiates and decides government policy at its weekly meetings in 10 Downing Street. Although this notion has weakened, there are still occasions when policy is thrashed out in cabinet. But, since the Prime Minister is responsible for Cabinet agendas and controls Cabinet proceedings, the Cabinet can become a 'rubber-stamp' or 'briefing room' for policies which have already been decided by the Prime Minister or smaller groups.

Much depends upon the personality of Prime Ministers and the way in which they avoid potential Cabinet friction. Some are strong and like to take the lead. Others work within the Cabinet structure, allowing ministers to exercise responsibility within their own ministerial fields. Much of our information about the operation of the Cabinet comes from 'leaks' or information divulged by Cabinet ministers. Although the Cabinet meets in private and its discussions are meant to be secret, the public is usually and reliably informed of Cabinet deliberations and disputes by the media.

The mass and complexity of government business and ministers' concern with their own departments suggest that full debate in Cabinet on every issue is impossible. But it is felt that broad policies should be more vigorously debated. The present system arguably concentrates too much power in the hands of the Prime Minister; overloads ministers with work; allows crucial decisions to be taken outside the Cabinet; and reduces the notion of collective responsibility.

Collective responsibility is that which all ministers, but mainly those in the Cabinet, share for government actions and policy. All must support a government decision in public, even though some may oppose it during private deliberations. If a minister cannot do this, he or she may feel obliged to resign.

A minister also has an individual responsibility for the work of his or her government department. The minister is answerable for any mistakes, wrongdoing or bad administration, whether personally responsible for them or not. In such cases, the minister may resign, although this is not as common today as in the past. This responsibility should also enable Parliament to maintain some control over executive actions because the minister is ultimately answerable to Parliament. But critics argue that such control today has weakened.

Government departments (or ministries) are the chief instruments by which the government implements its policy. A change of government does not necessarily alter the number or functions of departments. Examples of government departments are the Foreign Office, Ministry of Defence, Home Office and the Treasury (headed by the Chancellor of the Exchequer).

UK government departments are staffed by the *Civil Service*, consisting of career administrators (civil servants). They work in London and throughout Britain in government activities and are responsible to the minister of their department for the implementation of government policies. A change of minister or government does not require new civil servants, since they are expected to be politically neutral and to serve the government impartially. Restrictions on political activities and publication are imposed upon them in order to ensure neutrality. There are some 500,000 civil servants in Britain today. Nearly half of these are women, but few of them achieve top ranks in the service.

The heart of the Civil Service is the Cabinet Office, whose Secretary is the head of the Civil Service. The latter is responsible for the whole Civil Service, organizes Cabinet business and coordinates high-level policy. In each ministry or department the senior official (Permanent Secretary) and his or her assistants are responsible for assisting their minister in the implementation of government policy.

There have been accusations about the efficiency and effectiveness of the Service and civil servants do not have a good public image. There have been attempts to make the system more cost-effective and to allow a wider category of applicants than the traditional entry of Oxbridge graduates. Posts may now be advertised in order to attract older people from industry, commerce and the professions. Many aspects of departmental work have also been broken down and transferred to executive agencies in London and throughout the country, which have administrative rather than policy-making roles, such as the Driver and Vehicle Licensing Agency (DVLA) in Cardiff and social security offices. There have also been attempts to cut the number of civil servants and to restrict their policy-making role. Critics argue that the Civil Service has been politicized, lost its independence and become a delivery mechanism for targets initiated by unelected consultants, political advisers and 'spin doctors' in Downing Street.

On the other hand, it has been traditionally alleged that the Civil Service imposes a certain mentality upon its members, which affects implementation of government policies and which ministers are unable to combat. There is supposed to be a Civil Service way of doing things and a bias towards the status quo. But much depends upon ministers and the way in which they manage departments. There may be some areas of concern. But the stereotyped image of civil servants is not reflected in the many who serve their political masters and work with ministers for departmental interests. The Civil Service is highly regarded in other countries for its efficiency and impartiality.

UK parliamentary control of government

Most British governments (the executive) in the past governed pragmatically. The emphasis was on whether policies worked and were generally acceptable. Governments were conscious of how far they could go before displeasing their supporters and the electorate, to whom they were accountable at general elections. The combination of the two-party system, Cabinet government and party discipline in the Commons seemed to provide a balance between efficient government and public accountability. But both Conservative and Labour governments have become more intent on pushing their policies through Parliament.

Constitutional theory suggested that Parliament should control the executive government. But unless there is small-majority government, rebellion by government MPs or public protest, a government with an overall majority in the Commons (such as Labour since 1997) can carry its policies through Parliament, irrespective of Parliament's attempts to restrain it. Even the House of Lords has only a delaying and amending power over government legislation, although the Lords have effectively blocked some legislation in recent years. Critics argue for stronger parliamentary control over the executive, which has been described as an elective dictatorship. But there seems little chance of this without, for example, moving to a PR electoral system, more consensus politics, a strengthening of Parliament's constraining role and much more independent stances from MPs themselves.

Opposition parties can only oppose in the Commons and hope to persuade the electorate to dismiss the government at the next election. Formal devices like votes of censure and no confidence are normally inadequate when confronting a government with a large majority. Even rebellious government MPs will usually (if not always) support the party on such occasions, out of a self-interested desire to preserve their jobs and a need to prevent the collapse of the government and its policies.

Examinations of government programmes can be employed at Question Time in the Commons, when the Prime Minister (30 minutes on Wednesdays) is subjected to oral questions from the Leader of the Opposition and MPs. But the government can prevaricate in its answers and, while reputations can be made and lost at Question Time, it is a rhetorical and political occasion rather than an in-depth analysis of government policy. However, it does have a function in holding the executive's performance up to public scrutiny. The opposition parties can also choose their own topics for formal debate on a limited number of days each session, which can be used to attack the government.

A 1967 attempt to restrain the executive was the creation of the Parliamentary Commissioner for Administration (Ombudsman), who can investigate alleged bad administration by ministers and civil servants. But the office does not have strong watchdog powers and the public have no direct access to it, although its existence does serve as a warning.

In an attempt to improve the situation, standing committees of MPs were established, which examine bills during procedural stages. Such committees have little influence on actual policy. But in 1979 a new select committee system was created, which now has 14 committees. They comprise MPs from most parties, who monitor the administration and policy of the main government departments and investigate proposed legislation. MPs previously had problems in scrutinizing government activity adequately and party discipline made it difficult for them to act independently of party policy.

It is often argued that the real work of the House and parliamentary control of the executive is done in the select committees. Their members are now proving to be more independent in questioning civil servants and ministers who are called to give evidence before them (but who may refuse to attend). Select committees can be effective in examining proposed legislation and expenditure and their reports can be damaging to a government's reputation. Although opinions differ about their role, it does seem that they have strengthened Parliament's authority against government and critics would like to see their power enhanced. Nevertheless, although parliamentary scrutiny is important, a government is elected (or mandated) to carry out those manifesto policies on which it won the general election.

Attitudes to politics

Polls consistently reveal that British politicians and political parties do not rate highly in people's esteem. A National Opinion Poll (NOP) in 1997 found that politicians were the least admired group of professions (apart from journalists) and never answer the questions people put to them. In terms of trust, a MORI poll in March 2005 found that 75 per cent of respondents thought that politicians in general do not tell the truth and 71 per cent felt the same about government ministers. They are criticized and satirized in the media and allegations of sleaze, corruption and unethical behaviour in both Labour and Conservative Parties have led to stricter controls on politicians and their outside interests. The Labour government has faced accusations of 'cronyism' (favouring political supporters for public and official positions) since 1997.

Commentators frequently describe an increase in political apathy, particularly among the young, and a distrust in politicians to rectify social ills. This partly resulted in a 59 per cent turnout at the 2001 general election, the lowest in any general election since 1918 and only slightly better in 2005 at 60 per cent. A Populus poll in March 2005, prior to the general election, found that 66 per cent of respondents were disappointed with the Labour government's performance. Some 11 per cent said that they might not vote at all in the election because of their disillusionment with Labour. But disaffected Labour supporters would not vote for another party.

However, MORI opinion research in 2001 showed that in fact interest in politics has remained stable in Britain for 30 years; civic duty and habit are key motivators to voting (less so for the young); and people have positive attitudes to voting. They would prefer it to be made more convenient by phone/mobile phone, online and by post (the latter is now available, although there have been allegations of fraud). The research also found that low turnout is not a result of declining interest in politics or elections, but rather a failure of campaigns to connect with the electorate. This suggests that people want more accurate information and a greater focus on the issues that directly concern them.

People therefore appear to be more interested in the political process and issues than is popularly assumed. But the Independent Television Commission's Election 2001 survey found that interest in television election coverage fell to its lowest level; 70 per cent of viewers expressed little or no interest; and 25 per cent ignored all campaign coverage. None of the political parties, in spite of frequent drifts to the centre ground, individually encompass all the basic views and sense of contemporary reality of the people, who may vary between egalitarian economic views and authoritarian social and moral positions. They desire economic freedom and personal liberty but also want state interventionist policies in some social areas, such as education, health and law and order.

Exercises

Explain and examine the following terms:

Whigs	executive	'three-line whip'
constitution	minister	life peers
Cabinet	manifesto	Oliver Cromwell
Magna Carta	conventions	Question time
civil servant	secret ballot	backbenchers
Lords Spiritual	Tories	constitutional monarchy
the Speaker	legislature	'hung Parliament'
Whitehall	sovereignty	select committees
White Paper	'cronyism'	sleaze

Write short essays on the following topics:

1   Describe what is meant by the 'two-party system', and comment upon its effectiveness.

2   Does Britain have an adequate parliamentary electoral system? If not, why not?

3   Critically examine the role of the Prime Minister.

4   Discuss the position and powers of the monarch in the British constitution.

Further reading

1   Aughey, A. (2001) *Nationalism, Devolution and the Challenge to the United Kingdom State* London: Pluto Press

2   Bogdanor, V. (2001) *Devolution in the United Kingdom* Oxford: Oxford University Press

3   Childs, D. (2001) *Britain since 1945: A Political History* London: Routledge

4   Coxall, B., Robins, L. and Leach, R. (2003) *Contemporary British Politics* Basingstoke: Palgrave Macmillan

5   Foley, M. (2000) *The British Presidency* Manchester: Manchester University Press

6   Foster, C. (2005) *British Government in Crisis* London: Hart

7   Jones, B., Kavanagh, D., Moran, M. and Norton, P. (2004) *Politics UK* Harlow: Pearson Education Limited

8   Kavanagh, D. (2000) *British Politics: Continuities and Change* Oxford: Oxford University Press

9   Ludlam, S. and Smith, M.J. (2000) *New Labour in Government* London: Macmillan

Websites

UK government: www.open.gov.uk and www.ukonline.gov.uk
Houses of Parliament: www.parliament.uk
Monarchy: www.royal.gov.uk
Privy Council Office: www.privy-council.org.uk
Cabinet Office: www.cabinet-office.gov.uk
Prime Minister's Office: www.number-10.gov.uk
Wales Office: www.wales.gov.uk
National Assembly for Wales: www.wales.gov.uk
Scotland Office: www.scottishsecretary.gov.uk
The Scottish Parliament: www.scottish.parliament.uk
Northern Ireland Assembly: www.ni-assembly.gov.uk
Northern Ireland Office: www.nio.gov.uk

International relations

Britain's historical position as a colonial, economic and political power on the world stage was in relative decline by the early decades of the twentieth century. Some large colonies, such as Canada and Australia, had already achieved self-governing dominion status. The growth of nationalism and a desire for self-determination in African and Asian nations persuaded Britain to decolonialize further from 1945. The effects of global economic competition, two World Wars, the emergence of Cold War politics (dominated by the USA and the former Soviet Union) and domestic economic and social problems forced Britain to recognize its reduced international status.

It tried with difficulty to find a new identity and establish different priorities, particularly in relation to Europe. Some of the previous overseas links continue in the form of the Commonwealth (formerly the British Empire), traditional trading partners and the connection with the United States, while other relationships are new. But, in spite of these fundamental changes, Britain still experiences uncertainties about its potential international influence and appropriate role in global affairs.

PLATE 5.1 Commonwealth Day observance, Westminster Abbey, London, 8 March 2004. The Queen meets Commonwealth representatives and participants.
(*Tim Rooke/Rex Features*)

Foreign and defence policy

Britain's position in the world today is that of a medium-sized country which ranks economically in fourth place behind the USA, Japan and Germany. It is also facing increasing commercial competition from emergent powers such as China, India and other 'Asian rim' nations. Yet some of its political elite still believe that it can have an international influence and role. The Labour government since 1997 has developed a foreign policy which has shifted away from traditionally aggressive unilateral action to persuasive partnerships; embarked on coalition military actions around the world; and emphasized ethical and human rights in international and nationalist conflicts. Nevertheless, issues of national self-interest are still evident in these attempts at global cooperation and the concerted fight against terrorism.

Critics argue that Britain's foreign policy and self-image do not reflect the reality of its world position. It has engaged in recent wars and peacekeeping duties (for example in the Balkans, Afghanistan, Sierra Leone and Iraq). But, while military action in Iraq (from 2003) was initially supported by a majority of the British public, there has been increasing opposition over its aftermath and distrust of the Labour government's justification for the war. It is also felt that the current costs of defence expenditure and overseas commitments could be more profitably directed to the solving of domestic problems in Britain.

Britain's foreign and defence policies still reflect its traditional position as a major trading nation and finance centre. Consequently, it is self-interestedly concerned to maintain stable commercial, economic and political conditions through global connections. Britain is the world's sixth largest exporter of goods and the second largest exporter of services; has substantial overseas or outward investments; and imports some of its food and basic manufacturing requirements. It is therefore dependent upon maintaining global commercial links, although it is increasingly committed to Europe, where the 25 EU countries are Britain's biggest export and import markets. But other European countries, the USA, China, India, Japan, South America and Commonwealth nations are also important trading areas.

Britain's *foreign policy* and membership of international organizations is based on the principle that overseas objectives in the contemporary world can be best attained by persuasion and cooperation with other nations on a regional or global basis. The imperial days of unilateral action are now largely past, although Britain did take such action in the 1982 Falklands War. But its foreign policy can reflect particular biases, with support for one country outweighing that for another.

The USA has been Britain's closest ally in recent years. It is often considered that a 'special relationship' exists between the two based on a common language, cultural traditions, history and military partnership. But this association has varied according to circumstances, especially since 1945. Nevertheless, Britain is concerned to maintain the American military and security presence in Europe and

PLATE 5.2 Prime Minister Tony Blair with US President George W. Bush and Benjamin Mkapa at the G8 summit, Gleneagles, Scotland, 8 July 2005.
Britain chaired the summit and here Blair holds a press conference the day after suicide bomb attacks in London.
(*Sipa Press/Rex Features*)

NATO. The USA and the Labour government see Britain partly as a bridge to Europe, while Britain wants to maintain the Atlantic connection in its own bargaining with EU countries and for what it considers to be global stability.

An April 2003 Gallup poll found that 79 per cent of Americans regarded Britain as a close partner of the USA and a MORI research survey of the same date showed that 73 per cent of British respondents felt that the USA was Britain's most reliable ally. However, the latter poll also revealed that when asked which was most important to Britain, 34 per cent of British people chose the USA and 42 per cent preferred Europe, with the latter figure having dropped by 8 per cent since 1993.

Britain's membership of the EU means that it is to some extent dependent upon EU foreign policy. But, although the EU is moving to more unified policies (with a potential future constitution giving it legal negotiating status in world affairs, a president and a foreign minister), member states have conflicting interests and Britain also has its own policy priorities. EU foreign policy is still very much in its infancy and many critics doubt its validity and value.

Britain has diplomatic relations with 160 nations and is a member of some 120 international organizations, ranging from bodies for economic cooperation to the United Nations (UN). Support for the UN and the principles of its charter has been part of British foreign policy since 1945, although there has sometimes been (as over Iraq in 2003) a scepticism about its effectiveness as a practical and decisive body.

But, as a permanent member of the UN Security Council, Britain has a vested interest in supporting the organization. It sees a strong UN as a necessary framework for achieving many of its own foreign policy objectives, such as the peaceful resolution of conflict, arms control, disarmament, peacekeeping operations and the protection of human rights. UN agencies also provide forums for discussing issues in which Britain is involved, such as disaster relief, the use of the sea-bed, terrorism, the environment, energy development and world resources. Yet Britain, like other nations, is ready to ignore the UN when it sees its own vital interests challenged.

Britain's major *defence* alliance is with the North Atlantic Treaty Organization (NATO). This currently comprises 26 members (Belgium, Canada, Denmark, Iceland, Italy, Luxembourg, the Netherlands, Norway, Spain, Portugal, Britain, the USA, Greece, Turkey, Germany, Poland, Hungary, the Czech Republic, France, Bulgaria, Estonia, Latvia, Lithuania, Romania, Slovakia and Slovenia). Others may be admitted in the future. The justification for the original NATO was that it provided its members with greater security than any could achieve individually and was a deterrent against aggression by the now-defunct Warsaw Pact countries.

All the major British political parties are in favour of retaining the NATO link and, according to opinion polls, the public would not support any party which tried to take Britain out of the alliance. Membership of NATO also allows Britain to operate militarily on the international stage. Its defence policy is based on NATO strategies and it assigns most of its armed forces and defence budget to the organization.

Despite changes in Eastern Europe since 1989 and moves to transform NATO into a more flexible, leaner and high-technology military association, the British government has taken such developments cautiously and is concerned to maintain its own military defence with both conventional and nuclear forces. It recognizes that global instability, international terrorism and unstable states pose risks to its own security if it reduced its and NATO's armed defence capacity substantially. It also supports in principle the USA's proposed missile shield defence programme and will probably contribute early-warning facilities in Britain.

However, in 1998 Britain argued that the EU must also have a credible military and security capability to support its political role. The EU is now working towards the creation of its own 'rapid deployment force'. The problem is whether this should be seen as an independent force outside NATO or whether it should operate within NATO frameworks. It would respond to international crises, but without prejudice to NATO (which would continue to be the foundation of collective security). Some critics argue that this development has been inadequately planned and has cooperation problems. It could also weaken the NATO structure and lead to American withdrawal from Europe.

The British government's defence planning (6 per cent of state spending in 2004–5) has reduced the number of armed forces personnel, ships, aircraft and equipment, but has increased other priority areas, such as capabilities and structures. It aims to depend on leaner, fast-reaction and more flexible forces, although there have been strenuous objections to these policies (such as the reduction of old army regiments) from the military. The primary objectives of defence policy are to ensure the country's security and the NATO commitment and to allow British forces to engage in high-intensity war as well as in peace-keeping roles. However, defence spending is still higher than in other European countries and it is queried whether the money could be better spent in other areas of national life. At the same time, although the British armed forces are increasingly in demand for global commitments, they are undermanned and military equipment is often out-of-date and in short supply.

Nuclear weapons, which account for a large part of the defence budget, continue to be fiercely debated. Britain's independent nuclear deterrent consists mainly of long-range American-built Trident missiles carried by a fleet of four submarines (although only one is on patrol at any given time). Governments have committed themselves to upgrading nuclear weapons while critics want cheaper alternatives, or the cancellation of the nuclear system. But it seems that the British

PLATE 5.3 British troops in Basra, Iraq, April 2005.
British troops continue to serve as part of the coalition peace-keeping force following the Iraq war 2003.
(*Sabah Arar/Rex Features*)

nuclear strategy will continue. All the major political parties are multilateralist (keeping nuclear weapons until they can be abolished on a global basis).

Britain can operate militarily outside the NATO and European area, although this capacity is increasingly expensive and limited. Military garrisons are stationed in Brunei, Cyprus, the Far and Middle East, the Falkland Islands and Gibraltar. The 1982 Falklands War, the 1991 and 2003–4 Gulf Wars and Afghanistan in 2001 showed that Britain was able to respond to challenges outside the NATO area, although the operations did draw attention to defects and problems in such actions.

The total strength of the professional armed forces, which are now all volunteer following the end of conscription in 1962, was 207,020 in 2004. This was made up of 40,880 in the Royal Navy and Royal Marines, 112,750 in the Army and 53,390 in the Royal Air Force. Women personnel in the Army, Navy and Air Force are integral parts of the armed services. They were previously confined to support roles, but may now be employed in some front-line military activities. Reserve and volunteer forces, such as the Territorial Army (TA), perform a crucial role, support the regular forces at home and abroad, serve with NATO and coalition ground troops and help to maintain security in Britain.

The empire and Commonwealth

The British Empire was gradually built up over four centuries from the sixteenth century. But colonizing impulses had in fact begun with the attempted internal domination of the islands by the English from the twelfth century, together with military conquests in Europe. These were followed by trading activities and colonization in North and South America. Parts of Africa, Asia and the West Indies were also exploited commercially over time and many became colonies. Emigrants from Britain settled in colonies such as the USA, Australia, Canada, South Africa and New Zealand. By the nineteenth century, British imperial rule and possessions embraced a quarter of the world's population.

In the late nineteenth and early twentieth centuries large colonies such as Canada, Australia, New Zealand and South Africa became self-governing dominions and eventually achieved independence. Many of their peoples were descendants of those settlers who had emigrated from Britain in earlier centuries. They regarded Britain as the 'mother country' and nurtured a shared kinship. But this relationship has changed as national identities in these countries have become firmly established.

In 1931, the British Empire became the British Commonwealth of Nations and independence was gradually granted to other colonies. India and Pakistan became independent in 1947 (leading to the emergence of the modern Commonwealth in 1949), followed by African territories in the 1950s and 1960s and later many islands of the West Indies. Eventually, most of the remaining colonies became independent. They could choose whether to break all connections with the colonial past or remain within the Commonwealth as independent nations. Most of them decided to stay in the Commonwealth. Only a few small British colonies, dependencies and protectorates now remain and are scattered widely, such as the Falklands and Gibraltar.

The present Commonwealth is a voluntary association of some 53 independent states (including Britain). It does not have written laws, an elected Parliament, or one political ruler. There is evidence of past colonial rule in many of the countries, such as educational and legal systems. But few have kept the British form of parliamentary government. Some have adapted it to their own needs, while others are one-party states or have constitutions based on a wide variety of models, with varying records on civil and democratic rights.

The Commonwealth has nearly a third of the world's population and comprises peoples of different religions, races and nationalities, who share a history of struggles for independence from colonialism. The Commonwealth is often described as a family of nations. But there are occasional wars, tensions and quarrels between these family members.

The British monarch is its non-political head and has varying constitutional roles in the different countries. The monarch is a focal point of identification and has an important unifying and symbolic function, which has often kept the Commonwealth together in times of crisis and conflict.

The Prime Ministers, or heads of state, in Commonwealth countries meet every two years under the auspices of the monarch for Commonwealth Conferences in different parts of the world. Common problems are discussed and sometimes settled, although there seem to have been more arguments than agreements in recent years, with Britain having a minority position on some issues (such as opposing trade sanctions against the former apartheid regime in South Africa).

There is a Commonwealth Secretariat in London which coordinates policy for the Commonwealth, in addition to many Commonwealth societies, institutes, libraries, professional associations and university exchange programmes. Commonwealth citizens still travel to Britain as immigrants, students and visitors, while British emigration to Commonwealth countries continues in reduced amounts. English in its many varieties remains the common language of the Commonwealth and the Commonwealth Games (athletics and other sports) are held every four years. There are many joint British/Commonwealth programmes on both official and voluntary levels in agriculture, engineering, health and education, in which some vestiges of the old relationship between Britain and the Commonwealth are still apparent.

But British attempts to enter Europe from the 1960s reduced the importance to Britain of the organization. There is no longer the old sense of Commonwealth solidarity and purpose and Britain has little in common with some Commonwealth nations. It is argued that unless member countries feel there are valid reasons for continuing a somewhat moribund association which represents historical accident rather than common purpose, the long-term future of the Commonwealth must be in doubt. Opinion polls show that Europe and the USA are more important for Britons than the Commonwealth. Only 16 per cent of respondents in an April 2003 MORI research survey felt that the Commonwealth was the most important international partnership for Britain.

Britain had preferential trading arrangements with the Commonwealth before it joined the EU in 1973 and the Commonwealth question formed part of the debate on membership. EU entry was seen as ending the close relationship between Britain and the Commonwealth. But economic cooperation and trading between the two have continued, and Britain contributes a considerable amount of its overseas aid to countries in the Commonwealth. However, Britain has a declining share of the Commonwealth trading market and its economic priorities are now more with the EU and other world partners.

Nevertheless, the Labour government feels that the Commonwealth is a success and is committed to raising its profile. Indeed, a number of countries wish to join the organization, not all of whom have been previous British colonies. But it is argued that the value of the Commonwealth in the contemporary world must be based on a concrete and realistic role which is distinctive from other global organizations. For example, it might function as a worldwide political forum which emphasizes accountable government, democratic concerns, anti-corruption reform and civil and human rights.

The European Union (EU)

The ideal of a united Europe, strong in economic and political institutions, became increasingly attractive to some European statesmen after the Second World War (1939–45). There was a desire to create a peaceful and prosperous Europe after the destruction of two World Wars and after centuries of antagonism and mutual distrust between the European powers.

The foundations for a more integrated Europe were established in 1957 when six countries (West Germany, France, Belgium, the Netherlands, Luxembourg and Italy) signed the Treaty of Rome and formed the European Economic Community (EEC). Britain did not join, but instead helped to create the European Free Trade Association (EFTA) in 1959. Britain distanced itself from European connections in the 1950s and saw its future in the trading patterns of the Commonwealth and a 'special relationship' with the USA. It regarded itself as a commercial power and did not wish to be restricted by European relationships. An old suspicion of Europe also caused many British people to shrink from membership of a European organization, which they thought might result in the loss of their identity and independence.

PLATE 5.4 The European Parliament, Brussels.
The Parliament also meets in Strasbourg, France on a rotating basis.
(*Vidal/Rex Features*)

However, a European commitment grew among sections of British society in the 1960s, which was influenced by the country's increasing social and economic problems. But attempts by Britain to join the EEC were vetoed by the French President, Charles de Gaulle. He was critical of Britain's relationship with the USA (particularly on nuclear weapons policies), queried the extent of British commitment to Europe and arguably did not want Britain as a rival to the leadership of the EEC.

De Gaulle resigned from the French presidency in 1969, and new British negotiations on membership began in 1970 under the pro-European Conservative Prime Minister, Edward Heath. In 1972, Parliament voted in favour of entry, despite widespread doubts and the strong opposition of a politically diverse group of interests among the British people. Britain, together with Denmark and the Republic of Ireland, formally joined the EEC on 1 January 1973, having left EFTA in 1972.

But a new Labour government (1974) under Harold Wilson was committed to giving the British people a referendum on continued membership. After further renegotiations of the terms of entry, the referendum was held in 1975, the first in British political history. The pro-marketeers won by a margin of 2 to 1 (67.2 per cent in favour, 32.8 per cent against).

The EEC was based initially on economic concerns and instituted harmonization programmes such as common coal, steel, agricultural and fisheries policies, abolition of trade tariffs between member states and development aid to depressed areas within its borders. Britain's poorer regions have benefited considerably from regional funds. In 1986 the member-states formed an internal or Single European Market, in which goods, services, people and capital could move freely across national frontiers within what was then called the European Community. In 2004, 59 per cent of British exports went to the EU and Britain received 54 per cent of its imports from the EU countries.

Some politicians had always hoped that economic integration would lead to political initiatives and a more integrated Europe. The Maastricht Treaty (1992) was a step in this process as a result of which the European Community became the European Union (EU). The treaty provided for the introduction of a common European currency (the euro), a European Bank and common defence, foreign and social policies. Further treaties have also increased the integration momentum.

There are now 25 EU members with a total population of 450 million people (Britain, Denmark, Germany, Greece, Spain, Belgium, Ireland, Luxembourg, the Netherlands, France, Italy, Portugal, Sweden, Finland, Austria, Cyprus, the Czech Republic, Estonia, Hungary, Latvia, Lithuania, Malta, Poland, Slovakia and Slovenia). Since 1994, most of the EU single market measures have also been extended to Iceland, Norway and Liechtenstein through the creation of the European Economic Area (EEA). The actual and potential growth of the EU (to include other Eastern European nations and Turkey) has been seen as providing an important political voice in world affairs and a powerful trading area in global economic matters. Today, EU/EEA member states account for 40 per cent of world trade.

The institutions involved in the running of the EU are the European Council, the Council of Ministers, the European Commission, the European Parliament and the European Court of Justice.

The European Council consists of government leaders who meet several times a year to discuss and agree on broad areas of policy. The Council of Ministers is the principal policy-implementing and law-initiating body and is normally composed of Foreign Ministers from the member states.

The Commission (under an appointed President) is the central administrative force of the EU, proposing programmes and policy to the Council of Ministers. It comprises commissioners (with one from Britain) chosen from member states to hold certain portfolios, such as agriculture or competition policy, for a renewable five-year period. Their interests then become those of the EU and not of their national governments. It is argued that the unelected Commission has too much power and should be more democratically accountable.

The European Parliament (in which Britain has 78 seats – see Table 5.1) is directly elected for a five-year term on a party political basis from the EU-wide electorate. It advises the Council of Ministers on Commission proposals, determines the EU budget and exerts some control over the Council and the Commission. It is argued that the Parliament, as the only directly-elected body

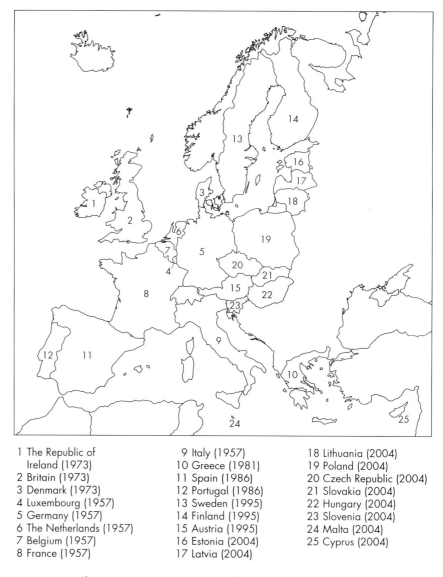

1 The Republic of
  Ireland (1973)
2 Britain (1973)
3 Denmark (1973)
4 Luxembourg (1957)
5 Germany (1957)
6 The Netherlands (1957)
7 Belgium (1957)
8 France (1957)

9 Italy (1957)
10 Greece (1981)
11 Spain (1986)
12 Portugal (1986)
13 Sweden (1995)
14 Finland (1995)
15 Austria (1995)
16 Estonia (2004)
17 Latvia (2004)

18 Lithuania (2004)
19 Poland (2004)
20 Czech Republic (2004)
21 Slovakia (2004)
22 Hungary (2004)
23 Slovenia (2004)
24 Malta (2004)
25 Cyprus (2004)

FIGURE 5.1 The European Union 2005 (with accession dates)

in the EU, should have more power and its veto over EU policy has now been
extended. In the 2004 British EU Parliament elections (held mainly under a partial
PR arrangement with party lists) the Labour Party did badly compared with the
Conservatives. The Liberal Democrats increased their seats slightly and the UK
Independence Party (which wants British withdrawal from the EU) did very well.

The Court of Justice comprises appointed judges from the member states. It
interprets EU laws and treaties, settles disputes concerning EU law and resolves

TABLE 5.1 European Parliament election results 2004 (Britain)

Party	Seats
Conservative	27
Labour	19
Liberal Democrats	12
UK Independence Party	12
Northern Irish parties	3
Scottish National Party	2
Plaid Cymru	1
Greens	2

conflicts between member-states and the EU. It is a very influential institution because it has built up a body of EU case law which is directly applicable in the domestic systems of the member states.

British membership of the EU continues to be difficult. It has complained about its contribution to the EU budget (which although reduced under Margaret Thatcher is now being reviewed); objected to the agricultural and fisheries policies; and opposed movements towards greater political and economic integration. On the one hand, Eurosceptic critics argue that Britain's sovereignty and independence are threatened by EU developments and want the repatriation of national rights from the EU back to Britain. They, and others, tend to see the EU as a free-trade area in which national legal rights and interests should be firmly retained. On the other, Europhile supporters want economic and political integration (possibly on federal lines), arguing that the EU enables governments to rationalize industrial and agricultural policies; allows European countries to operate effectively in a globalized world and run external policies which are beyond the capacity of a small or medium-sized country. In this view, membership of the EU means not a handing over of power to Brussels but a net increase in effective power.

All the major political parties are pro-European in the sense of wanting to be in Europe, although there are opposition groups in the Labour and (particularly the) Conservative parties. The country is now so closely tied to Europe in economic and institutional ways that withdrawal from the EU would be difficult in practical terms, although it is possible constitutionally.

There are divided views about the pace and direction of future developments. The Labour government wants a strong Europe in which Britain can play a central role; has supported enlargement of the EU; is backing the adoption of the proposed EU constitutional treaty (following a referendum of the British people); is in principle in favour of Britain entering the European common currency (euro);

and proposed a common defence and foreign policy for the EU. But it is against the concept of a federal 'superstate', favours the Council of Ministers as the key decision-making body and is against enhancing the powers of the European Parliament.

However, it did not take Britain into the first wave of the euro in 1999. Its policy is to wait until Britain's economy is in line with other members, see how the currency develops and then put the issue to a referendum. Polls in recent years have consistently suggested that a majority of Britons are against joining the euro. A MORI poll in February 2005 found that 57 per cent of respondents were against the euro and 55 per cent would not change their minds if the government strongly urged support.

Feelings in Britain about the proposed EU constitutional treaty have been volatile. A MORI poll in February 2005 found that 21 per cent of respondents were in favour of Britain adopting the constitution, but could be persuaded against if they thought it would be bad for Britain. Twenty-seven per cent were generally opposed to the constitution, but could be persuaded in favour if they thought it would be good for Britain. An earlier MORI poll in September 2004 put the situation in perspective, with 82 per cent of respondents saying that they did not have enough information about the issues involved to make a considered decision.

Among other things the proposed constitution would give legal identity and authority to the EU; create a legally-binding charter of rights; allow for a full-time president and foreign minister; and formally recognize the supremacy of EU law over national law. Since the French and Dutch rejected the Constitution in 2005, the question of its possible future has been placed on ice.

British support for the EU peaked in the 1980s but has since eroded and Britain is now the least enthusiastic of the EU countries. Some polls in recent years have suggested that only a slender majority of respondents wanted to stay in the EU while a majority wanted a referendum on Britain's continued membership and believed that Britons had not been given enough information about the arguments for and against membership. A 2003 MORI poll found that only 30 per cent of British respondents felt that EU membership was a good thing.

Public support for the EU tends therefore to be lukewarm and indifferent. The turn-out for British EU Parliament elections is the lowest in Europe and there is ignorance about, and little trust in, the EU, its benefits and its institutions. A MORI poll in September 2004 found that 32 per cent of respondents felt that the EU needs Britain more than Britain needs the EU; but 32 per cent also felt that Britain and the EU need each other equally. However, polls also show that 'Europe' is considered to be relatively more important to Britain than the USA and the Commonwealth. Europeanism (rather than an EU institutional entity) seems to be more easily and naturally accepted by people, particularly the young; large numbers of Britons live and work in European countries; people take their holidays in Europe; and there is considerable interchange at many levels between

Europeans and the British, so that increasing numbers of Britons regard themselves as Europeans.

The Republic of Ireland and Northern Ireland

Northern Ireland (also known as 'the six counties', or Ulster after the ancient kingdom in the north-east of the island) is constitutionally a part of the United Kingdom. But its (and British) history is inseparable from that of the Republic of Ireland. Historically, mainland Britain has been unable to accommodate itself successfully to its next-door neighbours. During the twentieth century, as Britain detached itself from empire and entered the EU, its relationship with Northern Ireland and the Republic of Ireland has been problematic. But the latter is now more closely involved politically with the UK as a result of the 1998 Good Friday Agreement on Northern Ireland and later legislation.

A basic knowledge of the island's long and troubled history is essential to understand the current role of the Republic of Ireland and the situation in Northern Ireland itself, for any solution to the problems there cannot be simplistic. Ireland was first controlled by England in the twelfth century. Since then there have been continuous rebellions by the native Irish against English colonial, political and military rule.

PLATE 5.5 Stormont, Northern Ireland.
The Parliament Building, known as Stormont because of its location in the Stormont area of Belfast. The seat of the Northern Ireland Parliament 1921–72 and now home to the Northern Irish Assembly following devolution in 1998.
(*Shout/Rex Features*)

The situation worsened in the sixteenth century, when Catholic Ireland refused to accept the Protestant Reformation, despite much religious persecution. The two seeds of future hatred (colonialism and religion) were thus sown early in Irish history. A hundred years later, Oliver Cromwell crushed rebellions in Ireland and continued the earlier 'plantation policy', by which English and Scottish settlers were given land and rights over the native Irish. These colonists also served as a police force to put down any Irish revolts. The descendants of the Protestant settlers became a powerful political minority in Ireland as a whole and a majority in Ulster. In 1690, the Protestant William III (William of Orange) crushed Catholic uprisings at the Battle of the Boyne and secured Protestant dominance in Northern Ireland.

Ireland was then mainly an agricultural country, dependent upon its farming produce. But crop failures were frequent and famine in the middle of the nineteenth century caused death and emigration, with the result that the population was reduced by a half by 1901. The people who remained demanded more autonomy over their own affairs. Irish MPs in the Westminster Parliament called persistently for 'home rule' for Ireland (control of internal matters by the Irish through an assembly in Dublin). The home rule question dominated late nineteenth- and early twentieth-century British politics. It led to periodic outbreaks of violence as the Northern Irish Protestant/Unionist majority feared that an independent and united Ireland would be dominated by the Catholics/Nationalists.

Eventually in 1921 Ireland was divided (or partitioned) into two parts as a result of uprisings, violence and eventual political agreement. This attempted solution of the historical problems has been at the root of troubles ever since. The twenty-six counties of southern Ireland became the Irish Free State and a dominion in the Commonwealth. This later developed into the Republic of Ireland, remained neutral in the Second World War and left the Commonwealth in 1949. The six counties in the north became known as Northern Ireland and remained constitutionally part of the United Kingdom. Until 1972, they had a Protestant-dominated Parliament (at Stormont outside Belfast), which was responsible for governing the province.

After the Second World War, Northern Ireland developed agriculturally and industrially. Urban centres expanded and more specifically Catholic districts developed in the towns. But the Protestants, through their ruling party (the Ulster Unionists) in Parliament, maintained an exclusive hold on all areas of life in the province, including employment, the police force, local councils and public services. The minority Catholics suffered systematic discrimination in these areas.

Conflicts arose again in Northern Ireland in 1968–9. Marches were held to demonstrate for civil liberties and were initially non-sectarian. But the situation deteriorated, fighting erupted between Protestants and Catholics and violence escalated. The Northern Ireland government asked for the British army to be sent in to restore order. The army was initially welcomed, but was soon attacked by both sides. Relations between Catholics and Protestants worsened and political attitudes became polarized. Violence continued after 1968 with outrages from both sides of the sectarian divide.

On one side of this divide is the Provisional wing of the Irish Republican Army (IRA) and other splinter nationalist groups, which are supported by some republicans and Catholics. The IRA is illegal in both the Republic and Northern Ireland and is committed to the unification of Ireland, as is its legal political wing, Provisional Sinn Fein. The IRA wants to remove the British political and military presence from Northern Ireland. Prior to the Peace Agreement in 1998, they had engaged in a systematic campaign of bombings, shootings and murders.

Protestant paramilitary groups and Unionist Parties, such as the Democratic Unionists under the hardline leadership of Ian Paisley, are equally committed to their own views. They are loyal to the British Crown and insist that they remain part of the United Kingdom. Protestant paramilitaries, partly in retaliation for IRA activities and partly to emphasize their demands, have also carried out sectarian murders and terrorist acts. British troops and the Police Service of Northern Ireland are supposed to control the two populations and to curb terrorism. But they are also targets for bullets and bombs and have been accused of perpetrating atrocities themselves.

From 1972, responsibility for Northern Ireland rested with the British government in London (direct rule) after the Northern Ireland Parliament was suspended. There have been various assemblies and executives in Northern Ireland, which were attempts to give the Catholic minority political representation in cooperation with the Protestant majority (power-sharing). But these efforts failed, largely because of Protestant intransigence, although most injustices to Catholic civil liberties were removed.

The level of violence in the province fluctuated from 1968. But emergency legislation and the reduction of legal rights for suspected terrorists continued. Moderates of all political persuasions, who were squeezed out as political polarization grew, were appalled by the outrages and the historical injustices. Outsiders often felt that a rational solution should be possible. But this was to underestimate the deep emotions on both sides, the historical dimension and the extremist elements. There was also little agreement over the cause of the problems, with views including ethnic, religious, political and economic reasons.

British governments have launched initiatives to persuade Northern Irish political parties to discuss the realistic possibilities of power-sharing in Northern Ireland. They have also tried to involve the Irish government and the Anglo-Irish Agreement of 1985 was a joint attempt to resolve the situation. It aimed to solve difficulties (such as border security and extradition arrangements) in order to achieve a devolved power-sharing government for Northern Ireland. The Republic of Ireland had to make some concessions as the price for the agreement, but was given a significant role to play in the resolution of the Northern Irish situation. However, the Republic's cooperation with Britain was seen by Northern Irish

Unionists as a step to reunification of the island and they opposed the agreement. The Republic now sees unification as a long-term aim and the British government insists that no change in Northern Ireland will take place unless a majority of the inhabitants there agree (consent). In this connection, the population of Northern Ireland is said to consist of Protestants (1,045,500 or 61.5 per cent in 2001) and Catholics (654,500 or 38.5 per cent).

The Downing Street Declaration of 1993 by the Irish and British governments was a further attempt to halt the violence and bring all parties to the conference table to discuss Northern Ireland's future. It largely restated existing positions. But, building on a Protestant paramilitary ceasefire, the Labour government in 1997 set out conditions and a schedule for peace talks between all the political parties. An IRA ceasefire also allowed Sinn Fein into the peace process.

Multi-party talks held in Belfast in April 1998 concluded with the 'Good Friday Agreement'. Legislation was passed in Dublin and London for referendums on the Agreement and provided for elections to a new Northern Ireland Assembly. In May 1998 referendums on the Agreement were held. Northern Ireland voted 71.1 per cent in favour and 28.8 per cent against, while in the Irish Republic the result was 94.3 per cent and 5.6 per cent respectively.

A new Northern Ireland Assembly of 108 members was elected by proportional representation (single transferable vote) in June 1998. A Northern Ireland Act sets out the principle of consent to any change in constitutional status in Northern Ireland, provides for its administration and contains arrangements for human rights and equality.

In December 1999, some political power was devolved by the Westminster Parliament to the Northern Ireland Assembly and its Executive. It has legislative and executive authority to make laws and take decisions in Northern Ireland, except for reserved UK powers over policing, security matters, prisons and criminal justice.

A North/South Ministerial Council, North/South Implementation Bodies, a British/Irish Council and a British/Irish Intergovernmental Conference were also established. These organizations bring together significant UK and Irish elements in the context of both islands. Critics argue that the British-Irish Council is a very positive step and a political expression of the mixed ethnic and cultural history of the islands. It comprises the UK and Irish governments, the Northern Ireland Assembly, the Welsh Assembly, the Scottish Parliament, the Isle of Man, the Channel Islands and provision for the English regions. It could potentially promote participation in one democratic, representative British-Irish body for the first time.

But in February 2000, following a report from the Independent International Commission on Decommissioning, the Northern Ireland Assembly was suspended due to a lack of progress on the decommissioning of illegally held weapons, mainly by the IRA. Direct rule from London was reimposed. Although periods of devolved power were later restored to the Assembly, obstacles appeared such as

Stormont spying allegations against the IRA, a large bank robbery attributed to the IRA and no significant progress on decommissioning. The Peace Agreement was in danger of collapse. The Assembly was suspended in 2004 and has not been restored (2005).

In 2005, the IRA announced that they would put all their weapons beyond use and ordered their members to stop military action. Critics reacted with scepticism and insisted that action follow these words. In the meantime, criminal activities continue to be carried out by both Unionist and Nationalist organizations, serious sectarian violence broke out again on Belfast streets in 2005 and dissident groups protested against the Good Friday Agreement.

Difficulties remain in the path of achieving the aims of the Agreement. The Protestant Unionists want to remain part of the United Kingdom, oppose union with the Republic of Ireland, insist upon the verifiable decommissioning of all IRA weapons and argue that any future solution for Northern Ireland must lie in consent by a majority of the people living there. Sinn Fein and the IRA are committed to a united Ireland and argue that a majority of all people (Northern Ireland and the Republic of Ireland) must consent to any eventual proposed solution. The 2005 British general election and the 2003 Northern Ireland Assembly election resulted in increased representation for Sinn Fein and the anti-peace agreement Democratic Unionist Party, with reduced support for the Ulster Unionists and the moderate SDLP. This could lead to more extreme and hardline positions being taken in Northern Ireland.

Opinion polls in recent years indicate a weariness by a majority of the mainland British population with both sides in Northern Ireland. They are in favour of Irish unification and do not accept the Labour government's strategy of British withdrawal only with the consent of the majority in Northern Ireland. A MORI poll in August 2001 of people in mainland Britain found that 26 per cent of respondents believed that Northern Ireland should remain in the UK and 41 per cent believed that the province should reunite with the Republic of Ireland.

Exercises

Explain and examine the following terms:

Commonwealth	Falklands	Treaty of Rome
decolonialization	Boyne	NATO
direct rule	Stormont	referendum
power-sharing	Trident	special relationship
Sinn Fein	Maastricht	European Commission
EFTA	IRA	pro-marketeer
euro	Unionists	EEA
'consent'	decommissioning	British-Irish Council

continued

Write short essays on the following topics:

1   Should Northern Ireland be united with the Republic of Ireland? Give your reasons.

2   Does the Commonwealth still have a role to play today?

3   Discuss Britain's relationship with the European Union.

4   Does Britain still have a world role?

Further reading

1   Chapters in Black, J. (2000) *Modern British History from 1900* London: Macmillan
2   Connolly, C. (2003) *Theorizing Ireland* London: Palgrave Macmillan
3   Dixon, P. (2001) *Northern Ireland: The Politics of War and Peace* London: Palgrave/ Macmillan
4   Marshall, P.J. (2001) *The Cambridge Illustrated History of the British Empire* Cambridge: Cambridge University Press
5   Moody, T.W. and Martin, F.X. (2001) *The Course of Irish History* Cork and Dublin: Mercier Press
6   Srinivasan, K. (2005) *The Rise, Decline and Future of the British Commonwealth* London: Palgrave Macmillan
7   Tonge, J. (2005) *The New Northern Irish Politics?* London: Palgrave Macmillan
8   Warner, G. (1994) *British Foreign Policy since 1945* Oxford: Blackwell
9   Watts, D. and Pilkington, C. (2005) *Britain in the European Union* Manchester: Manchester University Press
10   Young, J.W. (2000) *Britain and European Unity 1945–1999* London: Macmillan

Websites

Foreign and Commonwealth Office: www.fco.gov.uk
Department for International Development: www.dfid.gov.uk
The Commonwealth: www.thecommonwealth.org
Ministry of Defence: www.mod.uk
NATO: www.nato.int
European Union: http://europa.eu.int/

Chapter 6

The legal system

- ■ Legal history
- ■ Sources of British law
- ■ Court structures in England and Wales
- ■ Civil and criminal procedure in England and Wales
- ■ Law and order
- ■ The legal profession
- ■ Attitudes to the legal system and crime
- ■ *Exercises*
- ■ *Further reading*
- ■ *Websites*

Law and order and the workings of the legal system are of considerable concern to British people and directly affect individuals at different levels in their daily lives. In recent years, they have regularly appeared among the top issues in public opinion polls about the state of the country. In particular, they emphasize worries about the effects of crime, rising rates of anti-social behaviour, thuggery and yobbishness and the high incidence of these among youth groups. It is therefore necessary to appreciate how legal structures are attempting to cope with these public concerns.

Britain does not have a common legal system. Instead, there are three separate elements: those of England and Wales, Scotland and Northern Ireland. They sometimes differ from each other in their procedures and court names. Following devolution, some laws are only applicable to one of the nations although much Westminster legislation still applies to all of Britain.

In order to simplify matters, this chapter concentrates on the largest element – that of England and Wales, with comparative references to Scotland and Northern Ireland. The Northern Irish legal system is similar to that of England and Wales. But Scotland has historically maintained its independent legal apparatus.

British court cases are divided into civil and criminal law. Civil law involves private rights and settles disputes between individuals or organizations. It deals with claims for compensation (financial or otherwise) by a person (claimant) who has suffered loss or damage (like a breach of contract or a negligent act) at the hands of another (defendant). Civil cases may be decided by negotiation and settlement before trial or by a judge (and sometimes a jury) after trial.

Criminal law protects society by punishing those (the accused or defendants) who commit crimes against the state, such as theft or murder. The state usually prosecutes an individual or group at a trial in order to establish guilt. The result may be a fine or imprisonment. Such punishment is supposed to act as a deterrent to potential offenders, as well as stating society's attitudes on a range of matters.

Legal history

The legal system is one of the oldest and most traditional of British institutions. Its authority and influence are due to its independence from the executive and legislative branches of government. It is supposed to interpret and apply the law; serve citizens; control unlawful activities against them and the state; protect civil liberties; and support legitimate government.

But it has historically been accused of harshness; of supporting vested and political interests; favouring property rather than human rights; maintaining the isolation and mystique of the law; encouraging the delay and expense of legal actions; and showing a bias against the poor and disadvantaged. It has been criticized for its resistance to reform and the maintenance of professional privileges which can conflict with the public interest.

Some critics feel that the law today has still not adapted to changing conditions, nor understood the needs of contemporary society. Recent miscarriages of justice have embarrassed the police, government and judiciary (judges) and increased public concern about the quality of criminal justice. Similar misgivings are also felt about the expense and operation of the civil law.

But the legal system has changed over the centuries in response to changing social structures and philosophies. Contemporary consumer demands, professional pressures and government reforms are forcing it to develop, sometimes rapidly and sometimes slowly. Most people in the past were unaffected by the law. But it now involves citizens more directly and to a greater extent than before. Increased demands are made upon it by individuals, the state and corporate bodies. Concern about crime has emphasized the control role of the criminal law, while increased divorce, family breakdown and a more litigious society (or alleged 'compensation culture') have led to a heavier workload for the civil law.

To some extent, the structural differences in the UK legal system are due to the events of history and the internal, political development of the British state. Generally, however, English (and gradually British) legal history has been conditioned by two basic concerns: first that the law should be administered by the state in national courts and second that the judges should be independent of royal and political control.

State centralization of the law in England meant that the same laws should be applicable to the whole country. This was achieved by Anglo-Norman monarchs as they rationalized the existing common law and different legal codes. The early courts were therefore mainly based in London, where they dealt with canon (or church), criminal, civil and commercial law. But there was an increasing need for courts in local areas outside London to apply the national law. By the end of the twelfth century, London judges travelled throughout England and decided cases locally. In 1327, Edward III appointed magistrates (Justices of the Peace) in each county who could hold alleged criminals in jail until their later trial by a London judge. The powers of the magistrates were gradually extended and they ran a system of local criminal courts with the London judges. But there was no adequate provision for local civil courts. These were not established until 1846 and a more integrated apparatus of local civil and criminal law was only gradually established at a later stage.

Over the centuries, a growing population, an expanding volume of legal work and increased social and economic complexity necessitated more courts and specialization. But the number of local and London courts in this haphazard historical development resulted in diverse procedures and an overlapping of functions in England and Wales, which hindered implementation of the law. The two periods of major reform to correct this situation were in 1873–5, when there was a complete court revision, and in 1970–1, when further changes produced the present court system in England and Wales. Similar developments also occurred in Scotland and Ireland.

The second concern was that the judiciary should be independent of the executive and legislative branches of government. Monarchs were responsible for the law in earlier centuries, often interfered in the legal process and could dismiss unsympathetic judges. Judicial independence was achieved in 1701, when the Act of Settlement made judges virtually irremovable from office. This principle has now been relaxed for junior judges, who may be dismissed, and all judges who commit criminal offences are expected to resign. In recent years under both Labour and Conservative governments, there have been conflicts between judges and politicians, as the judiciary fights to maintain its traditional independence from the executive, its function of interpreting the law and its sentencing powers in individual cases.

Sources of British law

The three main sources of *English/Welsh* law are the common law, statute law and European Union law. The oldest is the *Common law*, based on the varied local customs of early settlers and invaders. After the Norman Conquest, it became a uniform body of rules, principles and law which was decided and written down by judges in court cases. The same rules still guide judges in their interpretation of statutes and in the expansion of the common law.

Common law decisions form precedents from which judges can find the principles of law to be applied to new cases. Normally today, the creation of new precedents in England and Wales lies with the House of Lords, as the supreme court of appeal. Its rulings state the current law to be applied by all courts. The tradition of following precedent maintains consistency and continuity. But it can result in conservative law and fail to take account of changing social conditions.

Statute law was originally made in various forms by the monarch. But the Westminster Parliament gradually became the legislating authority because of its growing power against the monarch. Statutes (Acts of Parliament which create new law) multiplied in the nineteenth and twentieth centuries because rules were needed for a changing, complex and larger society. Much British law today is in statute form and shows the influence of the state in citizens' lives. Acts of the Westminster Parliament are applicable to England, Wales and often the UK as a whole and are supreme over most other forms of law (except for some EU law).

European Union law became part of English (British) law following Britain's entry into the European Economic Community in 1973. EU law takes precedence

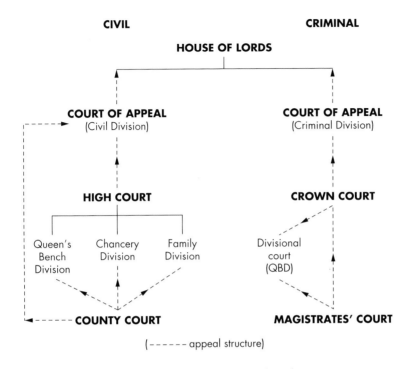

FIGURE 6.1 Civil and criminal courts in England and Wales

over British domestic law in certain areas and British judges must apply EU law when there is a conflict with Acts of Parliament. EU law and British domestic law therefore now coexist.

Scottish law derives from legal principles and rules modelled on both Roman and English law. The sources of Scots law are judge-made law, authoritative legal treatises, EU law and legislation. The first two are the common law of Scotland and are similar to the English common law. Legislation consists of relevant Westminster Acts of Parliament and Scottish Parliament Acts on devolved matters in Scotland.

Northern Ireland has a similar common law tradition to England and Wales. In addition to UK statutes affecting Northern Ireland, the Northern Ireland Assembly (when functioning) has legislative and executive authority for all devolved matters and can thus make laws in Northern Ireland.

Court structures in England and Wales

The court system is divided into criminal and civil courts (see Figure 6.1) under the central direction of the Department for Constitutional Affairs. Increasing numbers of British people have dealings with the different courts at various levels.

They are not, therefore, minority or abstract structures remote from the daily realities of British life and their activities are widely reported and commented upon.

Criminal courts

There are two levels of criminal courts. The lower and busiest is the magistrates' court, which deals with summary (less serious) cases and handles over 96 per cent of all criminal matters. The more serious (indictable) criminal offences, like murder, are tried by the higher court, the crown court.

Magistrates' courts serve local areas in England and Wales. Two types of officials try cases in the courts: Justices of the Peace (JPs) and District Judges.

Most magistrates' courts are presided over by 30,000 lay magistrates (JPs). They are part-time judicial officials chosen from the general public; hear cases without a jury; receive no salary for their services (only expenses); and have some legal training before sitting in court. Magistrates may be motivated by the desire to perform a public service or the prestige of the position. They sit daily in big cities and less frequently in rural areas. They date from 1327 and illustrate a legal system in which the ordinary person is judged by other citizens, rather than by professionals.

Magistrates are formally appointed by the Crown on the advice of the Lord Chancellor, who receives suitable names from advisory committees. Magistrates in the past were white middle- or upper-class males who were prominent in the local community, such as landowners, doctors, retired military officers and businessmen. But they are now recruited from wider and more representative social, ethnic and gender backgrounds.

The magistrates' court has an average of three JPs when hearing cases, composed usually of men and women. They decide a case on the facts and pronounce the punishment (if any). They are advised on points of law by their clerk, who is a legally qualified, full-time official and a professional element in the system. The clerk is restricted to an advisory role and must not be involved in the magistrates' decision-making, but is now able to handle some minor judicial tasks.

Everyone accused of a criminal offence (defendant) must usually appear first before a magistrates' court. The court can itself try summary offences and some indictable/summary offences ('either-way offences'). The magistrates also decide whether a person should be sent for trial at the higher crown court in serious cases.

Magistrates have limited powers of punishment. They may impose fines up to £5,000 for each offence, or send people to prison for six months on each offence up to a maximum of one year. They prefer not to imprison if a fine or other punishment is sufficient and the majority of penalties are fines. In either-way offences, they can send a person to the crown court for sentencing if they lack sufficient powers.

There is a need for uniform punishments in magistrates' courts. But sentences vary in different parts of the country. This factor, in addition to alleged bias and the amateur status of JPs, has led to criticism of the system. There have been proposals to replace magistrates with lawyers or other experts. But these suggestions are criticized by those who oppose the professionalization of the legal process and who argue that such changes would not necessarily result in greater competence or justice.

An important function of the magistrates' courts is to decide cases involving young persons under 18 in Youth Courts. Media reports of these cases must not normally identify the accused and there is a range of punishments for those found guilty. Youth Courts play a central role, particularly at a time when many crimes are committed by young people under 16. The Labour government has tried to encourage tougher treatment for young offenders. Magistrates' courts also handle limited civil matters involving family problems, divorce and road traffic offences.

District Judges in the magistrates' court are qualified lawyers and full-time officials, are paid by the state, usually sit alone to hear and decide cases and work

PLATE 6.1 The Old Bailey, London.
The scene of many famous trials in British legal history and now a Crown Court centre.
(*Alisdair MacDonald/Rex Features*)

mainly in the large cities. Since the magistrates' system is divided between amateur JPs and the professional District Judges, it is sometimes argued that the latter should be used to replace the former on a national basis. But this proposal has been resisted by those who wish to retain the civilian element in the magistrates' courts.

The higher *crown courts*, such as the Central Criminal Court in London (popularly known as the Old Bailey), are situated in about 78 cities in England and Wales and are centrally administered by the Department for Constitutional Affairs.

The crown court has jurisdiction over all indictable criminal offences and innocence or guilt after a trial is decided by a jury of 12 citizens. After it has reached its decision on the facts of the case, sentence is passed by the judge who is in charge of proceedings throughout the trial.

In *Scotland*, minor criminal cases are tried summarily by lay Justices of the Peace in District Courts (equivalent to English magistrates' courts). Sheriffs' courts deal with more serious offences where the sheriff sits alone to hear summary offences and is helped by a jury (15 members) for indictable cases. The most serious cases (such as murder and rape) are handled by the High Court of Justiciary in major urban centres and are heard by a judge and a jury of 15 lay people. *Northern Irish* criminal courts follow the system in England and Wales with lower magistrates' courts and higher crown courts (the latter generally with a judge and jury).

PLATE 6.2 A contemporary Crown Court.
Contains many of the traditional features such as the dock, judge's chair and bench, jury seats, and prosecution and defence benches.
(*Shout/Rex Features*)

Criminal appeal courts

The appeal structure (see Figure 6.1) is supposed to be a safeguard against mistakes and miscarriages of justice. But the number of such cases has increased, resulting in much publicity and concern. They have been caused by police tampering with or withholding evidence; police pressure to induce confessions; and the unreliability of some forensic evidence. Appeal courts are criticized for their handling of some appeals and an independent authority (the Criminal Cases Review Commission) was created (1995). It reviews alleged miscarriages of justice and directs some cases back to the appeal courts, which may quash convictions or order new trials.

Appeals to a higher court can be expensive and difficult and permission must usually be granted by a lower court. Appeals may be made against conviction or sentence and can be brought on grounds of fact and law. If successful, the higher court may quash the conviction, reduce the sentence or order a new trial. The prosecution can also appeal against a lenient punishment and a heavier sentence may be substituted.

Crown courts hear appeals from magistrates' courts and both may appeal on matters of law to a divisional court of the Queen's Bench Division. Appeals from the crown court are made to the Criminal Division of the Court of Appeal. Appeals may then go to the House of Lords as the highest court in England and Wales. But permission is only granted if a point of law of public importance is involved. Up to five Law Lords hear the case and their decision represents the current state of the law.

In *Scotland*, the High Court of Justiciary in Edinburgh tries criminal cases and is the supreme court for criminal appeals. *Northern Ireland* has its own appeal courts, but the House of Lords in London may also be used.

Civil courts

Civil law proceedings in England and Wales are brought either in the county court (which deals with 90 per cent of civil cases) or in the High Court (see Figure 6.1). Less expensive and complex actions are dealt with in the county court, rather than the High Court, and most civil disputes do not reach court at all.

England and Wales are divided into some 250 districts with a county court for each district. The county court handles a range of money, property, contract, divorce and family matters and a district judge usually sits alone when hearing cases.

The *High Court of Justice* has its main centre in London, with branches throughout England and Wales. It is divided into three divisions which specialize in specific matters. The *Queen's Bench Division* has a wide jurisdiction, including contract and negligence cases; the *Chancery Court Division* is concerned with commercial, financial and succession matters; and the *Family Division* deals with domestic issues such as marriage, divorce, property and the custody of children.

PLATE 6.3 The Royal Courts of Justice, the Strand, London.
Contains the High Court and the Courts of Appeal (civil and criminal).
(*Alisdair MacDonald/Rex Features*)

In *Scotland*, the sheriff court deals with most civil actions, because its jurisdiction is not financially limited, although the higher Court of Session may also be used for some cases. The *Northern Irish* High Court handles most civil cases.

Civil appeal courts

The High Court hears appeals from magistrates' courts and county courts. But the main avenue of appeal is to the Court of Appeal (Civil Division), which deals with appeals from all lower civil courts on questions of law and fact. It can reverse or amend decisions, or sometimes order a new trial.

Appeals from the Court of Appeal may be made to the House of Lords. The appellant must normally have obtained permission either from the Court of Appeal or the House of Lords. Appeals are usually restricted to points of law where an important legal issue is at stake. In *Scotland* at present, civil appeals are made first to a sheriff-principal, then to the Court of Session and finally to the House of Lords in London. The *Northern Irish* Court of Appeal hears appeal cases.

Civil and criminal procedure in England and Wales

Many features of civil and criminal procedure in England and Wales are similar to those in Scotland and Northern Ireland.

Civil procedure

A civil action in the county court or the High Court begins when the claimant serves documents with details of a claim on the defendant. If the defendant defends the action, documents are prepared and circulated to all parties and the case proceeds to trial and judgment. A decision in civil cases is reached on the balance of probabilities. The court also decides the expenses (damages) of the action, which may be considerable, and the loser often pays personal and the opponent's costs. Civil law procedures have been reorganized, streamlined and simplified since 1999 because of concern about the efficiency of the system, with its delays and expense. Much of the High Court's work has been transferred to the county court. Procedural rules between the two courts have been unified. Active court management is now in place with judges setting the pace of litigation and cheaper, quicker forms of settlement in other courts have been implemented, such as those dealing with smaller matters. Nevertheless, it is advisable that disputes be settled by negotiation and other avenues rather than by a court trial in order to avoid high costs and any uncertainty about a trial result. Most civil disputes are in fact decided out of court.

Criminal procedure

Crimes are offences against the laws of the state and the state usually brings a person to trial. Prior to 1985, the police in England and Wales were responsible for prosecuting criminal cases. But the Crown Prosecution Service (CPS) now does this job. It is independent of the police, financed by the state and staffed by state lawyers. There has been criticism of the performance of the CPS, which has suffered from understaffing and underfunding. The CPS and its head (the Director of Public Prosecutions – DPP) have the final word in deciding whether to proceed with cases. In *Scotland*, prosecution duties rest with the Crown Office and Procurator-Fiscal Service and in *Northern Ireland* with the police and the DPP.

Arrests for most criminal offences are made by the police, although any citizen can make a 'citizen's arrest'. After criticism of the police for their arrest, questioning and charging practices, they now operate under codes of practice, which lay down strict procedures for the protection of suspects. The police cannot usually interrogate people, nor detain them at a police station if they have not been arrested. Once persons have been arrested, had their rights read to them and been charged with an offence, they must be brought before a magistrates' court, normally within 24 hours. In serious cases and after arrest, a person can be held for up to 96 hours. After this period, the suspect must be released if no charges are brought.

When a person appears before a magistrates' court prior to a trial, the magistrates can grant or refuse bail (freedom from custody). If bail is refused, a person will be kept in custody in a remand centre or in prison. If bail is granted, the individual is set free until a later court appearance. The court may require certain assurances from the accused about conduct while on bail, such as residence in a specific area and reporting to a police station.

Application for bail is a legal right, since the accused has not yet been found guilty of a crime, and there should be strong reasons for refusing it. There is concern that people who are refused bail are, at their later trial, either found not guilty or are punished only by a fine. The system thus holds alleged criminals on remand to await trial and this increases overcrowding in prisons. But there is also great public concern about accused persons who commit further serious offences while free on bail.

Criminal trials in the magistrates' and crown courts are usually open to the public. But the media can only report the court proceedings and must not comment upon them while the trial is in progress (the *sub judice* or 'pending litigation' rule).

The accused enters the dock, the charge is read and he or she pleads 'guilty' or 'not guilty'. On a 'guilty' plea, the person may be sentenced after a statement of the facts by the prosecution. But sentencing can also be deferred to a later date. On a 'not guilty' plea, the trial proceeds in order to establish the person's innocence or guilt. An individual is innocent until proved guilty and it is the

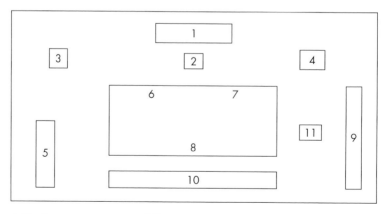

1 Magistrates   5 The press   9 Witnesses who have
2 Clerk to the Justices   6 Defending lawyer   given evidence
3 Defendant   7 Presecuting lawyer   10 The public
4 Witness   8 Probation officers   11 Court ushers

FIGURE 6.2 A typical magistrates' court in action

responsibility of the prosecution to prove guilt beyond a reasonable doubt. If proof is not achieved, a 'not guilty' verdict is returned by magistrates in the magistrates' court or by the jury in the crown court. In Scotland, there is an additional possible verdict of 'not proven'.

The prosecution and defence of the accused are usually performed by solicitors in magistrates' courts and by barristers and solicitor-advocates in crown courts. But it is possible to defend oneself. British trials are adversarial contests between defence and prosecution. Both sides call witnesses in support of their case, who may be questioned by the other side. The rules of evidence and procedure in this contest are complicated and must be strictly observed. The accused may remain silent at arrest, charge and trial and need not give evidence. However, the right to silence has now been limited. This means that the police must warn arrestees that their silence may affect their later defence. The judge at the trial may comment on silence and it may influence the decision of juries and magistrates.

It is argued that the adversarial nature of criminal trials can result either in the conviction of innocent people or the guilty escaping conviction. It is suggested that the inquisitorial system of other European countries would be better. This allows the prior questioning of suspects and establishing of facts to be carried out by professional impartial interrogators (or judges) rather than the police.

The judge in the crown court and the magistrates in the magistrates' court are controlling influences in the battle between defence and prosecution. They

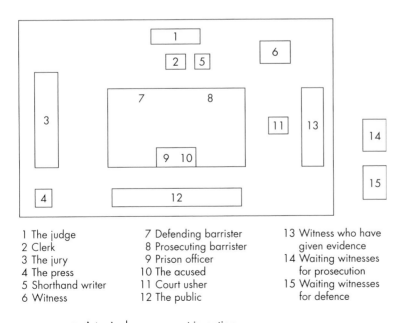

1 The judge	7 Defending barrister	13 Witness who have
2 Clerk	8 Prosecuting barrister	given evidence
3 The jury	9 Prison officer	14 Waiting witnesses
4 The press	10 The acused	for prosecution
5 Shorthand writer	11 Court usher	15 Waiting witnesses
6 Witness	12 The public	for defence

FIGURE 6.3 A typical crown court in action

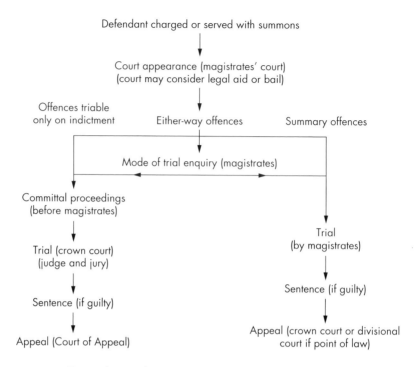

FIGURE 6.4 Criminal procedure

apply the rules of the court and give directions on procedure and evidence. But they should not interfere too actively, nor show bias. After the prosecution and the defence have concluded their cases, the magistrates decide both the verdict and sentence. In the crown court, the jury delivers the verdict after the judge has given a summing-up and the judge then pronounces sentence (which may be deferred).

The jury

Trial by jury is an ancient and important feature of British justice. It has declined in civil cases (except for libel and fraud), but is the main element in criminal trials in the crown court for indictable offences. Most British residents are obliged to undertake jury service when summoned.

Before the start of a criminal trial in the crown court, 12 jurors are chosen from a list of 30 names randomly selected from local electoral registers. They listen to the evidence at the trial and give their verdict on the facts, after having been isolated in a room for their deliberations. If a jury cannot reach a decision, it will be discharged and a new one sworn in. The accused can thus be tried twice for the same offence (as in appeals which order a new trial or in the re-hearing of cases where new evidence appears). Such results are an exception to the principle that a person can only be tried once for the same offence. In most cases, the jury reaches a decision. The judge accepts a majority (rather than a unanimous) verdict after the jury has deliberated for more than two hours, if there are no more than two dissentients (ten to two). The jury does not decide the punishment or sentence, except in some civil cases, where it awards damages.

The jury system is the citizen's link with the legal process. It is supposed to safeguard individual liberty and justice because a common-sense decision on the facts either to punish or acquit is taken by fellow citizens. But the system has been criticized because of high acquittal rates; allegedly unsuitable or subjective jurors; intimidation of and threats against jurors; and need to save time and expense. Some critics wish to replace the jury with 'experts' and the Labour government has reduced the right to jury trial in some 'either-way' offences. But it seems that the jury system, as an essential feature of British justice, will continue.

Legal aid and access to legal services

The British legal aid system was created in 1949 and was only the second of its type in the world. It was intended to help eligible persons who could not afford legal representation and advice in criminal and civil matters to have their bills paid by the state. Since then, eligibility for legal aid has been reformed and has become very complicated. The granting of legal aid now depends upon the merit of the case and income levels, so that, for example, families with an annual income of more than £27,500 are excluded from civil legal aid. Although criminal legal aid is available for anyone charged with a crime, a guilty person can be ordered to reimburse the aid. Recipients may also be asked to make contributions and meet charges.

Critics argue that legal aid has been effectively reduced and many legal firms (and barristers) have withdrawn from the system because it is unprofitable. In this view, access to legal services today is in practice restricted to the poorest members of society (for whom legal aid may be available without contribution) and the richest minority (who are able to pay their own legal fees). Most people on medium incomes will usually have to pay their own civil and criminal expenses in one form or another if they are caught up in legal actions.

Since fewer people are now eligible for state help at a time when demand is rising, it is argued that the provision of legal aid should be expanded and liberalized. But increased demand results in a more expensive system (costing £2 billion in 2005) and the Labour government seems to be increasing 'means testing' of legal aid by which any help is tied to income.

A recent reform may help those people who wish to start personal injury civil actions but who cannot afford the cost. Clients can enter into conditional agreements with lawyers, in which payment of legal fees on a percentage basis is only made if the client wins ('no win-no fee'). This scheme may be extended to most civil disputes which involve money or damages (and possibly criminal matters). But critics argue that such work only appeals to lawyers if there is a reasonable chance of winning and it will not solve the problem of insuring against the cost of losing.

Law and order

Crime and punishment

The total expense of the legal system and its protective services amounts to 6 per cent of government spending and the overall cost of crime to society is considerable. Law and order in Britain are serious issues, which are of great concern to people and on which political parties base their claims for public support.

Central problems in evaluating the extent of crime are that the government uses two sets of official crime statistics; there is significant non-reporting of offences such as assaults, burglary and rape; and unsolved crime remains high. Figures based on police data show that there was a 6 per cent decrease in overall reported crime for the year ending 2004 in England and Wales, but a 6 per cent rise in violent crimes like assaults, robberies and sexual offences and a 5 per cent increase in firearms offences. However, contrasting figures are found in supposedly more accurate victim-based statistics like the *British Crime Survey*, which covers people who actually experience crime but which does not cover all crimes or children. Figures for 2004 suggest a decrease of 11 per cent in overall crime, a 9 per cent decrease in violent crime and a falling trend in violent crime since its peak in 1995.

In terms of gun use, while the police figures show a 5 per cent rise in firearms offences, there has been a 5 per cent drop in serious injuries and a 15 per cent fall in handgun use. About one third of recorded offences also involve the use of imitation firearms (a 15 per cent increase), which are a persistent problem.

The police statistics suggest a fall in the overall level of crime, but a rise in the level of violent crime with an estimated 4 per cent of people experiencing a violent incident annually, half of which result in some injury. According to the government, these figures show that the risk of being a victim of crime is the lowest in more than 24 years. It attributes the rise in recorded violent crime to better reporting of low level thuggery, domestic violence and sexual offences. It argues that the crimes which affect most people, such as burglary, robbery and vehicle theft, have decreased significantly. However, although robbery represents only 2 per cent of the total, general street crime is a politically high profile issue, and 40 per cent of this type of crime occurs in London.

Other research surveys (such as the Offending, Crime and Justice survey) suggest that 10 per cent of offenders are responsible for 60 per cent of offences and that serious and prolific offenders amount to 1 per cent of the population. But it is estimated that only one in 50 crimes results in a conviction and only 23 per cent of all crimes are actually recorded by the police. Opinion polls regularly suggest that 50 per cent of victims do not report incidents to the police because they lack confidence that criminals would be caught.

Disturbing aspects of these statistics are the greater use of knives and firearms in criminal acts, particularly those connected to gang violence and serious organized crime (leading to demands that all police officers should be armed), the increased amount of drug- and alcohol-related crime and violence and the number of offences committed by young people. Britain has a serious problem with young offenders, the peak age for committing crime is 15 and 10 per cent of reported criminal offences are committed by teenagers under 16. There is a widespread membership of gangs in this group and adherence to gangster culture (allegedly encouraged by rap music lyrics) in which the carrying and use of guns and knives are prevalent. Binge-drinking in town and city centres has also increased and led to more violence on the streets. Critics argue that the Labour government's decision to extend drinking hours in pubs, clubs and restaurants from 2005 will only increase the problem.

Respondents to polls think that the causes of crime in Britain are lack of parental discipline and male role models; the breakdown of family and community structures; drugs; alcohol; lenient sentencing by the courts; gangs; unemployment; lack of school discipline; poverty; television; poor policing; teenage boredom; and lack of free-time facilities for young people. Tony Blair in 2005 laid the blame on parents and earlier in opposition had tried to ease public concern by promising 'zero tolerance' for crime and being 'tough on crime and the causes of crime'. The Labour government has introduced stricter punishment (particularly for young people), curfews and restrictions on persistent offenders, longer jail terms and greater protection for the public. But polls in the 2000s show that people do not think that the government has delivered on its law and order promises, despite its claim that its street crime initiatives are reducing street crime.

A person found guilty of a first criminal offence may receive no punishment, or be placed on probation for a period under the supervision of probation officers. Other punishments for adults are fines or imprisonment (for those over 21), which vary according to the severity of the offence and any previous convictions. Stricter sentencing will lead to more prisoners and 18 per cent of convicted persons are imprisoned, a higher rate than in other European countries. In 2003, the prison population in England and Wales (sentenced and remand prisoners) was 73,000 (including 4,400 women or 6 per cent); that for Scotland was 6,524 (280 women); and that for Northern Ireland was 1,160. These figures showed increases since the mid-1990s and were the highest in Europe. Prison overcrowding is a serious problem and prisons are now (2005) at full capacity.

Alternatives to prison are community rehabilitation orders (serving the community in some capacity for a number of hours over a number of months) and prison sentences which are suspended (dependent upon no further offences being committed for a specified period). A recent experiment is 'tagging' (arm or leg bracelets connected electronically to local police stations) whereby offenders are confined to a specific area and have to observe a curfew. The tag is activated if these conditions are broken. However, tagging has not proved to be a success according to reports in 2005 which suggested that re-offending after and even during tagging is very high. The latest attempt to control yobbish behaviour is the anti-social behaviour order (ASBO), which bans offenders from particular areas or prohibits various forms of thuggish behaviour.

Young people may be punished by fines (under 17), taken into local authority care, confined in a young offenders' institution (Youth Prison) for those between 17 and 20, or undergo supervision in the community. Re-offending among young people after a custodial sentence is high, but supervision outside institutions leads less often to re-offending.

The death penalty by hanging for murder was abolished in 1965. The House of Commons has since voted on several occasions against its re-imposition. Recent polls show that only one in four Britons want the restoration of the death penalty for murder (a much lower figure than previously). But the public do seem to support harsh treatment of criminal offenders and argue that more sympathy and aid should be given to the victims of crime. The government has supported such victims with financial compensation, but its programmes have not satisfied critics or the victims.

Many British people feel that the penalties for criminal offences are inadequate as deterrents to prevent crime. But many prisons are overcrowded, old and decayed, lack humane facilities, are unfitted for a modern penal system and their personnel are understaffed and overworked. Prison conditions have resulted in serious disorder and riots in recent years, low morale among prisoners and prison staff and an increase in suicides by prison inmates. Debates about punishment as opposed to the rehabilitation of offenders continue. But proposals to improve the situation usually encounter the problems of expense, although the government is building more courts and prisons. Some prisons and prison services (such as escorting prisoners to court) have now been privatized.

A majority of prisoners are not reformed by their sentences. Some 60 per cent are re-convicted for later offences, and fear of prison or punishment does not seem to act as a deterrent. Critics suggest that jail terms should be cut (with weekend-only prisoners) and that institutions should be humanized and prisoners given a sense of purpose. Alternatives to custodial sentences, such as supervised housing, probation hostels and supervised work projects are also advocated. But others argue that the main concern of the criminal system should be punishment and not rehabilitation.

Law enforcement and the police

The armed forces in Britain are subordinate to the civilian government and are used only for defence purposes. An exception has been the deployment of the army in Northern Ireland since 1969, where they supported the Royal Ulster

PLATE 6.4 British police at a demonstration during the G8 summit in Edinburgh, 4 July 2005. Demonstrators protesting against globalization, poverty and capitalism.
(*Ray Tang/Rex Features*)

Constabulary (now the Police Service of Northern Ireland). But there are proposals that the military could help the police to counter organized crime in drugs, illegal immigration and computer hacking.

The maintenance of law and order rests mainly with the civilian police. The oldest police force is the Metropolitan Police, founded in 1829 by Sir Robert Peel to fight crime in London, and from which the modern forces grew. Today there is no one national police force. Instead, there are 52 independent forces (43 in England and Wales), which undertake law enforcement in county or regional areas, with the Metropolitan Police being responsible for policing London from its headquarters at New Scotland Yard. Regional forces (which may be reduced in England and Wales through mergers) are under the political control of local police committees. Daily authority rests with the head of regional forces (Chief Constable), who has organizational independence and responsibility for the actions of the force.

There were 163,697 policemen and women in Britain in 2004, or one officer for every 364 people. Although these figures represent an increase over previous years, critics argue that the forces are under-manned and recruitment is difficult. Only a disproportionately small number are from non-white ethnic communities. Many of their members are hostile to or sceptical of the police, although there have been attempts to recruit more of them to the forces, with varying degrees of success. Community Support Officers and part-time special constables provide supplementary help to the regular police in security duties and give a greater street presence.

The police are not allowed to join trade unions or strike. But they do have staff associations to represent their interests. They are subject to the law, and can be sued or prosecuted for any wrongdoing in the course of their work. Individuals can complain about police actions to a new Independent Police Complaints Commission (2004) which, it is hoped, might provide a stronger role than previous models. However, critics still argue that complaints procedures are unsatisfactory and that democratic control of the police should be strengthened.

The police, with their peculiar helmets and lack of firearms, are often regarded as a typical British institution. They used to embody a presence in the local community by 'walking the beat' and personified fairness, stolidity, friendliness, helpfulness and incorruptibility. These virtues still exist to a degree and the traditional view is that the police should control the community by consent rather than force and that they should be visible in local areas.

But, in recent years, the police have been taken off foot patrols; put into cars to increase effectiveness and mobility; and more are now armed and trained in riot-control programmes. They have been accused of institutional racism, corruption, brutality, excessive use of force, perverting the course of justice and tampering with evidence in criminal trials. Some of these accusations have been proved. They have lowered the image of the police as well as their morale and have contributed to a loss of public confidence. Additionally, the Labour government is concerned to reform the police forces and what it sees as some of their 'inappropriate' practices.

The police tread a thin line in community activities, strikes and demonstrations. They are in the middle of opposing forces, much is expected of them and uncertain law often hinders their effectiveness. The problems of violent crime, organized criminality, gangs, relations with ethnic communities and an increasingly complex society have made their job more difficult. The police are trying to find ways of adequately and fairly controlling a changing society. They are concerned about their image, but insist that their primary duty is to maintain law and order.

The legal profession

The legal profession in England and Wales is divided into two types of lawyer: barristers and solicitors. Each branch has its own vested interests and jurisdiction and fiercely protects its position. This system is criticized because of duplication of services, delay and expense. But legal services have been reformed in order to benefit consumers, promote competition and give easier access to the law. Recent (2005) government proposals suggest further inroads into the profession's self-regulatory and representative status, the opening up of legal services and firms to commercial ownership and the sharing of functions with other professionals. Lawyers and their professional bodies will be regulated by an independent, lay-dominated Legal Services Board, which will control their accountability to clients and society. Such developments may lead to lawyers losing their traditional roles and exclusivity.

There are 100,000 *solicitors*, who practise mainly in private firms, but also in local and central government, legal centres and industry. Until proposed reforms, they were organized by their self-regulating and representative professional body, the Law Society. The solicitors' branch is a middle-class profession, but it is increasingly attracting members from relatively wide ethnic and gender spectrums of society.

Solicitors deal with general legal work, although many now specialize in one area of the law. Their firms (or partnerships) offer services such as conveyancing (the buying and selling of property); probate (wills and succession after death); family matters; criminal and civil litigation; commercial cases; and tax and financial affairs.

There are some 16,000 annual complaints by dissatisfied clients against solicitors. It was argued that the solicitors' existing supervisory body performed inadequately in investigating complaints although barristers' procedures functioned well. A single independent body will now be established under government proposals to oversee the way in which all consumer complaints are handled by solicitors, barristers and other legal professionals.

The client with a legal problem will first approach a solicitor, who can often deal with all aspects of the case. But solicitors were once only able to appear (rights of audience) for their clients in the lower courts (county and magistrates' courts) and cases in higher courts had to be handed to a barrister. This expensive practice has now been reformed and solicitor-advocates can appear in higher courts.

In order to become a solicitor, it is usual to have a university degree, not necessarily in law. After passing further professional examinations organized by the Law Society and other colleges, the student serves a practical apprenticeship as a trainee solicitor with an established solicitor for some two years. After this total period of about six years' education and training, the new solicitor can practise law.

There are 10,000 *barristers* in private practice, who have the right to appear before any court in England and Wales. They belong to the Bar, which is an ancient professional legal institution presently controlled by the self-regulating Bar Council and four Inns of Court in London (Gray's Inn, Lincoln's Inn, Middle Temple and the Inner Temple). Barristers have two functions: to give specialized advice on legal matters and to act as advocates in the courts. Historically, the general public could not approach a barrister directly, but must have been introduced by a solicitor. This regulation has now been relaxed for some clients.

In order to become a barrister, one must usually have a university degree, pass professional examinations and become a member of an Inn of Court. The student must dine in the Inn for a number of terms before being 'called to the Bar', or accepted as a barrister. He or she must then serve for a one-year period (pupillage)

PLATE 6.5 Staple's Inn, Holborn, London.
Originally a small Inn of Chancery attached to Gray's Inn, it now contains barristers' chambers in some of its buildings.
(*Andrew Drysdale/Rex Features*)

under a practising barrister. After this total training period of about five years, the new barrister can practise alone.

Barristers are self-employed individuals who practise from chambers (or offices), together with other barristers. The barrister's career starts as a 'junior' handling minor briefs (or cases). He or she may have difficulty in earning a living or in becoming established in the early years of practice, with the result that many barristers drop out and enter other fields. Should the barrister persist and build up a successful practice as a junior, he or she may 'take silk' and become a Queen's Counsel (QC). A QC is a senior barrister who can charge higher fees for his or her work, but who is then excluded from appearing in lesser cases. Appointment as a QC may lead to a future position as a judge and it is regarded as a necessary career step for the ambitious.

The *judges* constitute the judiciary, or independent third branch of the constitutional system. There are a relatively small number of judges at various levels of seniority, who are located in most large cities and in the higher courts in London. They are chosen from the ranks of senior barristers, although solicitors are now eligible for some of the lower posts. The highest appointments are made by the Crown on the advice of the Prime Minister and lower positions on the advice of the Lord Chancellor. This appointments procedure has been criticized because it rests with the Lord Chancellor and the senior judiciary, who consequently hold much power and patronage. In an attempt to combat 'elitism' and 'cronyism', more judgeships are now advertised for open competition and appointments, under present reforms, will be made by an independent Judicial Appointments Commission.

The Lord Chancellor is a political appointee of the sitting government in charge of the Department for Constitutional Affairs; effective head of the legal system and profession; a member of the Cabinet; presiding officer (or Speaker) of the House of Lords; and a law lord. It has been argued that this office should be abolished because of its political connections and the process of abolition is currently under way. Other judgeships are supposedly made on non-political grounds. Senior judges cannot be removed from office until retirement age of 75, although junior judges can be dismissed for good reasons before retirement age at 72. There have been proposals that complaints against judges and their dismissal should be handled by a complaints board and that judges should be more easily removable from office. But the existing measures have been designed to ensure the independence of the judiciary and its freedom from political involvement.

Critics feel that judges are socially and educationally elitist, remote from ordinary life and overwhelmingly male. They are seen as people who will not cause embarrassment to the establishment and who tend to support the accepted wisdom and status quo. However, they do rule against government policies and their powers of independence have arguably been increased by the Human Rights Act. They have increasingly argued publicly in the media and elsewhere and have been frequently in dispute with governments about their jurisdiction in areas such as the sentences for murder. The judiciary is gradually changing to admit more women, ethnic minorities and people with lower-class and educationally-diverse backgrounds. But, although over half of law students are female, there are few women judges (or QCs and senior partners in solicitors' firms).

The judiciary tends to be old in years because judgeships are normally awarded to senior practising lawyers and there is no career structure that people may join early in life. A lawyer's income may be greatly reduced on accepting a judgeship, but the honour and added security are supposed to be some compensation. There are promotional steps within the judiciary from recorder to circuit judge to High Court judge, and thence to the Court of Appeal and the House of Lords.

The legal professions in *Scotland* and *Northern Ireland* are also divided. Scotland has some 400 practising advocates (barristers) and 8,250 solicitors. Advocates practise as individuals, do not work from chambers and are independent of each other. Scottish solicitors usually operate in partnership with other solicitors. Northern Ireland has solicitors and about 450 barristers.

Attitudes to the legal system and crime

Britain historically has not been thought of as a litigious society. People usually avoid the difficulty and cost of legal actions if possible and regard the law and lawyers as a last resort in resolving their problems. But, in recent years, more Britons have been using the courts to gain satisfaction for what they consider to be their 'rights' and a 'compensation culture' has grown, aided by some lawyers ('ambulance chasers'). Large damages may be awarded in matters ranging from libel cases to complaints about schools, companies, doctors, hospitals and the criminal law system. The Human Rights Act (2000) is also being increasingly used by individuals to assert their 'rights', although the Labour government is introducing legislation to curtail the supposed 'compensation culture'.

MORI polls in the early 2000s revealed consistently that a majority of British people had little confidence in the legal system. Some 47 per cent of respondents in 2000 were dissatisfied with the courts, while 32 per cent were satisfied. Polls frequently show that while the police (perhaps surprisingly) are the most admired professional group after doctors and nurses, lawyers are the least admired. There was support for those legal reforms which had been completed (particularly in the civil courts from 1999) but a continuing desire to see more government action on the legal system's remaining delays, risks, costs, inefficiencies and lack of resources (2001).

Crime and violence are a main concern for many Britons, despite the Labour government's view (2005) that the risk of being a victim of crime is at its lowest for 24 years. In June 2001, a MORI poll showed that in a list of worries 33 per cent of respondents worried about law and order, an increase since 1996. A January 2005 poll by MORI found that crime, law and order, violence and vandalism occupied fourth place at 26 per cent in a list of the most important issues facing British society. But in May 2005, in the run up to the general election, these concerns had climbed to first place with 40 per cent.

In spite of the fact that fear of crime is arguably greater than its actuality, other polls in the 2000s reveal that many people (particularly the elderly) are afraid: feel unsafe walking alone after dark; believe that worries about crime affect their everyday life; and think that the police are handicapped in the fight against crime by the criminal justice system. The Crimestoppers Trust reported in September 2001 that three-quarters of British people believed that the country had become a more dangerous place to live in over the preceding ten years. In terms of neighbourhood crime, 56 per cent said they feared burglary and 35 per cent car crime; and 20 per cent would not go to the police if they had information about a crime. A NatWest survey in 1997 had indicated that 70 per cent of respondents would accept tax rises if significant cuts in crime would result.

In a 2000 MORI poll, 44 per cent of interviewees were fairly satisfied and 9 per cent very satisfied with the way their areas were policed. But when asked how confident they were that the police would arrive at an emergency within ten minutes, 37 per cent were fairly and 13 per cent very confident. But 44 per cent were not confident.

Some 72 per cent of respondents strongly agreed that people should have the right to defend their property and 24 per cent tended to agree. There has been heated debate on this issue in recent years with a large majority of people feeling that burglars are treated too leniently by the courts and that homeowners should be able to use force in self-defence proportional to their fear, rather than being judged by the legal test of reasonableness (in response to a perceived threat).

There continue to be mixed messages on crime and its effects in Britain, some of which are exaggerated by media campaigns and moral panics. The Labour government insists that crime is decreasing and that its crime-fighting measures are working. It argues that many people were less worried about crime in 2005 than in 2004 and that fewer people now feel that anti-social behaviour is a problem. Yet polls suggest that people are in fact very worried about a threatening culture of yobbishness and thuggery on British streets; drugs and drug-related offences; alcohol-fuelled anti-social behaviour; the abusive behaviour of some young people; the breakdown of community cohesion; muggings; and violent crime. All of these may impinge to varying degrees upon people's lives and create an atmosphere of threat. A popular reaction therefore is for people to demand zero tolerance for all crime; to insist that the police be allowed to do their job rather than engage in wasteful form-filling; to put more police on the streets to patrol neighbourhoods and reassure people; and to give strong punishments to convicted criminals.

Exercises

Explain and examine the following terms:

civil law	claimant	conveyancing
barrister	legal aid	Crown Prosecution Service
indictable	Inns of Court	common law
solicitor	Lord Chancellor	Metropolitan Police
jury	crown court	county court
JP	statute law	bail
'tagging'	summary	District Judge

Write short essays on the following topics:

1   Describe and comment critically on the structure of the legal profession in Britain.

2   How is the courts system in England and Wales organized?

3   Discuss the role of the police in law enforcement.

4   Examine British crime statistics in this chapter and comment on people's fear of crime.

Further reading

1 Baker, J.H. (2002) *An Introduction to English Legal History* London: Butterworths Lexis Nexis
2 Berlins, M. and Dyer, C (2000) *The Law Machine* London: Penguin
3 Emsley, C. (2005) *Crime and Society in England 1750–1900* London: Pearson Education Limited
4 Griffiths, J. (1997) *The Politics of the Judiciary* London: Fontana
5 Muncie, J. and McLaughlin, E. (2002) *The Problem of Crime* London: Sage Publications
6 Muncie, J. and McLaughlin, E. (2002) *Controlling Crime* London: Sage Publications
7 Partington, M. (2003) *Introduction to the English Legal System* Oxford: Oxford University Press
8 Robertson, G. (2000) *Freedom, the Individual and the Law* London: Pelican
9 White, R. (1999) *The English Legal System in Action: Administration of Justice* Oxford: Oxford University Press

Websites

Lord Chancellor's Department; www.lcd.gov.uk
Law Officers: www.lslo.gov.uk
Home Office: www.homeoffice.gov.uk
Police: www.police.co.uk
New Scotland Yard: www.open.gov.uk/police/mps/home.htm
Amnesty International: www.amnesty.org.uk
Scottish Executive: www.scotland.gov.uk
Northern Ireland Office: www.nio.gov.uk

Chapter 7

The economy

Fluctuations in the performance of the national economy affect British people directly in their daily lives and are of concern to them. Such changes influence interest and inflation rates, employment and unemployment levels, individual and corporate income, wealth creation, taxation, investment and government programmes.

Historically, the British economy has been conditioned by agricultural and industrial revolutions; a dramatic growth and later reduction of manufacturing industry; government policies and intervention; the expansion of service industries; and a relative decline in economic performance from the late nineteenth century as other competitor nations industrialized. The economy experienced alternating periods of recession and expansion throughout the twentieth century, but has grown strongly since 1994 with record levels of people in work and low inflation, unemployment and interest rates. It avoided the worst effects of a worldwide recession in the early 2000s, but from 2005 entered a slowdown in some areas. This coincided with increased global oil prices, high government (or public) spending and a fragile consumer market which was affected by higher interest rates and rising inflation.

Economic history

Britain was a largely rural country until the end of the eighteenth century and its economy was based on products generated by successive revolutions in agricultural practice from Neolithic times. But there had also been industrial and manufacturing developments over the centuries, which were mainly located in the larger towns. Financial and commercial institutions, such as banks, insurance houses and trading companies, were gradually founded in the City of London and throughout the country to finance and service the expanding and increasingly diversified economy.

The growth of a colonial empire from the sixteenth century contributed to national wealth as Britain capitalized on its worldwide trading connections. Colonies supplied cheap raw materials, which were converted into manufactured goods in Britain and exported. Overseas markets grew quickly because merchants and traders were protected at home and abroad. They exploited the colonial markets and controlled foreign competition. By the nineteenth century, Britain had become a dominant economic power. Its wealth was based on international trade and the payments that it received for its exported products. Governments believed that a country increased its wealth if exports exceeded imports.

PLATE 7.1 Wool industry.
The wool and textiles industry formed a basis of England's wealth from the 14th century and was an important part of the economy into the 20th century, but is now much reduced. (*Kudos/Rex Features*)

This trading system and its financial institutions benefited the major industrial revolutions, which began in the late eighteenth century. Manufacturing and industrial inventions, together with a rich supply of domestic materials and energy sources, such as coal, steel, iron, steam power and water, stimulated production and the economy. Manufacturers, who had gained by international trade and demand for British goods, invested in new industries and technology. Industrial towns expanded; factories were built and a transport system of roads, canals and railways developed. Efficient manufacturing produced competitively priced goods for foreign markets and Britain was transformed into an urban and industrialized country.

But industrialization was opposed by some people. The Luddites in the nineteenth century, for example, destroyed new machinery in an attempt to halt progress and preserve existing jobs. Industrial and urban development had negative effects, such as long working hours for low wages and bad conditions in mines and factories. They also resulted in the depopulation of rural areas and the decline of traditional home and cottage work. Industrial conditions caused social and moral problems in towns and the countryside and mechanization was often regarded as exploitative and dehumanizing. The situation was worsened by the indifference of many manufacturers, employers and politicians to the human cost of industrialization.

However, the industrial changes did transform Britain into a rich and powerful country, despite economic slumps, periods of mass unemployment, the growth of urban slums and significant social and economic hardship in the nineteenth century for many people. Manufacturing output became the chief generator of wealth; production methods and technology advanced; and domestic competition improved the quality of goods and services.

But this industrial dominance of world trade did not last. It declined relatively by the end of the nineteenth century as countries such as Germany and the USA rapidly developed their industrial bases and became more competitive. However, British financial expertise continued to be influential in global financial dealings.

The modern economy: policies, structure and performance

It is argued that British economic performance and world status declined further in the twentieth century, although some recent research queries whether decline has been as substantial in comparative terms as is popularly assumed. But Britain was affected by the economic problems created by two World Wars; international recessions; global competition; structural changes in the economy; a lack of industrial competitiveness; alternating government policies; and a series of 'boom-and-bust' cycles in which economic growth fluctuated greatly.

Economic policies

Although British governments have historically tended to be somewhat *laissez-faire* (letting things take their own course) in economic matters, they became much more involved in economic planning from the 1940s and the performance of the economy has been tied to their fiscal, monetary and political policies. All British governments thereafter have variously intervened in economic life in attempts to manage the economy and stimulate demand and growth, particularly as global competition has grown and domestic needs have become more complex.

Conservative governments have traditionally advocated a minimum interference in the economy and favoured the workings of the free market. But, in practice, they have also intervened whether out of necessity or changing ideology. Labour governments, on the other hand, initially argued that the economy must be centrally planned and its essential sectors should be owned and managed by the state.

Labour governments from 1945 consequently nationalized (transferred to public ownership) railways, road transport, water, gas, electricity, ship-building, coal-mining, the iron and steel industries, airlines, the health service, the Post

Office and telecommunications. These new public industries and services were run by the state through government appointed boards. They were responsible to Parliament and subsidized by taxation for the benefit of all, rather than for private owners or shareholders. But they were expensive to run and governments were expected to rescue any which had economic problems.

This policy was gradually reversed by the Conservatives. They argued that public industries and services were too expensive and inefficient; had outdated technology and bad industrial relations; suffered from lack of investment in new equipment; were dependent upon tax subsidies; and were run as state services with too little attention paid to profit-making, consumer demand or market forces. They denationalized some state industries and returned them to private ownership.

Conservative denationalization was later (1979–97) called 'privatization'. Ownership of industries such as British Telecom, British Airways, British Petroleum, British Gas, water and electricity supplies, British Coal and British Rail was transferred from the state to private owners mainly through the sale of shares. These industries are run as profit-making concerns and are regulated in the public interest by independent regulators. The aim was also to 'deregulate' the economy so that restrictions on businesses were removed to allow them to operate freely and competitively. For example, the stock market and public transport were deregulated, resulting in greater diversity in the City of London and local authority bus companies had to compete with private bus firms.

Conservatives believe that privatization improves efficiency, reduces government spending, increases economic freedom and encourages share ownership. The public bought shares in the new private companies and share-owning by individuals and financial institutions increased. But there was concern about privatization. Private industries became virtual monopolies (although there is now more competition) and there was criticism of the independent regulators' abilities to supervise them. There have been complaints about the private sector's services, prices and products, although many initial problems have been solved. But some areas, such as the railway system, still cause concern and attract criticism.

Recent Conservative governments also introduced a Public Finance Initiative (PFI) policy, by which the private sector is encouraged to invest in (and sometimes operate) public sector services such as schools and hospitals. This was intended to save public money, encourage cooperation on resources between the public and private sectors and also, for some critics, expand the privatization programme.

The Labour government accepted privatization on entering government in 1997, had dropped nationalization from its party manifesto in 1995 and has part-privatized concerns such as National Air Traffic Services and the London Underground. This development is part of its policy to introduce the private sector into public services such as transport, education and health. 'Public-private partnerships' (PPP) include PFI and can mean, for example, private companies either investing in and managing public concerns or building and running them.

The policy has been attacked by trade unions and a MORI poll in July 2001 found that only 8 per cent of respondents thought that hiring private sector managers to run public services would lead to big improvements. Only 11 per cent believed that using private companies to provide public services will improve them. A MORI poll in September 2001 showed that large majorities considered that schools, hospitals, trains, public utilities (water and electricity) and pensions should be provided and managed by the public sector. Independent surveys suggest that some private companies have found that PPP and PFI schemes do not generate the expected profits and that the quality of such initiatives is debatable. However, other private firms such as those involved in the Tube modernization programmes appear to be making a profit. It also seems that the Labour government intends to continue the policy.

The major political parties have now accepted free market (or liberal) economics, a closer relationship between the public and private sectors, deregulation and a mobile workforce. But a public or 'social sector market' still exists. The problem is how to manage the liberal economy effectively, while satisfying continuing demands for public services, such as the National Health Service and state school education, which are free of charge and funded from public taxation.

Economic structure

Government policies have created a mixed economy of public and private sectors. The public sector includes the remaining state-run industries and services which now amount to under one-third of the economy. Over two-thirds are in the private sector and this percentage will increase with further privatization (partial or full).

Unlike public-sector concerns which are owned by the state, the private sector belongs to people who have a financial stake in a company. It consists of small businesses owned by individuals; companies whose shares are sold to the public through the Stock Exchange; and larger companies whose shares are not offered for sale to the public. Most companies are private and small or medium-sized. They are crucial to the economy and generate 50 per cent of new jobs. Some 10 per cent of the economy is controlled by foreign corporations, which employ 10 per cent of the workforce. Britain (even outside the European common currency) has been seen as an attractive low-cost country for foreign investment in many areas such as electronic and high technology equipment, leisure facilities, hotels, finance and cars, although British-based production of the latter has decreased significantly in recent years.

The shareholders are the real owners of those companies in which they invest their money. However, the daily organization of the business is left to a board of directors under a chair person or managing director. In practice, most shareholders are more interested in receiving profit dividends on their shares from a successful business than in being concerned with its running. But shareholder power is occasionally mobilized if the company is performing badly.

PLATE 7.2 BMW Mini car plant, Oxford, 2003.
The once-flourishing British car industry is now much reduced, with increased foreign ownership and collapses (such as that of Rover in Birmingham in 2005).
(*Jonathan Player/Rex Features*)

National and foreign companies are sometimes involved in takeovers and mergers in the private sector. A takeover occurs when a larger company takes over (or buys) a smaller, often loss-making, firm. Mergers are amalgamations between companies of equal standing. Such battles for control can be fiercely fought and have resulted in sections of the economy, such as cars, hotels, media concerns and food products, being dominated by a relatively small number of major groups.

Takeovers and mergers can cause concern to the target companies and their workforces. A Competition Commission is supposed to monitor this situation by preventing any one group forming a monopoly or creating unfair trading conditions. It examines the plans and reports to the Director General of Fair Trading, who, in reporting to the government Secretary of State for Trade and Industry, may rule against the proposed takeover or merger. Some decisions have stopped undesirable developments. But others have allowed near-monopolistic situations and the performance of the Commission is criticized.

Economic performance

Since the Second World War, Britain has suffered from economic problems caused by domestic and global factors, which have resulted in alternating recessionary and expansionary cycles; high unemployment, inflation and interest rates; balance of trade weaknesses; a fluctuating pound; low growth rates; poor productivity; an often uncompetitive workforce; and industrial relations difficulties. These problems have sometimes coincided with enforced structural changes in the economy, such as a decline in industrial and manufacturing trades and a growth in service industries. However, since 1994, Britain's economic performance has been relatively successful, although encountering some difficulties in the early 2000s and from 2005.

The location of British industry, which was dictated by eighteenth- and nineteenth-century industrial revolutions, has been a factor in manufacturing and industrial decline. Industries were situated in areas where there was access to natural resources and transport systems and where there was often only one major industry. They could be easily damaged in a changing economic climate, unless they managed to diversify their product base. But even regions which had adapted successfully in the past were affected by further deindustrialization, increased global competition and recession from the 1970s to the early 1990s.

Many manufacturing industries did not adapt to new markets and demands; did not produce goods efficiently and cheaply enough to compete; and priced themselves out of the world market. In 1938, Britain produced 22 per cent of global exports of manufactured goods. This figure slumped to 6.5 per cent by 1989, due to world competition and the rundown of manufacturing industries.

Industrial decline badly affected northern England, the English Midlands, Scotland, Northern Ireland and South Wales. Traditional trades like textiles, steel, ship-building, iron and coal-mining were greatly reduced. Governments, helped by European Union grants, tried to revitalize depressed areas with financial aid and the creation of new businesses. These policies have slowly had a positive effect in places like Liverpool, Glasgow, Newcastle, Birmingham and Belfast, but other areas are still languishing. Nevertheless, structural change in industry and manufacturing forced adjustments to different markets. New production and research methods led to a growth in specialized industries (such as the high-technology sectors) and the service sector (banking, insurance, catering, leisure, finance and information).

The discovery of North Sea oil and gas in the mid-1970s contributed greatly to the British economy at a time of difficulty and also made it less dependent upon imported energy. But gas and oil are finite; Britain has problems in finding alternative sources; it already has to import some gas and oil; and must fill the financial gap with new revenues. It is argued that energy income has been unwisely spent on social targets, rather than being used more positively for investment in new industry and in creating a modern economic infrastructure.

Conservative governments (1979–97) addressed inherent weaknesses in the British economy, but opinions differ on their record. They tried to reduce inflation by high interest rates and cuts in public spending. Industry and commerce were expected to restructure themselves; increase their growth rates and productivity; cut down overstaffing in the workforce; and become more efficient under market forces. Privatization was also gradually applied in many areas of the public sector.

PLATE 7.3 The Lloyd's Building, London, 2005.
Lloyds is an association of individuals who are prepared to provide insurance for a
wide range of (often risky) activities, such as shipping.
(Alisdair Macdonald/Rex Features)

Such measures and a world recession resulted in the 1980 British economy
falling to very low levels with high interest rates, unemployment and inflation.
Although it improved by 1986, it overheated from mid-1988. There were record
balance-of-payments deficits, the pound was attacked, inflation increased, and
interest rates were raised. Domestic and international factors caused Britain to
have its worst recession (1989–93) since the 1930s world depression.

In an attempt to boost economic strength, Britain in 1990 joined the
European Exchange Rate Mechanism (ERM) which, by linking European currencies, was supposed to stabilize currencies and improve national economies. But,

after speculation against the pound in 1992, Britain withdrew from the ERM and allowed the pound to float. The economy recovered outside the ERM. At present (2005), the pound is strong, although this has created problems for British exporters and businesses.

In 1993–4, Britain came slowly out of recession, with improved manufacturing and financial performance and a fall in inflation, unemployment and interest rates. By 1997 the economy was one of the most successful in the world, which the Labour government inherited. It is continuing similar policies to the Conservatives; initially managed the economy prudently; and has largely avoided traditional boom and bust cycles. But Labour has had to spend considerably on services like health, education and transport, so that government or public spending is a growing concern. This illustrates the problem of trying to combine a 'market economy' with public services.

Britain in the early 2000s experienced mixed effects from a global economic downturn. Manufacturing was in recession and there was weakness in other sectors. Although consumer spending boosted the economy, consumer confidence was waning. Unemployment, after falling since 1993 rose in 2001. But interest rates were very low at 4.0 per cent, as was inflation at 2.6 per cent. Britain avoided the worst of an international recession and had above-average growth through 2002.

In 2004, the European Union forecast that Britain's growth would be the strongest in Europe in 2005–6. But the government's own growth figures and economic forecasts had to be scaled back significantly in 2005. The buoyancy of the economy was affected by heavy government spending; a drop in company profits; increases in oil and energy prices; rising inflation, interest and unemployment rates; a faltering housing market; higher indirect taxation and increased National Insurance contributions for workers; a decline in consumer confidence; and (economists alleged) a loss of control by the Treasury (the government finance ministry) over Britain's public finances. There were also other structural problems such as weak trade performance, a fluctuating manufacturing industry, a pensions deficit, the generally low UK personal savings rate and a continuing productivity gap between Britain and the USA, France and Germany. However, by November 2005 the inflation rate had improved on the Consumer Prices Index scale to 2.3 per cent, although unemployment continued to rise to 4.7 per cent or 890,100 people claiming benefit.

Britain is still the world's fourth largest economy and a significant industrial and manufacturing country, although facing challenges from China and India. It is the fifth largest exporter of goods and services, despite its reduced share of the global market and weaknesses in manufacturing since the 1980s. The gross domestic product (GDP) in 2005 was £1,043 billion (or $26,240 per head of population). GDP comprises the goods, services, capital and income which the country produces. Some 71.8 per cent arises from services and 27.3 per cent from industry (of which manufacturing amounts to 16.6 per cent), while agriculture

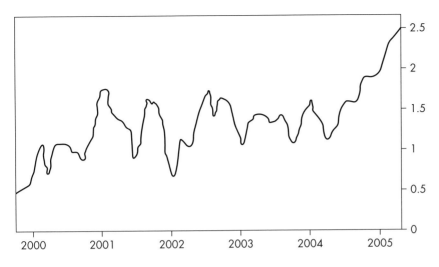

FIGURE 7.1 Inflation rate (%) 2000–5
Source: The Times, 19 October 2005

has 1 per cent. These figures dramatically illustrate the contemporary importance of the service sector and the corresponding decline of traditional sources of national wealth such as industry, manufacturing and agriculture.

Britain's trading patterns have also changed and its chief export partners are now (2005) the European Union (58.7 per cent), the USA (15.2) and other countries (24), with non-EU exports increasing. Its main import partners are the USA (13.7 per cent) and the European Union (53.7). Britain's principal exports and imports comprise finished manufactured products, semi-finished products, fuels, food, beverages, tobacco and basic materials. But it has had a balance-of-payments problem since 1983 and this increased significantly to record levels in 2005. A trade deficit results when exports do not exceed imports. However, 'invisible exports', such as financial, aviation and insurance services, are not calculated in this equation and contribute significantly to the economy.

The economy is also affected by fluctuations in the value of the pound. Devaluation (reducing the pound's exchange value) was used earlier by governments as an economic weapon. This boosted exports by making them cheaper on the world market, but raised the cost of imports and dissuaded people from buying foreign goods. Devaluation has not been used recently. Instead, the pound was allowed to 'float' from 1972 and find its own market value in competition with other currencies. Although Britain has not joined the European common currency (euro), the pound has performed successfully outside the eurozone (consisting of those EU countries which have adopted the euro).

Social class, the workforce and employment

Social class

Class in Britain has been variously defined by material wealth; ownership of the means of production as against the sellers of labour; education and job status; accent and dialect; birth and breeding; or sometimes by lifestyle.

Historically, the British class system was divided into upper, middle and working classes. Earlier, hierarchies based on wealth, the ownership of property, aristocratic privilege and political power were rigidly adhered to. But a middle class of traders, merchants and skilled craftsmen began to make inroads into this system. Industrialization in the nineteenth century further fragmented class divisions. The working class divided into skilled and unskilled workers and the middle class split into lower, middle and upper sections, depending on job classification or wealth. The upper class was still largely defined by birth, property and inherited money.

The spread of education and expansion of wealth to greater numbers of people in the twentieth century allowed more social mobility (moving upwards out of the class into which one was born). The working class was more upwardly mobile, the upper class (due to a loss of aristocratic privilege) merged more with the middle class. It was felt that the old rigid class system was breaking down as the proportions of people belonging to the various levels changed over time. But class structures still exist and the latest research (2005) suggests that Britain's social mobility rate is the lowest among western nations.

Some researchers now employ a six-class model based on occupation, income and property ownership, such as:

1   Higher-grade professional, managerial and administrative workers (e.g. doctors and lawyers)
2   Intermediate professional, managerial and administrative workers (e.g. school teachers and sales managers)
3   Non-manual skilled workers (e.g. clerks)
4   Manual skilled workers (e.g. coal miners)
5   Semi-skilled workers (e.g. postal employees)
6   Unskilled workers (e.g. refuse collectors, cleaners and labourers)

In addition, a further group (the underclass) has been used in recent years. This consists of people who fall outside the usual classes and includes the permanently unemployed, single-parent families, the very poor, the alienated and those with alternative lifestyles.

This model suggests two social/occupational groupings in contemporary Britain: a 'middle class' made up of classes 1, 2 and 3 and a 'working class' consisting of classes 4, 5 and 6. Research indicates that the British population today

PLATE 7.4 An open-plan office.
(*Eve Setch*)

largely consists of a middle class (60 per cent) and a working class (40 per cent). Despite a recent slackening in the social mobility rate, the working class has shrunk historically and there was more relative upward mobility, with people advancing socially due to economic progress and changes in occupational structures.

Polls suggest that the British themselves feel that they are becoming more middle class and it is argued that many people have the sort of lifestyle, jobs and income which classify them as middle class. It also seems that class is now as much a matter of different social habits and attitudes as it is of occupation and money. The old gaps between the classes have lessened and class today is a more finely graded hierarchy dependent upon a range of characteristics. But inequalities of wealth, difficulties of social mobility for the poorest in society, relative poverty and questions of prestige remain.

The workforce and employment

The potential workforce in 2004 was 29.7 million, of whom 28.3 million were in employment. The first figure also includes the self-employed (3.2 million), the unemployed (1.4 million), the armed forces and people on work-related training programmes. Of these workers, the large majority were employed in the services sector, a smaller percentage in industry (including manufacturing) and declining numbers in agriculture.

Despite twentieth-century occupational changes, the majority of British people, whether part-time or full-time, are employed by an organization. It may be a small private firm, a large company, a public sector industry or service, or a multinational corporation. Most people are workers who sell their labour in a market dominated by concerns which own and control production and services. The class-defining boundaries of employees and employers have remained constant and the top 1 per cent of British society still own more than 18 per cent of marketable wealth and the top 10 per cent have 56 per cent.

But the deregulated and mobile economy has created very different work patterns. Manufacturing has declined; service trades have increased; self-employment has risen; managerial and professional fields have expanded; and there are more part-time (7.4 million in 2004) and temporary jobs. Manual jobs have decreased in number; non-manual occupations have increased; the working-class has been eroded by salaried jobs; and the workforce has become more mobile, more 'white-collar' and better educated.

In 2004, some 70 per cent of working-age women were in employment; women in 2005 were 49 per cent of the total labour force; and women are the principal breadwinners in some 30 per cent of households. But a majority of female workers are low-paid, part-time and often unprotected by trade unions or the law. Although women form a 52 per cent majority of the population and are increasing their numbers in higher education (where they are a majority of students), the professions and white-collar jobs, they have problems in progressing to the senior ranks. Yet in 1996, for example, three out of every ten new businesses were started by women and in the service sector it was almost five out of ten.

Since the 1960s, women have campaigned for greater equality with men in job opportunities and rates of pay. Legislation has attempted to redress the balance with varying degrees of success. Equal Pay Acts stipulate that men and women who do the same or similar kinds of work should receive the same wages. The Sex Discrimination Act makes it unlawful for the employer to discriminate between men and women when choosing a candidate for most jobs. The Equal Opportunities Commission monitors this legislation and brings cases when there have been breaches of the Acts. But the average weekly wage of women is still only some 76 per cent of the average paid to men, particularly in industry and the service sector.

There has been a recent need for more women to enter the workforce at all levels, in order to compensate for a reduced birth-rate and shortage of labour. This situation requires improved financial, social and child-care benefits for women to enable them to work, as well as more flexible employment arrangements. Some employers and the government are responding positively in these areas and Britain now seems to be more egalitarian on women's work than it has been. However,

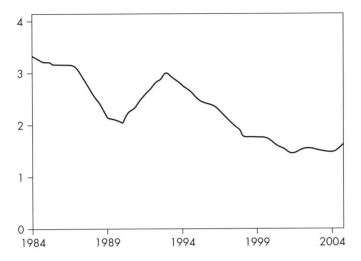

FIGURE 7.2 Unemployment rate (millions), 1984–2004
Source: Adapted from Labour Force Survey, Office for National Statistics 2004

flexible hours and part-time working (such as work-from-home schemes) for both sexes is increasingly being criticized by those workers in full-time jobs who feel that they have to bear the brunt of the work in the actual workplace.

More jobs have been created in the 2000s and unemployment has dropped steadily from 1993 (although rising in 2004 to 4.8 per cent of the workforce and continuing to rise in 2005). It remains proportionally high in Northern Ireland, the English Midlands, Merseyside, north-east England, Scotland and South Wales; in localized areas of the big cities and countryside; and among ethnic minorities such as Pakistanis and Bangladeshis. Since the late 1980s it has also affected the normally affluent south of England and includes professional and higher-grade workers.

The creation of jobs is important for political parties. The Labour government introduced (1997) a Welfare to Work programme. Companies willing to create jobs for the unemployed are given subsidies and the unemployed may also be placed in training and employment-related schemes under bodies like the Training and Enterprise Councils. These train the workforce, in the hope that permanent jobs may be found for them. Young people between the ages of 16 and 18, who become unemployed on leaving school, do not receive social security benefits and must undertake a training scheme or further education. The training programmes have been criticized and there is no guarantee that trainees will obtain a job afterwards. But the government argues that their policies have succeeded in getting more people into stable employment. Some critics disagree.

Although the British workforce is now more mobile and flexible, many vacant jobs are low-paid and part-time. Others are in technical and skilled areas, for which the educational systems have not adequately provided. Traditional apprenticeships have been greatly reduced and technical education suffers from a lack of investment and facilities. Although Conservative governments established technological colleges in the major cities (financed jointly by government and private companies), firms in the 2000s have experienced skills shortages and many had unfilled vacancies. Despite the success of some programmes, Britain lacks adequate vocational education and training schemes for the unemployed and young people in those technical areas which are essential for a modern industrial state. Reports on global competitiveness from bodies such as the World Economic Forum do not rank Britain highly for the quality of its employee training.

Traditional manufacturing industry has been progressively reduced in Britain. But an industrial infrastructure will continue to be important. It will not be as labour-intensive as in the past, because of technical advances. High-technology industry and service trades are set to expand. It is also likely that opportunities for professional and skilled workers in managerial, supervisory, personal and financial services will increase. But employment and a trained workforce will still be problems in this post-industrial society and will entail revisions of the work ethic and concepts of leisure, as well as more flexible employment and child-care arrangements. At present, although the situation is improving and more state aid is being delivered, only a small percentage of working parents can afford to use formal child-care services all the time and most parents themselves have to pay three-quarters of the cost of care.

Financial institutions

Financial institutions are central actors in the economy. In the 1980s, they responded to a deregulated and freer economy. Banks, building societies, insurance firms, money markets and the London Stock Exchange expanded, merged and diversified. They entered new fields and reorganized their traditional areas of expertise, as competition between institutions increased. But they also had problems when the economy fluctuated in the late 1980s, the early 1990s and 2000s. However, despite occasional unemployment in financial businesses, the periodically weak performance of the Stock Market and increasing European and international competition, London has retained its status as a global financial centre.

Many major financial institutions have their headquarters in London, with branches throughout Britain. The square mile of the *City of London*, with its banks, insurance houses, legal firms and financial dealers' offices, has always been a centre of British and world finance. Its resources have financed royal wars, military and colonial exploration and trading companies. Today it provides financial and investment services for commercial interests in Britain and overseas. Many City institutions were founded in the seventeenth and eighteenth centuries, as Britain's prosperity and overseas trade grew, such as the insurance firm Lloyd's (1680s),

PLATE 7.5 Canary Wharf, London.
Part of the Docklands redevelopment programme in East London, offering residential housing, hotels and financial offices. The Canary Wharf tower (centre) is the tallest building in Britain at 800 feet (244 metres) with 50 floors.
(*David Churchill/Arcaid/Rex Features*)

the London Stock Exchange (1773) and the Bank of England (1694). The City is now being seriously challenged in financial dealings by the London Docklands commercial redevelopment centred on Canary Wharf.

The Bank of England ('the old lady of Threadneedle Street') is the country's central bank. Although previously nationalized, it is now independent (1997) of government and has the vital role of setting interest rates to control inflation. Other institutions adjust their interest rates accordingly. It is organized by a governor and directors who are appointed by the government. It is the government's banker; the agent for British commercial and foreign central banks; prints money for England and Wales; manages the national debt and gold reserves; and supports the pound by buying pounds on foreign currency exchanges.

The other main banks which provide banking services throughout Britain are the *central clearing banks*, of which the most important are HSBC, Lloyds TSB, the Royal Bank of Scotland (including National Westminster) and Barclays. They provide their customers with current and deposit (savings) accounts, loans and financial advice. But they have been criticized for their banking charges to clients, the discrepancy between their savings and loan interest rates, their treatment of customers' complaints and their unwillingness to provide funds for small businesses. They are involved in international finance and have expanded their traditional activities. Building societies, which now offer banking facilities and Internet banking, provide competition to the high street banks.

In addition to these high street banks, there are the long-established *merchant banks*, which are mainly located in London. They give advice and finance to commercial and industrial businesses, both in Britain and overseas; advise companies on takeovers and mergers; provide financial assistance for foreign transactions; and organize a range of financial services for individuals and corporations.

The London Stock Exchange is a market for the buying and selling of quoted (listed) stocks and shares in British public companies and a few overseas. Dealings on the Stock Exchange reflect the current market trends and prices for a range of securities, which may go up as well as down. In recent years, the performance of the stock market has fluctuated under domestic and international pressures.

The Stock Exchange was revolutionized in 1986 by new developments, known popularly as 'Big Bang'. The changes deregulated the financial market and gave greater freedom of operation. New members were allowed; financial dealers were given greater powers of dealing and competition increased. However, some companies were too ambitious, over-expanded and suffered from the effects of the world stock market crash of 1987. The London market returned to earlier profitability levels only after many redundancies among dealers and closure of some companies. From 1997 financial transactions have been organized directly from computer screens in corporate offices by an order-driven system which automates the trading process, rather than traditional dealing on the floor of the Exchange.

The Foreign Exchange Market is also based in London. Brokers in corporate or bank offices deal in the buying and selling of foreign currencies. The London market is the largest in the world in terms of average daily turnover of completed transactions. Other money markets arrange deals on the Euromarkets in foreign currencies; trade on financial futures (speculation on future prices of commodities); arrange gold dealings on the London Gold Market; and transact global deals in the commodity, shipping and freight markets.

Lloyd's of London is a famous name in the insurance market and has long been active in the fields of shipping and maritime insurance. But it has now diversified and insures in many other areas. Lloyd's operates as a market, where individual underwriters (or insurers), who are all members of Lloyd's, carry on their business. Underwriters normally form groups to give themselves greater security, because they have to bear any loss which occurs. But many underwriters have suffered in recent years due to heavy insurance losses.

In addition to the Lloyd's market, there are many individual insurance companies with headquarters in London and branches throughout the country. They have international connections and huge assets. They play an important role in British financial life because they are the largest investors of capital. Their main activity has traditionally been in life insurance. But many have now diversified into other associated fields, such as pensions and property loans. However, their handling of customers' investments (particularly pension mis-selling and mismanagement of savings schemes) has been heavily criticized in recent years. Investors have lost money and some insurance companies have virtually collapsed.

British financial institutions have traditionally been respected for their honesty and integrity. But, as money markets have expanded and become freer, there have been fraud cases, collapse of financial organizations and financial scandals. These give the City a bad image and have forced it to institute self-regulatory provisions in order to tighten the controls on financial dealings. But consumer confidence and trust in the financial institutions continues to decline and there are often big differences between the promises contained in glossily advertised financial schemes and the actual service to customers.

Some critics have argued for stronger independent supervision of the City's business practices. The Labour government, although now more friendly towards the business world than in the past, created a watchdog (the Financial Services Authority) in 2000 and a Financial Ombudsman in 2001 to oversee all financial dealings. But these institutions have been criticized for their lack of adequate control. It is also argued that the City should be more nationally and socially conscious and forced to invest in British industry rather than overseas. The City insists that it should be allowed to invest how and where it likes in order to make a profit. However, it seems that City and financial organizations are conscious of the negative criticisms, although their attempts to put their houses in order are not always well-received.

The composition of those who create and control wealth in Britain has changed since the Second World War. Bankers, aristocrats, land-owners and industrialists were the richest people in the nineteenth and early twentieth centuries. Today the most affluent are retailers and those who service the con-sumer society, although holders of inherited wealth are still numerous. Many millionaires are self-made, with lower-middle-class and working-class back-grounds.

The Labour Party in opposition felt that anyone earning more than £27,000 a year should be classified as rich (and taxed accordingly), while polls suggest that the public considers earnings above £30,000 a year to be reasonable wealth. Talking about what one earns and about money generally has been traditionally regarded as unseemly in Britain and too much involved with the cruder elements of existence and survival. But this mentality has slowly changed, particularly since the expansion of the business and money markets.

Industrial and commercial institutions

The trade unions

Trade unions obtained legal recognition in 1871 after long and bitter struggles. The fight for the right of workers to organize themselves originated in the trade guilds of the fourteenth century and later in social clubs which were formed to give their members protection against sickness and unemployment.

The modern trade unions are associated (if no longer closely) with the Labour Party and campaign for better pay, working and health conditions for their members. The trade-union movement is highly organized, with a membership of 7.4 million people in 2003. But this is a fall from 12 million in 1978 and represents only 27 per cent of all individuals in employment.

Today there are some 243 trade unions and professional associations of workers, which vary considerably in size and influence. They represent not only skilled and unskilled workers in industry, but also white-collar workers in a range of businesses, companies and local and central government. Other professional associations like the Law Society, the Police Federation and the British Medical Association carry out similar representational roles for their members.

Members of trade unions pay annual subscriptions to their unions and frequently to the Labour Party, unless they elect not to pay this latter amount. The funding provides for union activities and services, such as legal, monetary and professional help. The richer unions are able to give strike pay to members who are taking part in 'official strikes', which are those legally sanctioned by members. Trade unions vary in their wealth and in their political orientation, ranging from the left to the right wing of the political spectrum.

Some unions admit as members only those people who work in a specific job, such as miners or teachers. Other unions comprise workers who are employed in different areas of industry or commerce, such as the Transport and General Workers' Union. Some unions have joined with others in similar fields to form new unions, such as Unison (public service workers) which is now the largest in Britain with 1.3 million members. Workers may choose, without victimization, whether they want to belong to a particular union or none at all.

Many trade unions are affiliated to the Trades Union Congress (TUC), which was founded in 1868, serves as an umbrella organization to coordinate trade-union interests and tries to promote worker cooperation. It can exert some pressure on government (although this has now decreased) and seeks to extend its contacts in industry and commerce and with employers as well as workers.

The influence of the TUC and trade unions (as well as their membership) has declined. This is due to unemployment; changing attitudes to trade unions by workers; the reduction and restructuring of industry; a deregulated economy; a more mobile workforce; and Conservative legislation. Laws were passed to enforce secret voting by union members before strikes can be legally called and for the election of union officials. The number of pickets (union strikers) outside business premises has been reduced, secondary (or sympathy) action by other unionists is banned and unions may be fined by the courts if they transgress legislation. Such Conservative laws (which the Labour government accept) and the economic climate have forced trade unions to be more realistic in their wage demands. But pay claims are escalating again and there is increasing (if sporadic) militancy among some union leaders. There are also arrangements for legal recognition of unions in those workplaces where a majority of workers want them and for consultation with workers in matters like redundancy.

Legislation has controlled extreme union practices and introduced democratic procedures into union activities. The grassroots membership has become more independent of union bosses and activists; is more determined to represent its own wishes; and is concerned to cure abuses in the labour movement. The initiative in industry has shifted to employers and moderate unions, who have been moving away from the traditional 'class-war' image of unionism and are accepting new technology and working patterns in an attempt to improve competitiveness and productivity.

Public opinion polls in the past found that, while a large majority of respondents believed that unions are essential to protect workers' interests, a sizeable number felt that unions had too much power in Britain and were dominated by extremists. Half of trade unionists themselves agreed with this latter point of view and half disagreed. The concern over trade unions and their close relationship with Labour governments has declined since the 'New' Labour election victory in 1997.

Strike action by unions can be damaging to the economy and has been used as an economic and political weapon in the past. In some cases, strikes are seen as legitimate and find public support. But others, which are clearly political, are unpopular and are rejected. Britain historically seemed to be prone to industrial disputes, with large numbers of strikes in the 1980s. However, statistics show that fewer working days are now lost in Britain each year than in other industrial nations, although the number has increased recently. On average, most manufacturing plants and businesses are free of strikes, and media coverage is often responsible for giving a distorted picture of industrial relations.

Industrial problems should be placed in the context of financial rewards. Britain has a low-wage economy, compared with other major European countries, although the Labour government has set a minimum wage of £4.85 an hour to help the lowest paid workers over 22 and £4.10 for those aged 18–21, to the dismay of many companies. The average gross weekly wage of workers in Great Britain in 2003 was £476 per week. Many workers (women at £396) receive less than this. Personal annual income is taxed at 10 per cent for the first £2,000 of taxable income, 22 per cent up to £28,000 and 40 per cent above this figure. The British tend to believe that they are over-taxed. But their basic and top rates of direct taxation are in fact lower than in many other Western countries.

However, direct income tax may have to increase in order to pay for public services and future state pension provision. The Labour government has also significantly raised indirect or 'stealth' taxes since 1997, such as increased National Insurance contributions for workers and employers. It has allowed stamp duty (on the purchase of property) and inheritance tax (on a deceased person's estate) to rise considerably in a rising house market and has not increased the bands for income tax allowances. Millions of Britons are now having to pay sharply increased amounts of various indirect taxes.

Employers' organizations

There are some 101 employers' and managers' associations in Britain, which are mainly associated with companies in the private sector. They promote good industrial relations between businesses and their workforces; try to settle disputes; and offer legal and professional advice.

Most are members of the Confederation of British Industry (CBI). This umbrella body represents its members nationally; negotiates on their behalf with government and the TUC; campaigns for greater investment and innovation in industry and technology; and is often more sympathetic to Conservative governments than Labour ones. However, it can be very critical of Conservative policies. It also acts as a public-relations organization; relays the employers' points of view to the public; and has considerable economic influence and authority.

Industrial relations

Complaints are often raised about the quality of industrial relations in Britain. Historically, this has tended to be confrontational rather than cooperative and based on notions of 'class-warfare' and 'us-and-them'. Trade union leaders can be extremist and stubborn in pursuing their members' interests. But the performance of management and employers is also criticized. Insensitive managers can be responsible for strikes arising in the first place, and relations between management and workers still leave much to be desired although industrial unrest is not as common as it once was. Opinion polls have suggested that a majority of respondents believe that bad management is more to blame than the unions for poor industrial relations and Britain's economic problems.

The Advisory, Conciliation and Arbitration Service (ACAS)

ACAS is an independent, government-financed organization, which was created in 1974 to improve industrial relations. It may provide, if requested, advice, conciliation and arbitration services for the parties involved in a dispute. But ACAS does not have binding power and the parties may disregard its advice and solutions. Industrial relations in Britain consist of free collective bargaining between employers and workers. It has been argued that arbitration should be made compulsory and that findings should be binding on the parties. However, strike action is not illegal for most workers if legally called and the government has no power to intervene. Nevertheless, ACAS has performed much valuable work and has been responsible for settling many disputes.

ACAS also oversees the operation of employment law and abuses of workers' legal rights. These may involve complaints of unfair and unlawful dismissal; claims under Equal Pay Acts; grievances under Sex Discrimination Acts; and unlawful discrimination under Race Relations Acts. There is now a large body of employment and regulatory law, which makes conditions of work more secure and less arbitrary than they have been in the past, particularly in the cases of women, ethnic minorities and the low-paid. But there is still concern about the real effectiveness of such legislation.

Consumer protection

In a competitive market, consumers should have a choice of goods and services; information to make choices; and laws to safeguard their purchases. Statutory protection for consumers has grown steadily in Britain and is harmonized with European Union law. The public can complain to tribunals and the courts about unfair trading practices, dangerous and unsafe goods, misrepresentation, bad service, misleading advertising and personal injuries resulting from defective products.

The Office of Fair Trading is a government department which oversees the consumer behaviour of trade and industry. It promotes fair trading, protects consumers, suggests legislation to government and has improved consumer awareness. It has drawn up codes of practice with many industrial and commercial organizations; keeps a close watch for any breaches of the codes; and publishes its findings, often to the embarrassment of the manufacturers and companies concerned.

Organizations which provide help on consumer affairs at the local level are Citizens Advice Bureaux, Consumer Advice Centres and consumer protection departments of local councils. Private consumer-protection groups, which investigate complaints and grievances, may also exist in some localities.

The independent National Consumer Council monitors consumers' attitudes, although its effectiveness is queried. A more active body is Which? (formerly the Consumers' Association). Its magazine *Which?* champions the consumer and applies rigorous tests to anything from television sets to insurance and estate agents. *Which?* is the 'buyers' bible' and its reports have raised the standards of commercial products and services in Britain.

Much still needs to be rectified in the consumer field, such as cowboy builders and other trades people preying on gullible consumers, commercial incompetence and mis-selling of products by financial organizations, to achieve minimum standards and adequate protection. But there are signs that a British reticence to complain about goods and services is breaking down as litigation and financial claims increase. This attitude is associated with what is seen as a growing 'compensation culture' in Britain. Some critics doubt its existence, although the Labour government believes that it is a problem and is introducing legislation to curb it.

Attitudes to the economy

The changing economic climate is reflected in opinion polls which itemize the public's views on both national and personal levels. Although Conservative governments have been traditionally trusted to manage the economy efficiently and had delivered a booming economy in 1997, the electorate was dissatisfied with them in the mid-1990s for political reasons. General elections in 1997, 2001 and 2005 showed that voters were willing to trust the Labour Party to run the economy competently because it had adopted centrist and pragmatic policies and promised not to increase direct taxation. It is accepted that the Labour government managed the economy prudently from 1997, at least initially. The British economy has been the most successful in Europe in recent years with relatively strong growth, but suffered a slowdown in 2005 which some economists attribute to government failings.

Divided public opinions on the British economic performance were reported in a Populus poll in March 2004. This found that men were more optimistic than women about the economic outlook both for the country as a whole and personally for their families. But satisfaction with the economy for both sexes had risen faster and higher among professionals and managers than among manual workers.

A later Populus poll in April 2005 prior to the general election also revealed divided views among voters. A majority thought that the national economy was doing well; were more optimistic about the economy than in 2004; thought that the Labour government was managing the economy well overall; and believed positively in its future progress. Such optimism was common to supporters of all political parties and floating voters. But voters were much more cautious and worried about their own and their families' personal prospects, and optimism on this score had fallen since 2004.

One year later, a GfK survey of consumer confidence in November 2005 showed a drop in general economic optimism and the lowest dissatisfaction since 2003. Economists suggested that high petrol and utility (energy) bills, rising unemployment and inflation, the possibility of higher interest rates on loans, increased direct and indirect taxation, problems of personal debt and future pensions, as well as anxiety about the national economic outlook in general had curtailed consumer spending. People did not see any immediate change for the better.

These findings suggest that the economy concerns Britons in those areas which affect them directly and adversely on a personal level, such as unemployment, industrial decline, inflation, interest rates, savings, pensions, public spending, prices, taxation and the provision of public services. In 2005, these were tied to concerns about the slump in industry, an abrupt fall in economic growth, rising oil prices on the world market and economic turbulence following a period of stability since 1994.

Polls in recent years suggest that, in a mobile and deregulated market, job security (or the ability to get another job if one is lost) is a priority of job seekers, ranked ahead of work satisfaction, promotion and working conditions. Britain also has a reputation as a country of workaholics, where people work the longest hours in Europe (despite an EU maximum working week of 48 hours). This may be out of choice, enjoyment, ambition, coercion or desperation not to lose one's job. However, it seems that a majority of British people are very or fairly satisfied with their jobs and only a small minority are either fairly or very dissatisfied.

A CBI poll in 2001 showed that flexible working was now a key part of British employment patterns, despite the problems of finding adequate child-care provision: 81 per cent of businesses use part-time workers; 62 per cent operate subcontracting; and 39 per cent use teleworking to allow their employees to work at home for at least some of the time. But there are also negative responses to part-time, flexible or home workers from those full-time employees who have to provide cover in the workplace.

Respondents to polls also still tend to believe that business and economic arrangements in Britain are unfair: the values of managers and workers continue to be opposed in many companies; the country's wealth is unfairly distributed which favours the owners and the rich at the expense of employees and the poor; the gap between rich and poor is growing; there are no longer 'jobs for life' and businesses do not care about the community, the environment or customers. It is felt that workers should be given more control over and say in the organization of their workplaces (now covered by the Social Chapter of the Maastricht Treaty).

A MORI Corporate Image survey in August 2001 showed that public hostility towards profitability and business success had waned slightly after rising from 1980 to 1999. In 1999 only 25 per cent of respondents supported corporate profit while 52 per cent were against. In 2001 the figures were 29 per cent and 43 per cent respectively. Stakeholders or shareholders wanted their companies to make a profit but not at the expense of their staff or the community. The public thought that caring for employees should be the top priority for business. Providing more jobs, the safety of workers and the training of the workforce were also emphasized.

It is often argued that Britain's historical economic ills were due to cultural factors and attitudes. Traditionally, educated and upper-class people were reluctant to enter trade and industry; the workforce had a lower productivity rate than comparable competitors; there had been insufficient investment in industry and training; management was weak and unprofessional; and there had been too little investment in and encouragement of the technical, scientific and research fields. These views still have some validity. For example, it is felt that Britain lacks adequate technical education and training facilities. This leads to a lack of applicants for vacancies in vital technical trades, manufacturing and industry.

Exercises

Explain and examine the following terms:

diversify	privatization	GDP	invisible exports
merger	Lloyd's	shares	balance of payments
private sector	deficit	TUC	service industries
ACAS	Canary Wharf	HBSC	'market economy'
the City	inflation	*Which?*	mixed economy
devaluation	Stock Exchange	CBI	deregulation
monopoly	PPP	ERM	deindustrialization

Write short essays on the following topics:

1   Examine modern British economic policies and performance.

2   Discuss the role of the trade unions in British life.

3   Consider the financial institutions in Britain. Should they be more closely regulated by government? If so, why?

4   What is the relationship between the performance of the national economy and Britons' personal life situations?

Further reading:

1   Booth, A. (2001) *The British Economy in the Twentieth Century* London: Palgrave
2   Buxton, T., Chapman, P. and Temple, P. (1997) *Britain's Economic Performance* London: Routledge
3   Gregg, P. and Wadsworth, J. (eds) (1999) *The State of Working Britain* Manchester: Manchester University Press
4   McIlroy, J. (1995) *Trade Unions in Britain Today* Manchester: Manchester University Press

Websites

Department of Trade and Industry: www.dti.gov.uk
HM Treasury: www.hm-treasury.gov.uk
National Statistics: www.statistics.gov.uk
British Trade International: www.brittrade.com
Bank of England: www.bankofengland.co.uk
Financial Services Authority: www.fsa.gov.uk
Lloyds of London: www.lloydsoflondon.co.uk
Confederation of British Industry: www.cbi.org.uk

Trades Union Congress: www.tuc.org.uk
Business in the Community: www.bitc.org.uk
The Industrial Society: www.indsoc.co.uk
Populus opinion polls: www.populuslimited.com

Chapter 8

Social services

- Social services history
- Changing family and demographic structures
- Social security
- The National Health Service (NHS)
- The personal social services
- Housing
- Attitudes to the social services
- *Exercises*
- *Further reading*
- *Websites*

State (or public) sector provision for social security, health care, personal social services and council (or social) housing are very much taken for granted by many Britons today. They also feature prominently in lists of people's concerns and directly affect the daily lives of individuals of all ages. But it was not until the 1940s that the state accepted overall responsibility for providing basic social help for all its citizens. Previously, there had been few such facilities and it was felt that the state was not obliged to supply them. British social services developed considerably from the mid-twentieth century as society and government policies changed. Reflecting this historical context, they are now divided between state (public) and private sectors.

The state provides services and benefits for the sick, retired, disabled, elderly, needy and unemployed. They are organized by devolved and local authorities throughout Britain under the central direction of the UK Department of Health and the Department of Work and Pensions. The costs of this system are funded mainly by general taxation and partly by a National Insurance Fund to which employers and employees contribute. This means that although many social services, such as health care, are provided free at the point of need, most people will have contributed to them during their working lives through income tax and National Insurance contributions.

In the private sector, social and health services are financed by personal insurance schemes, company occupational plans and by those people who choose to pay for such facilities out of their own income or capital. But most of these people are eligible for public sector care if they wish. There are also many long-established voluntary organizations which continue the tradition of charitable help for the needy and largely depend for their funding upon donations from the public.

Conservative governments (1979–97) introduced reforms in the state sector in order to reduce expenditure, eradicate fraud, improve efficiency, encourage more self-provision and target benefits to those most genuinely in need. Such policies were widely attacked and it was argued that they were based on a market orientation and a return to the old mentality of personal responsibility for social needs.

The Labour government since 1997 has also tried to reform the very expensive welfare state by encouraging people to insure themselves against unemployment and sickness and to provide for their own pensions and care in old age. It has introduced reforms to help families, reduce poverty and exclusion, and made efforts to return the unemployed to work. But it has had to increase public spending in these areas (such as the National Health Service) in order to prevent their decay and possible collapse.

These developments suggest that the state in future may be unable (or unwilling) to meet the financial costs of public social services without increases in personal income tax or alternative funding schemes. People are consequently being encouraged to build their own welfare plans and government's role in the future may lie in directing aid rather than its funding and provision. This shows the difficulty of reconciling public services demand with a 'free market economy' and of deciding how much dependence there should be upon the state. The Labour government also intends to involve the private sector more in the provision and management of public services. But there is public and trade union opposition to this policy, which is generally perceived as the privatization of 'free' social services.

Social services history

Historically, state social services were non-existent for most of the British population. The churches, charities, the rural feudal system and town guilds (organizations of skilled craftsmen) did give some protection against poverty, illness and unemployment. But this help was limited in its application and effect. Most people were thrown upon their own, often minimal resources in order to survive.

In Elizabeth I's reign (1558–1603), a Poor Law was established in England, by which the state took over the organization of charity provisions from the church. Similar schemes existed in Wales, Scotland and Ireland. They operated at the local level and parishes were responsible through taxation for their poor, sick and unemployed, providing housing, help and work relief. The Poor Law was the start of state social legislation in Britain. But it was grudging, limited in its effects and discouraged people from relying on it. Poverty and need were considered to be the result of an unwillingness to work and provide for oneself. The state was not supposed to have extensive responsibility for social services.

These attitudes persisted in later centuries. But urban and rural poverty and need continued. Conditions worsened in the eighteenth and nineteenth centuries under the industrial revolutions as the population increased rapidly. The urban workforce had to work long hours in often bad conditions in low-quality factories for low wages. Families frequently inhabited slums of overcrowded, back-to-back dwellings which lacked adequate sewerage, heating or ventilation. The situation of many rural agricultural workers was just as bad.

Public health became an inevitable problem and the poor conditions resulted in infectious epidemics in the nineteenth century, such as diphtheria, typhoid, tuberculosis and smallpox. Some diseases remained endemic in the British population into the twentieth century because of bad housing and the lack of adequate health and social facilities.

The old Poor Law was replaced by the Poor Law Amendment Act of 1834 in England and Wales (later in Scotland). This was designed to prevent the alleged abuse of parish social relief and to reduce the high taxes needed to service the system. It created a system of workhouses in which the destitute and needy could work and live. But the workhouses were unpleasant places and people were discouraged from relying upon them. They were dreaded by the poor and accepted as a last alternative only when all else failed. Since nineteenth-century Britain was subject to economic slumps and unemployment, the workhouse system often resulted in misery and the separation of families.

Successive governments until the nineteenth century also refused to allow workers to organize themselves into trade unions, through which they might agitate against their working and living conditions. This forced some workers into establishing their own social and self-help clubs in order to provide basic protection for themselves. Some employers were more benevolent than others and provided good housing and health facilities for their workforces. But these examples were few and life continued to be harsh for many people in the towns and countryside.

The social misery of the nineteenth century persuaded some towns to establish local boards to control public health and initiate health schemes. But a public health apparatus was not created until 1848 and an effective national system was not in place until 1875. Other legislation was passed to clean up slum areas, but large-scale clearance was not achieved until the middle of the twentieth century. Reforms in housing, health, factory and mine conditions, sanitation and sewerage, town-planning and trade unionism were implemented in the nineteenth century. But they were limited in their effects and have been described as paternalistic in their intention.

The social welfare problems of the nineteenth century were considerable and the state's failure to provide major help against illness, unemployment and poverty made the situation worse. Social reformers, who promoted legislation which gave some relief from the more negative effects of industrialization, had to struggle against the apathy and hostility of vested interests in Parliament and the country.

However, small victories had been won and it was slowly admitted, if not universally, in the early twentieth century that the state had social responsibility for the whole of society. Progressive Liberal governments between 1905 and 1922 introduced reform programmes on old age pensions, national insurance, health, employment and trade unionism. These formed the basic structures of the future welfare state. But they affected only a minority of people, and the state was unwilling or unable to introduce further provisions in the early twentieth century. The financial and physical exhaustion resulting from the 1914–18 War and the economic crises of the 1920s and 1930s halted social services expansion.

But the underlying need for more state help continued as the population increased. The model for a welfare state appeared in the Beveridge Report of 1942. It recommended that a comprehensive system of social security and free health care for all should be established to overcome suffering and need 'from the cradle to the grave'. It was intended that the system would be largely financed by a national insurance scheme, to which workers would contribute, and out of which they and their families would receive benefits when required. Although Conservative governments passed some of the legislation to implement these proposals, it was the Labour government from 1945 to 1951 that radically altered the social and health systems and created the present welfare state. It was also gradually realized that most of the cost of the system would have to be provided for by general taxation.

Changing family and demographic structures

The provision of contemporary social services, in both public and private sectors, is conditioned by changes in family structures, demographic factors (such as birth rates and increases in life expectancy), governmental responses to social needs and the availability and cost of services.

It is argued that, as new social structures have emerged, the traditional British family either as a nuclear (two parents and children living together) or extended unit is falling apart; failing to provide for its elderly and disabled; suffering from social and moral problems; lacking parenting skills; and looking automatically to the state for support. In 2004, there were 24.1 million private households in Great Britain (an increase of 30 per cent since 1971) as illustrated in Table 8.1. These bare statistics have to be interpreted.

Marriage, for example, has decreased in popularity in Britain by 20 per cent since 1971. In 2002 it accounted for some 54 per cent of the population over 16

TABLE 8.1 Types of household, Great Britain 2004

Couple with children (married and unmarried)	28%
Couple with no children (married and unmarried)	29%
One person household	29%
Single parent with children	10%
Other (Two or more unrelated adults or containing more than one family)	4%

Source: Adapted from Labour Force Survey, Office for National Statistics 2004

and two in five of these unions were remarriages of one or both parties. Only a quarter of first marriages now have a religious ceremony, while most remarriages are civil. More people are delaying marriage until their late twenties (average age 28 for men and 26 for women) for career and other reasons.

Statisticians predict that married couples will in future be outnumbered by those people who never marry. The number of married adults will fall to 48 per cent by 2011 and 45 per cent by 2021. The proportion of unmarried men will increase more than that of unmarried women; the rise in cohabiting couples (couples of the same or different genders living together outside marriage) will not compensate for the decrease in married couples; and divorce rates may decline correspondingly.

This suggests that many more adults will be living alone in the future. There has already been a significant increase in one-person households with no children. These are people of all ages who may be single by choice, divorced, separated, widows or widowers. They are nearly one in three (29 per cent) of all households, more than double the proportion in 1961.

Four out of ten marriages end in divorce with a total increase to 160,700 in 2002. Britain has the highest divorce rate in the European Union; remarriages are at greater risk than first marriages; and people who marry under 21 are the most susceptible to divorce. The average length of marriages ending in divorce in England and Wales was 11.1 years in 2002; the average divorce age is 37 for women and 39 for men; and divorce affects a considerable number of children under 16. The trauma is increased by the confrontational nature of the divorce system, with conflicts over property, financial support and custody of children.

Given the rate of divorce, there has been, over the past 20 years, a big increase in cohabitation. In 2004, 12 per cent of 16–59-year-olds in Great Britain were cohabiting. This percentage translates into some 1.6 million cohabiting couples in England and Wales and the number is expected to rise to 2.93 million over the next 25 years. Many of these relationships are stable and long-term and eight out of ten resulting births are registered by both parents, rather than one as previously.

Non-marital (illegitimate) births arising from cohabitation and single mothers are 39 per cent of live births. This figure (particularly the number of under-18 single mothers which is the highest in Europe) has caused controversy on moral and cost grounds. Illegitimacy retains some of its old stigma. But the legal standing of such children has been improved by removing restrictions in areas like inheritance.

The British population was some 59.6 million in 2003 and projections suggest that it will increase to 65 million by 2050, after which it will decline. There were 695,600 live births in 2003 which outnumbered deaths at 611,800. But average family size has declined and is below 2.1 children per family. Between 1971 and 2003 there was an 18 per cent decrease in the number of children aged under 16 and a 28 per cent increase in the number of people aged 65 and over. Family size is expected to decline to 1.8 children per woman for women born after 1970 and people over 65 will exceed the number of children under 16 in the population by 2013. Some one in six of the population are now over 65 and 7 per cent are over 75. Life expectancy of men is 75.7 years and women 80.4 years, so that there are more women among the elderly. However, the number of older people in the population is expected to grow less quickly than in recent years.

There are several reasons for the low birth rate. Child-bearing is being delayed, with women in Britain having their first child on average at 28, seven years older than in 1971. Some women are delaying even longer for educational and career reasons and there has been an increase in the number of single women and married/unmarried couples who choose to remain childless, or to limit their families. Contraception has become more widespread; voluntary sterilization of both sexes is more common and legal abortions have increased.

Increased divorce and individual lifestyles have led to a threefold growth in the number of one-parent families with dependent children since 1961. It is estimated that some 2 million children are being raised in 1.3 million one-parent units (or 10 per cent of all households), where 89 per cent of the parents are women. Of the women bringing up one-parent families 16 per cent are single, 34 per cent are divorced, 22 per cent are separated and 17 per cent are widowed. Many of these families (with the highest proportion being in inner London) often have reduced living standards and are dependent upon social security benefits.

The proportion of married women in employment is now some 49 per cent. More women are returning to work more quickly after the birth of a child and women make up 45 per cent of the workforce. But although Britain has a high percentage of working mothers and wives, provisions for maternity leave and child-care are low in European terms.

The various family and single units have to cope with increased demands upon them, which may entail considerable personal sacrifice. Families carry out most of the caring roles in British society, rather than state professionals. Only 5 per cent of people over 65 and 7 per cent of disabled adults live in state or private institutions. Most disabled children and adults are cared for by their families and most of the elderly are cared for by families or live alone. This is a saving to the state without which the cost of state health and welfare care would rise. But the burden upon families will grow as the population becomes more elderly, state provision is reduced and the disabled (6 million adults) and disadvantaged increase. There are demands that more government aid should be given to carers, families and local authorities to lighten their burden.

The picture that emerges from these statistics is one of smaller families; more people living alone; an increase in one-parent families and non-marital births; high divorce rates; more people living longer and contributing to an ageing population; more working mothers and wives; more cohabiting couples; and a decline in marriage. These features influence the contemporary state and private provisions for social security, health, social services and housing.

Social security

The social security system provides benefits for British people and is operated by Department of Work and Pensions agencies throughout the country. It is the government's single most expensive programme (28 per cent of public spending or £138 billion in 2004–5) and is financed from general taxation and contributions by employers and workers over 16 to the National Insurance Fund.

This means that social security gives benefits to workers who pay contributions to the National Insurance Fund and income tax system; income-related benefits to people who have no income or whose income falls below certain levels and who need assistance; and other benefits which are conditional on disability or family needs, such as non-contributory Disability and Attendance Allowances.

The contributory system gives, for example, relatively low state retirement pensions for employed women at 60 and men at 65 (to be equalized at 65 for all from 2010); maternity pay for pregnant working women; sick pay or incapacity benefit for people who are absent from work because of illness or who become incapable of work; and a Jobseeker's Allowance for those who become unemployed (dependent upon people actively seeking work).

Income-related benefits are also provided by the state, usually after means-testing (examination of financial position). For example, *Income Support* depends upon savings and capital and is given at various levels of eligibility to some 5.6 million people in financial need, such as one-parent families, the elderly, long-term sick and unemployed. It covers basic living requirements, although the sums are relatively low. It also includes free prescription drugs, dental treatment, opticians' services and children's school meals. The *Working Families' Tax Credit* is a benefit whereby families with children and at least one parent in low-paid work receive a tax credit through workers' pay packets to increase their earnings. It includes the same extra benefits as Income Support and is dependent upon income, savings and capital. A *Child Tax Credit* is a payment to support families with children and is dependent upon income and the number of children in a family unit. *Housing Benefit* is paid to people on Income Support and other low-income claimants (4.2 million in 2001) and covers the cost of rented accommodation. A tax-free *Child Benefit* (£15 per week for the eldest child and £10 for other children) is paid to all mothers for each of her children up to the age of 18, irrespective of family income.

In the past, people in great need were also able to claim non-contributory single payments, such as the cost of clothes, cookers and children's shoes, in the form of grants or loans. But these have been sharply cut and replaced by a Social Fund, to which people have to apply. The fund is applied restrictively and has been widely attacked as an example of government's alleged reduction of social security aid.

Social security does provide a degree of security. It is supposed to be a safety-net against urgent needs, but this does not prevent hardship. Some 27 per cent of British people are on different kinds of income-related benefits. It is also estimated that a quarter of the population (including 4.5 million children) exist on the poverty line, which is sometimes measured as half the average national income. But accurate figures of poverty are difficult to find, because of the variable presentation of official statistics; because there are different definitions of what constitutes poverty; and because poverty today tends to be seen in relative rather than absolute terms.

Social security is very expensive and will become more so as the population ages and as the numbers of the sick, poor, disadvantaged and unemployed persist. It is very complicated with its array of benefits and subject to fraud, particularly in the cases of Income Support, Disability Allowance and Housing Benefit.

The Labour government intends to reform the system, attack fraud, cut expense and reduce benefits while still preserving the safety-net commitment and targeting those people with the greatest needs. It is committed to reducing poverty and exclusion. It is argued that such reforms will mean a real reduction in social security, particularly the Social Fund, Housing Benefit, Income Support, Disability Allowance and unemployment aid. The young unemployed between 16 and 18 are now ineligible for benefits until they are 18 and must follow training or education programmes. The government argues that the cost of social security is unsustainable and encourages greater self-provision through work rather than dependency. But it is difficult to create a simple and fair system which protects the genuinely needy and also encourages people to become more self-reliant and independent.

Conservative and Labour governments are concerned that people should look after themselves more, without automatic recourse to the state for help and that they should seek employment more actively. They are encouraged to take out private pensions (such as the government-backed stakeholder pension) to add to their low state pensions and to insure privately against health and other costs. But the inadequate record of the insurance companies in these areas has been criticized.

The value of occupational pensions operated by private companies has effectively been reduced by a movement from final-salary pensions to different forms of subscription and some firms have gone out of business leaving workers without the pensions to which they have contributed. It is argued that a predicted state and private pension crisis in Britain can be solved only by increased taxation to pay for state pensions at a time when the labour force is decreasing or by workers working longer and saving more for their retirements (or by a mixture of the two).

The National Health Service (NHS)

A Labour government created the National Health Service (NHS) in 1947. It was based on the Beveridge Report recommendations and replaced a private system of payment for health care by one of free treatment for all at the point of need. The medical profession wished to retain private medicine and opposed the establishment of the NHS. But this was countered by the Labour government.

The NHS was originally intended to be completely free for those needing medical help, irrespective of income. This ideal, to a large extent, has been achieved, although most people fund the system through their taxes and National Insurance contributions while working. Hospital and most medical treatment under the NHS is free for British and EU citizens. The NHS provides a range of medical and dental services for the whole country based on hospitals, doctors, dentists, nurses, midwives, ambulance services, blood transfusion and other health facilities.

But some charges are now made. For example, prescriptions (written notes from a doctor enabling patients to obtain drugs from a chemist) have to be paid for, as do some dental work, dental checks and eye tests. Payments are dependent upon employment status, age and income. Children under 16, people on social security benefits and old age pensioners receive free prescriptions. But NHS dental treatment is in serious trouble and many dentists have left the NHS for private practice.

The NHS is financed from taxation and National Insurance. It cost £81 billion per year or 17 per cent of government spending in 2004–5 and is the biggest single employer of labour in Western Europe. Yet, despite increased government spending, state health expenditure in Britain is only 7.3 per cent of the gross domestic product (GDP) and lower than other major Western countries, which have a higher combination of the public and the private in their total health spending.

The UK government is responsible for the NHS through the Department of Health in England and devolved bodies in Wales, Scotland and Northern Ireland. At a lower level, the NHS used to be administered by local health authorities in England and Wales and health councils in Scotland and Northern Ireland. They identified the general health care needs of the people living in their area and secured hospital and community health services. But their functions are being changed.

The structure has been localized and the Labour government has created Primary Care Trusts, controlling two-thirds of NHS budgets at local level. These bodies comprise health professionals (such as doctors) and hospitals; work with local health authorities; and determine patient services. The aim is to achieve a system of integrated care by frontline medical professionals which is direct and effective.

Doctors

Most people who require health care will first consult their local NHS-funded doctor, who is a GP or non-specialist general practitioner: of these there are about 35,000 in Britain. Doctors have an average of 2,000 registered patients on their panel (or list of names), although they will see only a small percentage of these on a regular basis. The majority of GPs are now members of group practices, where they share larger premises, services and equipment, which also allow for some minor surgery. However, a patient will usually be on the panel of one particular doctor, who will often be a personal choice. An alternative to seeing a doctor is to make use of the NHS Direct service, which allows one to seek advice on the telephone from nurses. There are conflicting reports on this service's effectiveness.

Hospitals

If patients require further treatment or examination, the GP refers them to specialists and consultants, normally at local NHS hospitals or NHS Trusts. NHS Trust hospitals are funded by contracts with the local Primary Care Groups. But they are 'self-governing' to a large extent, while new, controversial Foundation Hospitals are supposed to run their own independent budgets and services.

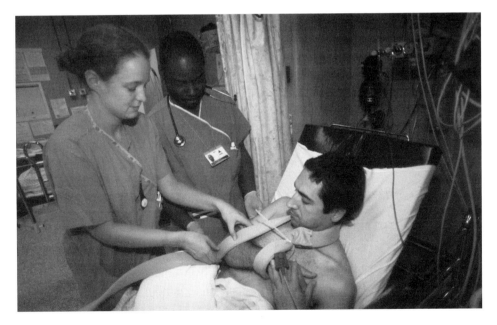

PLATE 8.1 Hospital care.
NHS doctor and nurse attend a patient with a dislocated shoulder.
(*Shout/Rex Features*)

PLATE 8.2 University College Hospital, London.
One of the new NHS hospitals which are being constructed in many areas of Britain.
(*Paul Brown/Rex Features*)

Hospitals have about 370,000 beds and provide medical, dental, nursing and midwifery staff. Britain has some very modern hospitals and facilities and more hospitals are being constructed. But it also has many buildings which were erected in the nineteenth century and which are in urgent need of modernization and repair. There is a shortage of beds in some hospitals. Wards and hospitals are being closed. Waiting times for consultancy visits and admission to hospital for operations as well as for treatment in accident and emergency departments are still a source of concern, despite a large infusion of government funds into the system.

The state of the NHS

The NHS has an ambivalent position in the public mind. On one hand, it is praised for its work as a free service and its achievements. It is considered a success in terms of consumer demand. Today people are in general receiving help when they need it and many who would previously have died or suffered are surviving and being cared for. Standards of living and medicine have risen; better diets have been devised and there is a greater health awareness in the population at large.

On the other hand, the NHS is criticized for its alleged inefficiency, inadequate standards, treatment discrepancies throughout the country and bureaucracy. Its objectives are considered too ambitious for the money spent on

it. The media constantly draw attention to shortcomings (such as hygiene problems and infectious disease outbreaks in hospitals) and forecast breakdown.
Workers in the NHS, such as doctors, nurses and non-medical staff, complain
about low pay, long hours, management weaknesses, levels of staffing (with a
shortage of doctors and nurses), and cuts in services. In the past, it was suggested
that such problems could be solved simply by injecting more money into the
NHS. But increased spending by the Labour government has not eradicated what
many critics see as a managerial inability to organize the funds competently at the
point where they are needed.

Rising costs and increased demand provoke cries for more finance and
resources. The NHS is in many ways a victim of its own success and of the
demands that the British place upon it as of right. It is inevitable that a free,
consumer-led service will require increasing levels of expenditure, better management of existing resources or alternative funding. Yet despite problems, such
as increasing physical assaults upon health professionals in hospitals and surgeries,
and undoubted pressures, much of the NHS works well and gives value for the
money spent on it.

There are many suggestions as to how the NHS can be improved, but each
can have unfortunate results. Increased government spending on the NHS may
increase personal taxation. Charges could be made for some services, but this hits
the principle of free health care, although a MORI poll in May 2001 showed that
66 per cent of respondents were prepared to pay for some NHS care if it meant
an overall better service. Better management of existing funds might make some
savings, but possibly not enough. Combining a public service with private
insurance would not include poorer people, who would still depend upon a free
NHS. The Labour government is trying to involve the private sector more closely
in the running of the NHS through Public-Private Partnerships and paying
for patient care in private hospitals. But many people regard these devices as
privatization of the NHS.

The government is committed to raising NHS spending to European levels;
cutting down management costs; transferring money to medical care and staff; and
reorganizing NHS administration. But the public see little actual improvement
and according to MORI polls in May and July 2005 are disillusioned with Labour's
attempts to revitalize the NHS and are very concerned about health facilities.
However, the World Health Organization in August 2001 had ranked Britain as
twenty-fourth out of 191 countries in terms of the efficiency of its health system,
above countries such as Germany, the USA and Denmark.

The private medical sector

It is argued that health care should not be a question of who can pay for it, but a
responsibility of the state. However, the public sector has problems and attempts
have been made to involve the private sector in providing health care.

The previous Conservative government encouraged the growth of private health institutions, private medical insurance and partnership between the public and private sectors on a commercial basis. Its Private Finance Initiative allowed new health facilities to be built, maintained and owned by the private sector. These are then leased to the NHS, which provides clinical services and controls planning and clinical decisions. The Conservatives saw the private sector as complementary to the NHS. It would release pressure on state funds; give choice to patients; allow the sharing of medical resources; provide flexible services; result in cost-effective cooperation with the NHS; and allow treatment of NHS patients at public expense in the private sector.

The Labour government, in a reversal of old Labour ideology, has embraced these ideas. It has agreements with private health care providers to enable the NHS to make better use of facilities in private hospitals. Some NHS hospitals share expensive equipment with private hospitals, and NHS patients are treated (at public expense) in the private sector when it represents value for money. But the scale of private practice in relation to the NHS is small. Much private treatment is confined to minor medical cases and expensive, long-term care is still carried out by the NHS.

A quarter of patients pay for private health care out of their income or capital. Some 6.9 million other individuals and 4.8 million people in company plans are covered by private medical insurance taken out with businesses such as the British United Provident Association (BUPA). Concern about waiting lists and standards of health care in the NHS persuade many to take out such insurance. The insurance policy pays for private care either in private hospitals and clinics, or in NHS hospitals which provide 'pay-beds' (beds for the use of paying patients, which still exist in NHS hospitals and were a concession in 1946 to those doctors who agreed to join the NHS but who wished to keep a number of private patients). A Consumers' Association report in August 2001 found that 40 per cent of respondents would consider going private to avoid lengthy NHS queues, although 84 per cent did not have medical insurance. Many people today are also likely to be deterred by the rising costs of insurance premiums and private treatment.

The personal social services

The social services provide facilities in the local community for assisting people, such as the elderly, the disabled, the mentally handicapped, families, children and young people. Trained staff, such as district visitors and social workers, cater for these personal needs. The services are organized by local government authorities with central government funding (£22 billion or 5 per cent of government spending in 2004–5). While it is argued that social services need extra public money to address growing problems, there are signs that the Labour government may privatize at least parts of the sector.

An increasing pressure is being put upon the social services, families and carers as the elderly population grows and the ranks of the disadvantaged rise. For example, the number of public residential and nursing homes for the elderly is insufficient for the demand, and some private homes close because of cost. In both cases, people may be forced to sell their homes to cover some or all of their expenses in England, Wales and Northern Ireland, unlike Scotland where residential and medical care is free under devolved legislation. Care services for the elderly and infirm face a severe staff shortage unless higher pay and better training for care workers are introduced and the system operates on a better foundation.

The previous Conservative government introduced a 'Care in the Community' programme, parts of which are being continued by the Labour government. The aim is to give financial and material support to families and carers looking after elderly or disabled relatives in the latters' own homes or for children and adults with disabilities in the family home. It also allows psychiatric patients who do not need constant care to be moved to the community under social services supervision and for some elderly and disabled people to be cared for in their own homes by social services. The aim is to prevent the institutionalization of people and to give them independence.

But the scheme has had difficulties, such as mentally handicapped and disabled patients becoming homeless or housed in inadequate temporary accommodation and elderly people receiving poor attention and help. It is argued that local authorities need more support and that a greater awareness of implementation problems is required if the policy is to be more successful.

The personal social services also cater for people with learning disabilities, give help to families and provide day care facilities for children. Children in need are also supposed to be protected in residential care accommodation and local authorities facilitate fostering and adoption services. But there have been a number of serious cases in recent years which have focussed on abuse in children's care homes.

The private social services (voluntary) sector

While there have been substantial improvements in state social services in the twentieth century, there is still a shortage of finance and resources to support all the needy in a comprehensive fashion. It is therefore important that voluntary charities and agencies have continued. They are a complementary welfare service to the state and private facilities and provide an essential element in the total aid pattern. The state system would be unable to cover all needs without them.

Most of the voluntary agencies have charitable status, which means that they receive tax concessions on their income, but receive no (or very little) financial support from the state. However, some groups, such as those dealing with drug and alcohol addiction, do receive financial grants from central and local government. There are many thousands of voluntary organizations in Britain, operating at national and local levels and varying considerably in size. Some are small and collect limited amounts of money from the public. Others are very large, have professional staffs and receive millions of pounds from many different sources. Some groups, such as Oxfam (for the relief of famine) and the Save the Children Fund, have now become international organizations.

The following are examples of the voluntary agencies. Barnado's provides care and help for needy children; the Church of England Children's Society cares for children in need and is Britain's largest adoption agency; the Cancer Research Fund gathers finance and carries out research into potential cures for cancer; the People's Dispensary for Sick Animals (PDSA) provides veterinary aid for people's pets; the Samaritans give telephone help to the suicidal; women's groups have founded refuges for abused women; and Help the Aged campaigns for the concerns of the elderly.

Housing

Housing in Britain is divided into public and private sectors. Of the 25 million domestic dwellings, the majority are in the private sector, with 68 per cent being owner-occupied and 11 per cent rented out by private landlords. Some 21 per cent

PLATE 8.3 Detached house on suburban housing estate, 1997.
Detached houses command the highest prices on the British housing market.
(*Gregg Watts/Rex Features*)

are in the public, subsidized sector and are rented by low-income tenants from local government authorities or housing associations (non-profit-making bodies which manage and build homes for rent and sale with the aid of government grants).

In both public and private sectors, over 80 per cent of the British population live in houses or bungalows (one-storey houses) and the remainder in flats and maisonettes. Houses have traditionally been divided into detached (22 per cent), semi-detached (30) and terraced housing (28), with the greater prices and prestige being given to detached property.

Public-sector or social housing in England is controlled centrally by the Department of the Environment and by devolved bodies in Wales, Scotland and Northern Ireland. Much of this housing has historically been provided by local authorities with finance from local sources and central government. But the provision and organization of such properties by local government has declined in recent years and more has been taken over by housing associations.

The previous Conservative government (1979–97) encouraged the growth of home ownership in the housing market, as part of its programme to create a property- and share-owning democracy in Britain. In the public sector, it introduced (1980) a right-to-buy policy by which local government sells off council housing to sitting tenants at below-market prices. This policy has increased the number of home-owners by over 1 million and relieved local authorities of the

PLATE 8.4 Terraced housing, Muswell Hill, London, 2005.
Terraced housing (often from the Victorian and Edwardian periods) is prominent throughout Britain and can attract high prices depending on location and condition.
(*Richard Gardner/Rex Features*)

expense of decoration, upkeep and repair. The Labour Party, after initially opposing the policy, accepted it, mainly because it proved attractive to tenants. The current Labour government has ploughed back the revenue from council sales into local government (which previously had not been able to spend it) so that it can provide more low-cost social accommodation. It is also sceptical of tenants who buy council properties to quickly sell on for profit on the open market. Government spending on housing amounted to £17 billion or 3 per cent of total spending in 2004–5.

The Conservatives were critical of local government housing policies. They wanted local authorities to divest themselves of housing management. Instead, they would work with housing associations and the private sector to increase the supply of low-cost housing for rent without providing it themselves. However, the Labour government has returned some control over housing policies to local government.

But the construction of new publicly funded houses has declined in real terms and the private sector is not building enough low-cost properties. Critics argue that Conservative government housing policies contributed to a serious shortage of cheap rented accommodation in towns and rural areas for low-income groups, single people and the unemployed, at a time when demand was (and is) growing. The biggest increase in this demand is expected to be in the number of one-person

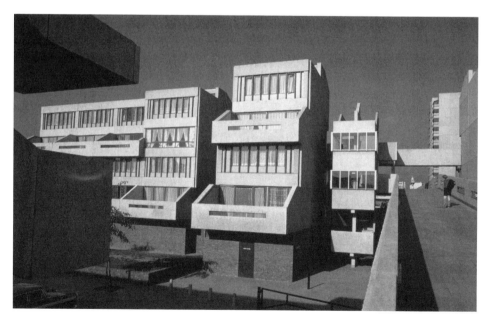

PLATE 8.5 A concrete council estate, Thamesmead, London.
Council or social housing built by local government authorities (here on the south bank of the River Thames) for rent to low-income tenants.
(*Adam Woolfitt/Corbis*)

households which are projected to grow from 5.8 million in 1996 to 8.5 million by 2021 or 71 per cent of the total increase in the number of households.

Home ownership in the private sector has increased by 10 per cent since 1979. The normal procedure when buying a house or flat is to take out a loan on the security of the property (a mortgage) from a building society, bank or other financial institution. The amount of money advanced on a loan depends mainly on the borrower's salary and it is usual to borrow three times one's gross annual salary. This long-term loan is usually paid off over a 25-year period and includes interest.

House prices can vary considerably throughout the country, with London and south-east England having the highest prices and northern England, Scotland and Wales having the lowest. Prices increased dramatically at the beginning of the 1970s and much property speculation occurred. Price increases then stabilized for some years. But there was a price boom from 1986 to 1988, followed by high interest rates and an increase in mortgage foreclosures. This means that, when people cannot afford to continue their repayments on the loan, the lending institution takes over the property and the occupier becomes homeless. There was also a fall in house prices, a property slump and a growth in negative equity which was only slowly reversed from 1994 as interest rates were reduced and the property market recovered. Since then, house prices have increased spectacularly again throughout Britain, and critics argue that properties are overvalued. Interest rates have increased to counter the property boom. Foreclosures have increased, but house prices have only slowly moderated.

British homes still have variable construction standards. Many are old and cold; are frequently badly built; and lack central heating and adequate insulation. But there has been some improvement in housing quality in recent years and most new houses have a high percentage of the basic amenities. Greater attention has been paid to insulation and energy saving. However, as building costs rise and available land becomes scarcer, the trend in new property construction has been towards flats and much smaller rooms in houses.

Nevertheless, there are still districts, particularly in the centres of the big cities, where living conditions are bad and the equivalent of contemporary slums. Nearly half of the property in the inner-city areas was built before 1919 and, in spite of large-scale slum clearance in the 1950s and 1960s, much existing housing here is in barely habitable shape. Some recently completed high-rise blocks of council flats and estates in the public sector have had to be demolished because of defective and dangerous structures. According to the National Housing Forum, one in 13 British homes (or 1.8 million) are unfit for human habitation.

Twentieth-century town renovation and slum clearance policies from the 1930s were largely devoted to the removal of the populations of large city-centres to new towns, usually located in the countryside, or to new council estates in the suburbs. Some of the new towns, such as Crawley and Stevenage, have been seen as successes, although they initially had their share of social and planning problems. The same cannot be said of many council estates, which have tended to degenerate very quickly. The bad design of some housing estates, their social deprivation and lack of upkeep are often blamed for the crime and vandalism which affect many of them. Some local councils are now modernizing decaying housing stock, rather than spending on new development, in an attempt to preserve local communities, although the Labour government currently seems intent on demolishing old properties, particularly in northern England. Renovation work is also being done by housing associations (with government grants) and by private builders.

The provision of sufficient adequate and varied housing in Britain, such as one-bedroom properties for young and single persons, has been a problem for many years. People on low (and even medium) wages, whether married or single, are often unable to afford the cost of a mortgage for suitable private property in the current market. One of the factors (in addition to high property prices) causing the difficulty for young people in affording first homes, particularly in rural areas with (ever-increasing) commuting distance of London, is the desire of affluent people for homes – or second homes – in the country. It is also difficult for them to obtain council housing because of long waiting lists, which contain people with priority over them. The right-to-buy policy has reduced the number of available council houses and flats for low-income groups and the unemployed. Alternatives for many are to board with parents (as many young people – including professionals on reasonable salaries – increasingly do), house-share with others or rent property in the private sector.

The previous Conservative government tried to encourage landlords and other agencies to provide more privately rented accommodation by lessening the effects of rent legislation and introducing new lease structures. But the relaxations have led to accusations of exploitation of tenants by landlords. The Labour government wants to see a healthy private rented sector. It is trying to improve the rights of leaseholders to purchase their freehold and protect themselves against abuse by unscrupulous landlords. At the same time, there has been a growth in individuals purchasing 'buy-to-rent' properties which, until recently proved to be attractive investments.

In an attempt to cope with the demand for housing, the Labour government has embarked on large-scale building plans in the English south midlands, southeast and along the south coast. This policy has aroused criticism since some houses will be built on flood plains with the consequent threat of flooding, as well as environmental damage and increased traffic congestion in other areas. The government also permits local councils to build high-density housing in urban areas and in some Green Belts.

Inadequate housing provision has also partly contributed to the number of homeless people, particularly in London and other large cities, which in turn has led to increased social problems. Officially, there are some 105,000 homeless people, who must be housed in temporary accommodation, which is usually

PLATE 8.6 Homeless man begging, Oxford Street, London.
The Labour government claims that the number of homeless people and 'rough sleepers' has been reduced.
(*Alex Segre/Rex Features*)

inadequate. But unofficial figures put the real homeless total for all age groups at about 300,000 and some of them are visible on the streets of Britain's large cities, particularly London. The Labour government has established programmes and funds to combat 'rough sleeping' (people who sleep in the open) and there had been a reduction of one-third in the numbers of rough sleepers by 2000. The causes of homelessness are complex and affect all age groups and types of people, but it is suggested that the problem could be better handled. There are some 700,000 homes (mainly in the Midlands and the north of England but increasingly in southern England) in both the private and public sectors which remain empty and unoccupied for various reasons. Critics argue that these could eradicate the problem of homelessness and the housing shortage if they were properly refurbished and utilized.

Charities such as Shelter and religious organizations like the Salvation Army provide accommodation for the homeless for limited periods and campaign on their behalf. Local organizations, such as Housing Advice Centres and Housing Aid Centres, also provide help. But the problem of housing in Britain is still a major one and a focus of public concern. The high prices of many private houses and the inadequacies of the public sector market suggest that the problem will remain. The number of new starts for construction in both the public and private sectors has decreased and continues to stagnate (2005).

Attitudes to the social services

Recent opinion polls have consistently shown that a majority of British people feel concern about and dissatisfaction with the public social services in general. MORI polls in 2005, before and after the general election, reported that the National Health Service (including hospitals) was near the top of a list of worries. But state pensions, social security and public housing had also climbed up the list. A problem with these views is whether they accurately portray the reality of the social services, since the personal experiences of many other individuals in their dealings with the system are positive. The culture of complaint can become self-perpetuating.

Respondents to polls feel that there should be greater public spending on the National Health Service and medical resources (such as more doctors and nurses) and do not believe that there has been a great improvement in these areas despite increased funding by the Labour government since 2001. They do not consider that the NHS is as well run as other institutions and there has been growing support for a comprehensive, better-funded and more efficient state health care service. However, doctors and nurses always head the lists of those professionals with whom Britons are most satisfied, despite recent scandals about medical negligence.

Concern is also felt about the provision of public housing, social security benefits, state pensions, the personal social services and community care. Most people, at least in response to poll questions, indicate that they would be willing to pay higher taxes in order to ensure better social and health welfare. There is also some support for the idea that a proportional amount of income tax could be earmarked or ring fenced as directly applicable to the public services.

The Public-Private Partnership schemes favoured by the Labour government, which involve the private sector in the provision and organization of public services, are not supported by a majority of the public, who see them as a form of gradual privatization. There is also opposition to other government reforms. There are plans for a controversial reorganization of Primary Care Trusts, which could involve some health professionals being transferred to the private sector. There has been much disquiet about the functions and responsibilities of new Foundation Hospitals which, while being state hospitals, are independent, free from government control, and open up public medical services to private sector finance and possible control. Critics argue that such developments establish a market for health care which will be extended to the rest of the welfare state.

A MORI poll in July 2001 found that only one in nine respondents believed that extending private sector involvement would improve public services. A later MORI poll in September 2001 found that 64 per cent of respondents felt that public services, such as health, should be entirely or mostly provided by the public sector.

On being asked how public services could be improved, 64 per cent of respondents thought that better pay and conditions should be given to public sector workers as an aid to recruitment; 43 per cent believed that there should be more public sector workers; and 42 per cent considered that there should be more investment in new buildings and equipment for public services.

These results show that a majority of British people support the idea of free public services funded by taxation. Trade union leaders suggested that the Labour government could be on a collision course with the public if it pushed ahead with public-private partnerships in the public services. A MORI poll in October 2001 found that only 42 per cent of respondents felt that Labour government policies in general would improve the state of public services, despite the government's increased funding.

Exercises

Explain and examine the following terms:

welfare state	chemist	flats	social services
Social Fund	benefits	GP	nuclear family
'pay-beds'	rent	Shelter	council housing
workhouses	landlord	Oxfam	Beveridge Report
Poor Law	bungalow	mortgage	Income Support
charities	homeless	cohabitation	building society

Write short essays on the following topics:

1   Describe the structure and condition of the National Health Service.

2   Does the social security system provide a comprehensive service for the needy in Britain?

3   Discuss the different types of housing in Britain and the mechanics of buying property. What are some of the problems that affect property buying today?

Further reading

1   George, V. and Wilding, P. (1999) *British Society and Social Welfare* London: Palgrave/Macmillan

2   Glennester, H. (2000) *British Social Policy since 1945* Oxford: Blackwell

3   Ham, C. (1999) *Health Policy in Britain* London: Palgrave/Macmillan

4   Harris, B. (2004) *The Origins of the British Welfare State: Social Welfare in England and Wales, 1800–1945* London: Palgrave/Macmillan

5   Lowe, R. (2004) *The Welfare State in Britain since 1945* London: Palgrave/Macmillan

6   Ludlam, S. and Smith, M.J. (eds) (2000) *New Labour in Government* London: Macmillan

7   Mullins, D. and Murie, A. (2005) *Housing Policy in the UK* London: Palgrave/Macmillan

8 Page, R. and Silburn, R. (eds) (1999) *British Social Welfare in the Twentieth Century* London: Palgrave/Macmillan

9 Willman, J. (1998) *A Better State of Health* London: Profile Books

Websites

Department of Work and Pensions: www.dwp.gov.uk
Department of Health: www.doh.gov.uk
Home Office: www.homeoffice.gov.uk
Charity Commission: www.charity-commission.gov.uk
Women's Unit: www.womens-unit.gov.uk
National Assembly for Wales: www.wales.gov.uk
Northern Ireland Executive: www.nics.gov.uk
Scottish Executive: www.scotland.gov.uk

Education

British education operates on three levels: schools, higher education and further/adult education. Schools are divided into state (maintained from public funds) and independent (privately financed) sectors (the latter mainly in England). But there is no common educational organization for the whole country and England/Wales, Northern Ireland and Scotland have somewhat different school systems. To simplify matters, this chapter concentrates on the largest school element, that of England and Wales, with comparative references to Scotland and Northern Ireland. Further/adult and higher education generally have the same structure throughout Britain and are mostly state-funded. Following devolution, the individual countries of the United Kingdom have greater degrees of self-government in educational matters at all these levels.

The quality of contemporary British state school education is of great concern to parents, employers, politicians and students. School inspectors have criticized standards in English, Mathematics, Technology and writing/reading skills. In recent years, international comparisons by organizations such as the OECD and World Economic Forum, have suggested that Britain does not rank highly for the quality of its secondary schools (defined by good passes in national examinations) and that British 13-to-14-year-olds lag behind comparable pupils in most European countries. British pre-school and primary education have had a poor reputation in international terms, with a lack of high-quality nurseries and low-qualified and underpaid staff and poor working conditions at primary school levels. In 2005, figures from Ofsted (the Office for Standards in Education) reported that almost half of children were leaving state primary schools without the basic skills of reading, writing and arithmetic. It is argued that this results in some functionally illiterate pupils passing on to the secondary level of education. A National Skills Task Force in 2000 reported that 7 million adults (one in five) in Britain were functionally illiterate, although some think tank reports suggest that this could now be higher. It is argued that low standards of literacy and numeracy stem from decades of inadequate state school education.

But the OECD has nevertheless reported that Britain leads the world in higher education, defined as the highest proportion (35.6 per cent) of university graduates aged 21, largely because of short (three-year) degree courses. However, in Britain itself there is criticism of degree standards and the content of some university courses, varying performances between different universities and the declining quality of students entering university from secondary school.

In spite of these reports, British education should not be seen in a wholly negative light. The Labour government in 1997 prioritized education, promised to focus on its quality and to make it a life-long learning experience. Primary school literacy has improved, although not as much as expected. National school examination and test results have improved in recent years, although some critics attribute this to lower standards. Many schools, teachers and students in the state and independent sectors produce excellent work, as do some universities. It is the failing and underperforming state schools and universities which catch the media headlines. But state school education still has weaknesses and the public are dissatisfied with Labour's progress in raising educational standards or creating an adequate structure of schools. Education appears consistently in opinion polls as a main concern of the British public in terms both of its declining quality and its socializing influence.

School history

The complicated nature of British (particularly English) schooling and current educational controversies have their roots in school history. State involvement in education was late and the first attempt to establish a unified system of state-funded elementary schools came only in 1870 for England and Wales (1872 for Scotland and 1923 for Northern Ireland). But it was not until 1944 that the state provided a comprehensive and national apparatus for both primary and secondary state schools, which were free and compulsory.

However, some church schools have long existed. After England, Scotland, Ireland and Wales were gradually converted to Christianity by the fifth and sixth centuries, the church's position in society enabled it to create the first schools. These initially prepared boys for the priesthood. But the church then developed a wider educational role and its structures influenced the later state system.

Other schools were also periodically established by rich individuals or monarchs. These were independent, privately-financed institutions and were variously known as high, grammar and public schools. They were later associated with both the modern independent and state educational sectors. But such schools were largely confined to the sons of the rich, aristocratic and influential. Most people received no formal schooling and remained illiterate and innumerate for life.

In later centuries, more children benefited as the church created new schools; local areas developed secular schools; charity schools were provided by wealthy industrialists and philanthropists for working-class boys and girls; and some other poor children could attend a variety of schools organized by voluntary societies, women (dames), workhouses and the Ragged School Union. But the minority of children attending such institutions received only a very basic instruction in reading, writing and arithmetic. The majority of children received no adequate education.

By the nineteenth century, Britain had a haphazard school structure (except for Scotland). Protestant churches had lost their monopoly of education and competed with the Roman Catholic Church and other faiths. Church schools guarded their independence from state and secular interference and provided much of the available schooling. The ancient high, grammar and public schools continued to train the sons of the middle and upper classes for professional and leadership roles in society. But, at a time when the industrial revolutions were proceeding rapidly and the population was growing strongly, the state did not provide a school system which could educate the workforce. Most of the working class still received no formal or adequate education.

However, local and central government did begin to show some regard for education in the early nineteenth century. Grants were made to local authorities for school use in their areas and in 1833 Parliament funded the construction of school buildings. But it was only in 1870 that the state became more actively involved. An Education Act (the Forster Act) created local school boards in England and Wales, which financed and built elementary schools in their areas. Such state schools supplied non-denominational training and the existing religious voluntary (or church) schools served denominational needs.

By 1880 the state system provided free and compulsory elementary schooling in most parts of Britain for children between the ages of five and ten (12 in 1899). The Balfour Act (1902) abolished the school boards, made local government responsible for state education, established some new secondary and technical schools and funded voluntary schools. But, although state schools provided education for children up to the age of 14 by 1918, this was still limited to basic skills.

Adequate secondary school education remained largely the province of the independent sector and a few state schools. But generally people had to pay for these services. After a period when the old public (private) schools had declined in quality, they revived in the nineteenth century. Their weaknesses, such as the narrow curriculum and indiscipline, had been reformed by progressive head-masters like Thomas Arnold of Rugby and their reputations increased. The private grammar and high schools, which imitated the classics-based education of the public schools, also expanded. These schools drew their pupils from the sons of the middle and upper classes and were the training grounds for the established elite and the professions.

State secondary school education in the early twentieth century was marginally extended to children whose parents could not afford school fees. Scholarships (financial grants) for clever poor children became available; some state funding was provided and more schools were created. But this state help did not appreciably expand secondary education, and by 1920 only 9.2 per cent of 14-year-old children in England and Wales were able to enter secondary schools on a non-fee-paying basis. The school system in the early twentieth century was still inadequate for the demands of society; working- and lower middle-class children lacked extensive education; and hard-pressed governments avoided any further large-scale involvement until 1944.

The 1944 Education Act

In 1944, an Education Act (the Butler Act) reorganized state primary and secondary schools in England and Wales (1947 in Scotland and Northern Ireland) and greatly influenced future generations of schoolchildren. State schooling became free and compulsory up to the age of 15 and was divided into three stages: primary schools (5–12 years old), secondary schools (12–15) and further post-school training. A decentralized system resulted, in which a Ministry of Education drew up policy guidelines and local education authorities (LEAs) decided which forms of schooling would be used in their areas.

Two types of state school resulted from the Act: county and voluntary. Primary and secondary county schools were provided by LEAs in each county. Voluntary schools were mainly those elementary schools which had been founded by religious and other groups and which were now partially financed or maintained by LEAs, although many retained a particular religious affiliation. Non-denominational schools thus coexisted with voluntary schools.

Following the 1944 Act, most state secondary schools in England/Wales and Northern Ireland were divided into grammar schools and secondary modern schools. Some grammar schools were new, while others were old foundations, which now received direct state funding and were known as grant maintained schools. Placement in this secondary system depended upon an examination result. The eleven-plus examination was adopted by most LEAs, consisted of tests which covered linguistic, mathematical and general knowledge and was taken in the last year of primary school at the age of eleven. The object was to differentiate between academic and non-academic children and introduced the notion of 'selection' based on ability. Those who passed the eleven-plus went to the grammar school, while those who failed went to the secondary modern school.

Although schools were supposed to be equal in their respective educational aims, the grammar schools were equated with a better (more academic) education; a socially more respectable role; and qualified children (through national examinations) for better jobs and entry into higher education and the professions. Secondary modern schools emphasized practical schooling, initially without national examinations. A third type of school (technical school) educated more vocationally-inclined pupils.

The intention of the 1944 Act was to provide universal and free state primary and secondary education. Day-release training at local colleges was also introduced for employed people who wanted further education after 15 and local authority grants were given to students who wished to enter higher education. It was hoped that such equality of opportunity would expand the educational market, lead to a better-educated society, encourage more working-class children to enter university and achieve greater social mobility.

However, it was felt in the 1950s that these aims were not being achieved under the selective secondary school system. Education became a party-political battlefield. The Labour Party and other critics maintained that the eleven-plus examination was wrong in principle; was socially divisive; had educational and testing weaknesses; resulted in middle-class children predominating in grammar schools and higher education; and thus perpetuated the class system.

Labour governments from 1964 were committed to abolishing the eleven-plus, selection and the secondary school divisions. They would be replaced by non-selective 'comprehensive schools' to which all children would automatically transfer after primary school. These would provide schooling for children of all ability levels and from all social backgrounds in a local area on one school campus.

The battle for the comprehensive and selective systems was fierce. Although more schools became comprehensive under the Conservative government from 1970, it decided against legislative compulsion. Instead, LEAs were able to choose the secondary education which was best suited to local needs. Some decided for comprehensives, while others retained selection and grammar schools.

But the Labour government in 1976 intended to establish comprehensive schools nationwide. Before this policy could be implemented, the Conservatives came to power in 1979. The state secondary school sector thus remains divided between the selective and non-selective options since a minority of LEAs in England/Wales do not have comprehensives and there are some 166 grammar schools left. Scottish schools have long been comprehensive, but Northern Irish schools are divided into selective grammars and secondary moderns.

The comprehensive/selection debate continues. School education is still subject to party-political and ideological conflict. Opinion polls suggest that only a minority of parents support comprehensive education and a majority favour a selective and diverse system of schools (including grammars) with entry based on continuous assessment, interviews and choice. It is often argued that the long-running arguments about the relative merits of different types of schooling in Britain have not benefited schoolchildren or the educational system. But reforms to the state school system are still being made by the Labour government (see below).

The state school sector

State education in the UK is free and compulsory for children between the ages of five and 16. Schools are mainly mixed-sex, although some are single-sex. The vast majority of children (94 per cent) receive free education in state primary and secondary schools. But the state system is complicated by remnants of the 1944 Act and a diversity of school types throughout the country.

In England and Wales, the Department for Education and Skills (DfES) initiates policy (with Wales having some devolved responsibility). Today, state non-denominational schools are controlled by LEAs and are called community schools; foundation schools include many former grant-maintained schools; and

PLATE 9.1 Pupils in a primary school class, Tooting, London.
Ethnic minority pupils can form a majority in state schools in areas of minority group concentration.
(*Ilpo Musto/Rex Features*)

voluntary (faith) schools are divided into state-controlled and aided, with many being connected to specific religious groups. The LEAs retain decentralized choice to organize school planning in their areas for many of these schools with finance provided by central government. They are responsible for employing staff and for admission procedures in non-denominational, community and voluntary controlled schools. School governing bodies (composed of local citizens and parents) perform this role in foundation and voluntary aided (formerly grant maintained) schools. The academic organization of schools has been traditionally largely left to headteachers and staff.

Following Conservative and Labour reforms, headteachers now have greater financial responsibility for school budgets, management and academic organization; school governors in some schools have greater powers of decision-making; and parents are supposed to have a greater voice in the actual running of schools; as well as a legal right to choose a particular school for their children (not always successfully accomplished). These changes have meant a shift from purely educational to management roles within state schools and involve increased burdens of time and administration. The LEAs have lost some of their earlier authority in some areas in the state school sector and may lose more under new Labour reforms.

State schooling before the age of five is not compulsory in Britain and there is no statutory requirement on the LEAs to provide such education. But more parents (particularly those at work) are seeking school provisions for young children and there is concern about the lack of opportunities. At present, 65 per cent of three- and four-year-olds benefit from a state nursery or pre-school education, while others attend private playgroups. The Labour government wants to expand state pre-school education and child-care opportunities for working parents.

Pupils attend primary school (divided usually into infants and junior levels) in the state sector from the age of five and then move to secondary schools normally at 11 until the ages of 16 to 18. Over 87 per cent of state secondary pupils in England and most state secondary pupils in Wales attend comprehensives. There are only a small number of grammar (166) and secondary modern schools left in the state system. The continued existence of these schools depends partly upon local government decisions, partly upon parent power and partly upon Labour government policy. Although the Labour government is ideologically against increasing the number of grammar schools, many critics and parents argue for their retention and expansion. These schools achieve very good national examination results and provide a disciplined academic background.

Comprehensive school pupils are of mixed abilities and come from a variety of social backgrounds in the local area. There is still much argument about the quality and performance of the system. Some critics maintain that bright academic children suffer, although 'setting' (formerly called 'streaming') divides pupils into different ability and interest classes and examination results can be excellent. Arguably, therefore a form of 'selection' continues within the comprehensives, although not on entry. There are some very good comprehensive schools, which are not necessarily confined to privileged and affluent areas. But there are also some very weak and failing ones, which suffer from a variety of social, economic and educational problems and are usually associated with the deprived inner cities.

In an attempt to encourage diversity in the state comprehensive system, the former Conservative government established secondary level state-funded privately-sponsored City Technology Colleges specializing in science, technology and mathematics. The Labour government from 1999 has also promoted school diversity and standards rather than having only one type of comprehensive

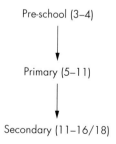

FIGURE 9.1 The state school sector

school and has involved the private sector in school organization. It has created (and wants to expand) a system of publicly-funded, part privately-sponsored and managed City Academies which replace failing and underperforming schools and were intended to revitalize deprived areas; some 530 secondary level Specialist Schools which may concentrate on the sciences, modern foreign languages, sports or the arts; and Beacon Schools which are singled out as best performing schools and are supposed to serve as examples of best practice for other schools. It also intends to increase the number of voluntary schools controlled by faiths (for example, Church of England, Roman Catholic, Methodist, Jewish, Muslim and Sikh). It seems as if selective criteria for entry to some schools (particularly the specialist and faith schools) will be necessary. Critics argue that these movements to diversity and choice represent a withdrawal from monolithic comprehensive principles and the inevitable creation of a two-tier secondary school educational system, in which some state schools may become self-governing independent trusts freed from LEA control.

Scotland has its own ancient educational system, with schools, colleges and universities which are among the oldest in Europe. Its state school system is comprehensive and non-selective. Children transfer from primary to secondary education at 12 and may continue until 18. The Scottish 'public schools' are state and not private institutions (although a few independent schools do exist).

In *Northern Ireland* the state schools are mostly divided on religious grounds into Catholic and Protestant and are often single-sex. However, there are some tentative movements towards integrated co-educational schools. The comprehensive principle has not been widely adopted and a selective system with an examination at eleven gives entrance to grammar schools, which 40 per cent of the age group attend. Performances at these schools are generally superior to their counterparts in England and Wales, although examination results in the other secondary schools are poor.

The independent (fee-paying) school sector

The independent school sector operates mainly in England, is separate from the state school sector and caters for some 6 per cent of all British children, from the ages of four to 18 at various levels of education. There are 2,400 independent schools of varying size and status with over 563,500 pupils.

The sector is defined by payment for education. Its financing derives from investments and the fees paid by the pupils' parents for their education, which vary considerably between schools and can amount to many thousands of pounds a year. The independent sector is dependent upon its charitable and tax-exempt status to survive. This means that the schools are not taxed on their income if it is used only for educational purposes. A minority of children are scholarship holders, whose expenses are covered by their schools.

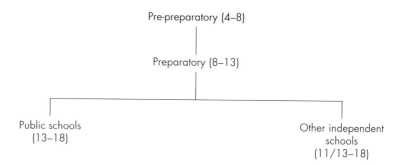

FIGURE 9.2 The independent school sector

Some 246 so-called public schools (private, not state), like Eton, Harrow and Winchester, are the most famous of the independent schools and are usually defined by their membership of the Headmasters' and Headmistresses' Conference. Many were originally created (often by monarchs) to provide education for the sons of the rich and aristocratic although some were under public management and offered free schooling to the public. Today, such schools are mainly boarding establishments, where the pupils live and are educated during term time, although many of them now take day pupils who do not board.

PLATE 9.2 Schoolboys at Eton College (public school).
Photo taken in 1990 at the school's 550th anniversary celebrations.
(*David Hartley/Rex Features*)

Public and other independent schools play a significant role in British education and many leading figures have been educated at them. Entry today is competitive, normally by an entrance examination, and is not confined to social class, connections or wealth, although the ability to pay the fees is important. Independent preparatory schools (primary level) prepare their pupils for independent secondary school entrance and parents who decide to send their children to an independent school will often give them a 'prep school' education first.

Independent schools can vary considerably in quality and reputation. The sector has grown and has an attraction despite its small size and increasing school fees. Insurance schemes for the payment of fees give opportunities for independent education to the less affluent. But some parents make great financial sacrifices so that their children can be independently educated. Opinion polls often suggest that many parents would send their children to an independent school if they could afford it because of the quality of many (if by no means all) of the schools and because such schooling may give social advantages in later life.

The independent sector is criticized for being elitist, socially divisive and based on the ability to pay for education. In this view it perpetuates the class system. The Labour Party in opposition historically argued for the abolition of independent schools and the removal of their tax and charitable status. A recent Labour government evaluation concluded that the sector should continue but that its charitable position would be more rigorously defined to include aid to neighbouring state schools, such as the sharing of teaching and sporting facilities. Short of government abolition, the independent schools are now firmly established and for many provide choice in what would otherwise be a state monopoly on education.

School organization and examinations

The school day in state and independent schools usually runs from about 9.00 a.m. until 4 p.m. and the school year is divided into three terms (autumn, spring and summer), although there have been proposals to reorganize this system. Classes in British schools used to be called 'forms' and in secondary schools were numbered from one to six. But most primary and secondary schools have now adopted year numbers from 1 to 11, which include a two-year 'sixth form' for advanced work.

A reduced birth rate in recent years led to a decrease in the number of schoolchildren, resulting in the closure of schools in rural and urban areas. Numbers have since increased but average class size for primary schools has been reduced to 26, although many secondary schools have classes with over 30 pupils.

Most teachers are trained at the universities and other colleges. There is a serious shortage of teachers in Britain in all subjects, but especially in mathematics, technology, physics and foreign languages, and there is an increasing use of

PLATE 9.3 Secondary school playground activity.
School children skipping in playground of a secondary (comprehensive) school during a break in classes.
(*Steve Lyne/Rex Features*)

unqualified teaching assistants to take some of the burden from classroom teachers. Potential teachers increasingly see the profession as unattractive and many practising teachers leave for better-paid jobs or retire early. Teachers at present are suffering from low morale after battles with the government over pay, conditions, prescribed targets and educational reforms, and from what they perceive as the low status afforded them by government and the general public. The teaching profession has become very stressful and subject to greater pressures, such as physical assaults upon teachers by pupils, increased bureaucracy, pupil indiscipline and a lack of support for teachers from local authorities and the government. The quality of teaching in state schools has also attracted much criticism in recent years and the Labour government is committed to raising standards, removing incompetent and underperforming teachers and closing 'failing schools'.

However, the effect of alleged earlier spending cuts in education has been considerable, with GDP public expenditure on education in Britain being below that of many comparable countries. This has prevented the building and modernization of schools, especially in inner-city areas. It has also resulted in reduced services and a shortage of books and equipment for pupils, teachers and libraries. The Labour government has increased spending on schools, but teachers and parents argue that they have not seen visible results from such investment.

Previous Conservative governments introduced school reforms, which still remain under Labour. Attainment tests were set to establish what children should be reasonably expected to know at the ages of 7, 11 and 14. The progress of each schoolchild can then be measured against national standards, assessed and reported. But many teachers were opposed to the extra work involved and doubted the validity of the tests.

Another radical reform was the creation of a National Curriculum in England and Wales (with similar developments in Northern Ireland but not Scotland). The aim was to create a curriculum which was standardized, centrally devised and appropriate to the needs and demands of the contemporary world. In England, for example, it covers all age groups, is structured into Key Stages 1–4 and includes at all stages the 'compulsory subjects' of English, mathematics, science, design and technology, physical education and information and communications technology. History, geography, music and art are taught in the earlier stages of the curriculum before becoming optional; a modern foreign language is added later before controversially becoming optional; and a 'citizenship' subject to encourage civic knowledge has been recently added. These reforms have generated controversy,

PLATE 9.4 Secondary school science class.
Schoolgirls and teacher at secondary (comprehensive) school practise a chemistry experiment.
(*Simon Townsley/Rex Features*)

opposition, difficulties of implementation and problems about the content and scope of course material.

The National Curriculum (which is not applicable to independent schools although they follow the subject structure) is tied to a system of examinations at the secondary level. They may be taken at all types of schools in England, Wales and Northern Ireland. The main examinations are the General Certificate of Secondary Education (GCSE), which is taken usually by 16-year olds; Advanced Subsidiary (AS) qualifications in the first year of the sixth form; and the General Certificate of Education at Advanced Level (GCE A-level), which is normally taken at the end of the second year in the sixth form by 18-year olds. Results in all exams at all levels tend to be better in single-sex girls' schools.

The GCSE is taken in a range of subjects, the questions and marking of which are undertaken by independent examination boards whose standards have attracted criticism in recent years. In addition to written examinations, project work and continuous assessment of pupils are also taken into account in arriving at a final grade. It can be taken in any subject(s) according to individual choice. But most candidates will attempt six or seven subjects and the basic subjects required for jobs and further education are English, mathematics (or a science) and a foreign language. The GCSE was intended as a better evaluation of pupils' abilities than pure examinations and would give prospective employers some idea of the candidate's ability. But, although standards continue to improve, a third of students did not achieve high passes and some 8 per cent did not pass a single subject in 2002–3.

The GCE A-level is associated with more academic children, who are aiming for entry to higher education or the professions and who spend two years on their studies in the sixth form or at sixth-form colleges. Good passes are now essential because the competition for popular courses at the universities and other colleges has become stiffer. This system was controversially changed in 2000 by the Labour government, which wanted to broaden the syllabus. Four AS (Advanced Subsidiary) level subjects are taken in the first year in addition to key skills tests, before a concentration on three A2 (A-level) subjects and pupils may mix arts and science subjects. AS subjects may serve as a lower-level alternative for students who do not wish to go on to A2 levels.

The standards achieved and examination results continue to rise. But there is continuing discussion about the format and content of A-levels and the new system has been criticized for over-examining students, creating less time for other school activities and leading to teacher overwork. The Labour government has reviewed the examination structure and has decided on a continuation of GCSEs and A-levels rather than a diploma-type structure which would include academic and vocational courses for 14–19-year-olds.

Alternative examinations are vocational GCSEs which are mainly taken by young people in full-time education between the ages of 16 and 19 and provide a broad-based preparation for a range of occupations and higher education; and National Vocational Qualifications (NVQs) which are job-specific examinations.

Scotland does not have a statutory national curriculum and pupils take the National Qualification (NQ) at the age of 16. Those between 16 and 18 take the reformed Scottish Highers (Higher and Advanced Higher).

GCSE, AS, A-level and alternative examination results by pupils are the basis of school 'league tables', instituted by the previous Conservative government. Examination results and marks at individual schools are published so that parents and pupils can judge a school's performance. The exercise has been criticized for its methodology and creating a 'results mentality'. But it is now firmly established and influential and parents use it as a guide to enrol their children in good schools.

Higher education

Should a pupil obtain the required examination results at A- or alternative levels, and be successful at interviews, he or she may go on to an institution of higher education, such as a university or college. The student, after a prescribed period of study and after passing examinations, will receive a degree and become a graduate of that institution. In the past only a small proportion of the age group in Britain proceeded to what was an elitist higher education, in contrast to the higher rates in other major nations. But, following a rapid increase in student numbers from the 1990s (with the ratio of female to male students being three to two), the rate was some 44 per cent in 2005. The Labour government wishes to raise this figure to 50 per cent of students aged between 18 and 30 by 2010.

The universities

There were 23 British universities in 1960. After a period of expansion in the 1960s and reforms in 1992 when existing institutions such as polytechnics were given university status, there are now some 89 universities and 60 institutions of higher education. In 2003, there were 1.2 million full-time undergraduate students (690,000 part-time) and 207,000 full-time postgraduate students (292,000 part-time) in higher education. The Open University and the independent University of Buckingham are additional university-level institutions.

The universities can be broadly classified into four types. The ancient universities of Oxford and Cambridge (composed of their many colleges) date from the thirteenth century. But until the nineteenth century they were virtually the only English universities and offered no places to women. However, other older universities were founded in Scotland, such as St Andrews (1411), Glasgow (1450), Aberdeen (1494) and Edinburgh (1583). A second group comprises the 'redbrick' or civic universities such as Leeds, Liverpool and Manchester, which were created between 1850 and 1930. The third group consists of universities

PLATE 9.5 Kings College, Cambridge.
Kings College is a college of Cambridge University. Bicycles are the most common form of transport for students and townspeople in Cambridge.
(*Nils Jorgensen/Rex Features*)

founded after the Second World War and in the 1960s. Many of the latter, like Sussex, York and East Anglia are in rural areas. The fourth group are the 'new universities' created in 1992 when polytechnics and some other colleges attained university status.

The competition to enter universities is now very strong in popular subjects, and students who do not do well at A- or equivalent levels may be unable to find a place. Some 17 per cent of students drop out of higher education because of work, financial or other problems. But the majority aim for a good degree in order to obtain a good job, or to continue in higher education by doing research (master's degrees and doctorates). The bachelor's degree (Bachelor of Arts or Bachelor of

Science, BA or BSc) is usually taken in final examinations at the end of the third year of study, although some degree courses do vary in length in different parts of Britain (such as Scotland with a four-year MA Honours degree). The degree is divided into first-, second- and third-class honours. Some degrees depend entirely upon the examination results, while others include continuous assessment over the period of study.

Universities are supposed to have uniform standards, although there are centres of excellence in particular subjects and there has been recent criticism about levels in some universities and some subjects. Students can choose from an impressive array of subject areas and teaching is mainly by the lecture system, supported by tutorials (small groups) and seminars. The student–lecturer ratio at British universities has increased because of expanded recruitment. Most students tend to live on campus in university accommodation, while others choose to live in rented property outside the university. Until recently few British students chose universities near their parents' homes and many seemed to prefer those in the south of England. But financial costs now persuade many students to live at home or locally.

Universities are independent institutions created by royal charter, enjoy academic freedom, appoint their own staff, award their own degrees and decide which students to admit. But they are in practice dependent upon government money. This derives mainly from finance (dependent upon the number of students recruited and research performance) given by government to Universities Funding Councils for distribution to the universities through university Vice-Chancellors who are the chief executive officers of the universities.

Both Conservative and Labour governments have been concerned to make the universities more accountable in the national interest; tightly controlled their budgets; and encouraged them to seek alternative private sources of finance from business and industry. The universities have lost staff and research money; have been forced to adopt more effective management and accounting procedures; must market their resources more efficiently; must attract and recruit students in order to obtain government finance; pay greater attention to teaching and research performance; and must justify their positions financially and educationally.

Government consequently intervenes more closely in the running of the universities than in the past. Such policies have provoked considerable opposition from the universities, which argue that the recent large expansion of student numbers has not seen an equivalent rise in funding, salaries or new staff appointments. But they are being forced to adapt rather than continue to lose staff, finance and educational programmes. It is also argued that expansion has led to universities taking poorly qualified students to fill their places, who then drop out because of work and other pressures. Some educationalists feel that British universities will decline in quality if they are not better funded. Since governments seem unwilling to do this, critics argue that the universities (or at least those able to do so) should break away from the state, market their own services and attract their own finance.

Other higher education colleges

The 1970s saw the creation of colleges (or institutes) of higher education, often by merging existing colleges with redundant teachers' training colleges or by establishing new institutions. They now offer a wide range of degree, diploma and certificate courses in both science and the arts, and in some cases have specifically taken over the role of training schoolteachers. They used to be under the control of their local authorities, but the Conservative government granted them independence and some have achieved university status.

A variety of other institutions also offer higher education. Some, like the Royal College of Art, the Cranfield Institute of Technology and various Business Schools, have university status, while others, such as agricultural, drama and art colleges like the Royal Academy of Dramatic Arts (RADA) and the Royal College of Music, provide comparable courses. All these institutions usually have a strong vocational aspect to their programmes and fill a specialized role in higher education.

Student finance

In the past, British students who gained a place at an institution of higher education were awarded a grant from their local education authorities. The grant was in two parts: first, it covered the tuition fees of a first degree course (paid directly to the institution); and second, it covered, after means-testing of parents' income, maintenance expenses like the cost of rent, food and books of a course during term time. This system meant that higher education was largely free for many students.

The Labour government radically changed this situation from 1998 by abolishing the student grant. Instead, students had to pay tuition fees for each year of their course (£1,125 in 2004–5) except in Scotland. They are means-tested on their parents' income and those from less affluent backgrounds may not have to pay the full or any tuition fees (some 50 per cent). Students must also provide for their own maintenance expenses, usually through loans from the Student Loan Company. They start to pay back their loans after graduation when they reach certain salary levels. Consequently, most students now have to finance their own higher education; some are in financial difficulties; and most will finish their studies with an average debt of about £15,000. But these changes in funding have not resulted in a marked reduction of students applying for university entry, except for mature students.

The Labour government increased the tuition fees with effect from 2006. This means that universities will be able to charge variable fees up to £3,000 provided that they pursue 'fair access' policies by encouraging greater number of students from lower-income households. Such students will also be eligible for government maintenance grants and financial aid from those universities which charge the higher tuition fees.

The Open University

The Labour Party broached the idea of the Open University in the 1960s. It would be a non-residential service, which used television, radio, specially produced books, audio/video cassettes and correspondence courses to teach students of all ages. It was intended to give opportunities (or a 'second chance') to adults who had been unable to take conventional higher education. It was hoped that the courses might appeal to working-class students who had left school at the official school-leaving age and who wished to broaden their horizons.

The Open University opened in 1969 and its first courses started in 1971. It now caters for undergraduate, postgraduate and research students in a wide range of subjects. About 7,000 students of all ages and from very different walks of life receive degrees from the Open University each year. First degrees (bachelor's) are awarded on a system of credits for each course completed and now include students from the European Union, Gibraltar, and Switzerland.

Dedication, stamina and perseverence are necessary to complete the long, part-time courses of the Open University. Students, who are often employed, follow their lessons and lectures at home. Part-time tutors in local areas mark the students' written work and meet them regularly to discuss their progress. There are also special weekend and refresher courses throughout the year, which are held at universities and colleges, to enable students to take part in intensive study. The various television programmes and books associated with the Open University programmes are widely exported throughout the world. The Open University is generally considered to be a cost-effective success, has provided valuable alternative educational opportunities for many people and has served as a model for other countries.

Further, adult and lifelong education

An important aspect of British education is the provision of further and adult education, whether by colleges, universities, voluntary bodies, trade unions or other institutions. The present organizations and their offerings originated to some degree in the thirst for knowledge which was felt by working-class people in the nineteenth and early twentieth centuries, particularly after the arrival of elementary state education and growing literacy. Today a wide range of educational opportunities is provided by self-governing state-funded colleges of further education and other institutions. These offer vocational and academic subjects at basic levels for part- and full-time students. Some part-time students over 16 may study in the evenings or on day-release from their employment and their studies are often work-related, include government training programmes and have close ties with local commerce and industry. Some 5 million full- and part-time students of varying ages are taking a wide spectrum of further education courses.

Adult education is provided by these colleges, the universities, the Workers' Educational Association (WEA), evening institutes, local societies and clubs. Adult courses may be vocational (for employment) or recreational (for pleasure), and cover a variety of activities and programmes.

In the past a relatively low percentage of the 16–24-age group in Britain were in further and higher education, compared to the much larger percentages in Japan, the USA and West Germany. The figures have now improved considerably, with almost three-quarters of 16- to 18-year-olds in Britain remaining in full-time education after this age, either in school or in further education colleges. But the Labour government feels that even more people should be educated or trained further after the age of 16. This is particularly true at a time when there will be an increasing shortage of well-qualified people in the future workforce, especially in the vocational, trade and technical fields.

Nevertheless, there has been a recent expansion of continuing-education projects and a range of programmes specifically designed for employment purposes and to provide people with access qualifications for further training. The Labour government sees further and adult education as part of a lifelong learning process, which it wants to prioritize. The aim is to encourage the continuous development of people's skills, knowledge and understanding as well as creating skills and improving employment prospects in a changing labour market.

Attitudes to education

Concerns about the quality of British education and educational policy at all levels are consistently voiced by a majority of respondents to public opinion polls. They think that state schools are not run well; that more money should be spent on education generally; and that people's wishes about their children's education are not taken seriously by politicians. The Labour government has responded by giving more funding to the system and by tinkering with its structures. But serious dissatisfaction continued to be voiced in polls leading up to the general election in 2005 and education is likely to continue as a problem and concern in British life.

However, despite the Labour government's promises, the money spent on education in Britain is in fact proportionally much less than that spent on health and transport over a period of time, only marginally more than that on law and order and considerably less than that spent by other European countries and other advanced economies. Some critics therefore query whether the government is totally committed to raising quality, whether education has the same political priority as other areas of expenditure and whether many parents are actually as concerned about the state of the schools as they say they are.

There have been continuous and vigorous debates about the performance and goals of British education at all levels since the 1960s, although much on this discussion was (and is) ideological rather than objectively educational. Traditionalist critics, who wanted disciplined learning programmes, felt that state comprehensive schools and 'creative/progressive' methods of child-centred teaching were not producing the kind of people needed for contemporary society. It was argued that pupils lacked the basic skills of numeracy and literacy and were unprepared for employment and the realities of the outside world. Today, employers frequently criticize both schools and higher education for the quality of their products, and only 37 per cent according to SIF UK in 2005 believed that today's graduates leave university with the necessary skills for employment.

The previous Conservative government's reforms from 1986 were based on centralized and consumer-choice policies. They were an attempt to rectify the educational situation and aimed at producing accountability, improved standards and skills in schools and higher education by more formal learning programmes. The government attempted to reform the teaching profession, improve pupil performance, emphasize science and modern language studies and increase parental choice.

The Labour government is continuing this process by stressing compulsory homework, contracts with parents, 'literacy hours', concentration on the '3 Rs' (reading, writing and arithmetic) and grouping children by ability ('setting'). Progressive 'child-centred' practices are dismissed and funds are being provided for school fabric repairs and computers in every school. There is also a move away from having only one type of state secondary school (comprehensive) to embracing diversity and specialism through the expansion of specialist and faith schools and City Academies. The government also wants more impecunious and working-class students to enter university.

Some critics argue that an educational system should not be solely devoted either to elitist standards or to market considerations. It should provide a choice between (and ideally a mixture of) the academic/liberal tradition, the technical and the vocational. The lack of adequate vocational/technical education and training is creating big problems for employers, who argue that they cannot find competently-trained staff to fill vacancies. The future of British education will depend in large part on how government reforms work and how they are perceived by teachers, parents, students and employers. But successive polls reveal that a majority of respondents say they are dissatisfied with the Labour government's 1997 promise to prioritize education.

On the other hand, a 1999 MORI/British Council poll of overseas respondents found that 76 per cent regarded the British as well-educated. Higher education was particularly well respected with 88 per cent of respondents rating it as 'good'.

Exercises

Explain and examine the following terms:

public schools	grammar schools	WEA
comprehensives	eleven-plus	tutorial
GCE A level	Open University	scholarships
LEAs	tuition fees	student finance
Eton	GCSE	'prep school'
the Butler Act	degree	vocational
streaming/setting	'3 Rs'	literacy
faith schools	AS levels	specialist schools

Write short essays on the following topics:

1   Critically examine state secondary education in Britain, analysing its structures, aims and achievements.

2   Describe the structure of British higher education and its roles.

3   Comment upon the desirability, or otherwise, of the division of British schools into state and independent sectors.

4   Should schoolchildren attend technical, vocational or academic schools, depending on their choices and abilities? Or should they all attend one common type of school?

Further reading

1   Abercrombie, N. and Warde, A. (2000) *Contemporary British Society* Oxford: Polity Press, Chapter 14.

2   Chitty, C. (1992) *The Education System Transformed* London: Baseline Books

3   Ryan, A. (1999) *Liberal Anxieties and Liberal Education* London: Profile Books

4   Walden, G. (1996) *We Should Know Better: Solving the Education Crisis* London: Fourth Estate

Websites

Department for Education and Skills: www.dfes.gov.uk

Independent education: www.isis.org.uk

The Times Higher Education Supplement: www.thes.co.uk

The Times Educational Supplement: www.tes.co.uk

Scottish Executive: www.scotland.gov.uk

National Assembly for Wales: www.wales.gov.uk

Northern Ireland Assembly: www.ni-assembly.gov.uk

Office for Standards in Education: www.ofsted.gov.uk

Chapter 10

The media

- The print media
- The broadcasting media
- Media ownership and freedom of expression
- Attitudes to the media
- *Exercises*
- *Further reading*
- *Websites*

The term 'media' may include any communication system by which people are informed, educated or entertained. In Britain it generally refers to the print industries (the press or newspapers and magazines) and broadcasting (cable and satellite television, radio and terrestrial or earth-based television). These systems overlap with each other and with books, video, DVD, film, the Internet and mobile phones; are profitable businesses; and tied to advertising, sponsorship, commerce and industry.

The media have evolved from simple methods of production, distribution and communication to their present sophisticated technologies. Their growth and variety have greatly improved information dispersal, news availability and entertainment opportunities. They cover homes, places of business and leisure activities and their influence is very powerful and an inevitable part of daily life. Surveys indicate that 69 per cent of Britons obtain their daily news from television, 20 per cent from newspapers and 11 per cent from radio. Electronic technology, such as the Internet and television, is an important part of business and education, while the British use of home-view videos and DVDs is the highest in the world.

But the media provoke debates about what is socially and morally permissible in their content and methods. Questions are asked about the role of advertising and sponsorship, the quality of the services provided at a time of rapidly expanding and diversifying media outlets, the alleged danger of the concentrated ownership of media resources, media influence on politics, legal restraints upon media 'free expression' and the ethical responsibilty of the media to individuals and society. The following sections examine the historical growth of the print and broadcasting media and discuss contemporary debates and developments.

The print media

The print media (newspapers and magazines) began to develop in the eighteenth century. Initially, a wide circulation was hindered by transportation and distribution problems, illiteracy and government licensing or censorship restrictions. But, over the last 200 years, an expanded educational system, abolition of government control, new print inventions and Britain's small physical size have eliminated these difficulties and created a free, outspoken and often controversial print media.

The growth of literacy after 1870 provided the owners of the print media with an increased market. Newspapers and magazines, which had previously been limited to the middle and upper classes, were popularized. They were used for news and information, but also for profit and entertainment. Ownership, new types of print media and financially rewarding advertising increased in the highly competitive atmosphere of the late nineteenth and early twentieth centuries. Owners also realized that political and social influence, as well as the dissemination of combative ideology, could be achieved through control of the means of communication.

National newspapers

National newspapers are those which are mostly published from London (with some regional versions) and are available in all parts of Britain on the same day, including Sundays. Many are delivered direct to the home from local newsagents by newsboys and girls. The good internal distribution systems of a compact country enabled a national press to develop and Internet online copies of newspapers now offer updated news and immediate availability everywhere.

The first British newspapers with a limited national circulation appeared in the early eighteenth century and were followed by others, such as *The Times* (1785), the *Observer* (1791) and the *Sunday Times* (1822). Most of these were 'quality' papers, catering for a relatively small, educated market.

In the nineteenth century, the growth and diverse composition of the population conditioned the types of newspaper which were produced. The first 'popular' national papers were deliberately printed on Sundays, such as the *News of the World* (1843) and the *People* (1881). They were inexpensive and aimed at the expanding and increasingly literate working class. In 1896, Alfred Harmsworth produced the *Daily Mail*, which was targeted at the lower middle class as an alternative to the 'quality' dailies. Harmsworth then published the *Daily Mirror* in 1903 for the working-class 'popular' market. Both the *Mail* and the *Mirror* were soon selling more than a million copies a day.

The early twentieth century was the era of mass-circulation papers and of owners like Harmsworth and Arthur Pearson (press barons). There was fierce competition between them as they fought for bigger shares of the market. Pearson's *Morning Herald* (later the *Daily Express*) was created in 1900 to compete with the *Daily Mail* for lower middle-class readers.

The *Daily Mirror* was the largest-selling national daily in the early twentieth century. It supported the Labour Party and was designed for quick and easy reading by the industrial and increasingly politicized working class. The *Daily Herald* (1911) also supported the Labour Party, until it was sold in 1964, renamed the *Sun* and developed different political and news emphases. The competition between the *Sun* and *Mirror* continues today, with each aiming for a bigger share of the mass daily market. Battles are still fought between dominant proprietors, since newspaper ownership is concentrated in a few large publishing groups, such

PLATE 10.1 News International Plant, Wapping, London, 1986.
The newspaper plant after the company's move from Fleet Street in central London and site of confrontation with the print unions in the 1980s. Situated in the East London Docklands redevelopment area near Tower Bridge.
(*Rex Features*)

as Rupert Murdoch's News International (which has large media holdings in Britain, Australia and the USA) and Trinity Mirror (see Table 10.1).

The success of the early popular press was due to growing literacy; a desire for knowledge and information (as well as entertainment) by the working class; and political awareness among workers caused by the rise of the Labour Party. Newspaper owners profited by the huge market, but they also satisfied demand. The price and content of mass papers reflected lower middle- and working-class readerships and tastes. This emphasis attracted large consumer advertising, and owners were able to produce cheaply by using modern printing methods and a nationwide distribution network.

The circulation of national papers rose rapidly, with 5.5 million daily sales by 1920. By 1973 these increased to 17 million. But newspapers had to cope first with the competition of radio and films and later with television. Although they have survived, there has, since the 1970s, been a continuing decline in sales and in the number of national and other newspapers.

Surveys suggest that some 50 per cent of people over 15 read a national daily paper and 70 per cent read a national Sunday newspaper. The main national newspapers have sales of some 13 million on weekdays and 14 million on Sundays, but it is estimated that on average two people read each paper purchased.

The main national press in Britain today consists of 11 main daily morning papers and nine main Sunday papers. It is in effect a London press, because most national newspapers have their bases and printing facilities in the capital, although editions of some nationals are now published outside London, in Europe and the USA. Most of them used to be located in Fleet Street in central London. But all have now left the street and moved to other parts of the capital or outside London. The reasons for these moves were high property rents, fierce competition between papers and opposition from trade unions to the introduction of new printing technology. Newspapers and magazines have also had to cope with the expense of newsprint, declines in advertising revenue, rising production and labour costs and competition from other media outlets, such as the Internet.

Heavy labour costs were due to the overmanning and restrictive practices of the trade unions. Owners were forced into new ways of increasing productivity while cutting costs. Regional owners outside London had in fact pioneered the movement of newspapers and magazines into new print technology and London newspapers had to follow in order to survive.

New technology meant that journalists' 'copy' could be printed directly through computers, without having to use the traditional intermediate 'hot-metal' typesetting by printers. This gave owners flexibility in their printing and distri-bution methods and cheaper production costs. It allowed them to escape from trade-union dominance and the concentration of the industry in London. But it also resulted in job losses, trade-union opposition and bitter industrial action such as picketing.

New technology, improved distribution methods and cuts in labour and production costs have increased the profitability of print industries. Despite the attraction of other media, they still have a considerable presence, although sales are declining. The business is very competitive and papers can suffer from a variety of problems. However, the high risks involved have not stopped the introduction of new newspapers. The quality national daily, the *Independent*, was published in October 1986 and survives despite circulation losses. Sunday nationals, like the *Independent on Sunday* (1990), have also appeared. But other dailies have been lost.

Most national papers are usually termed either 'quality' or 'popular' depend-ing on their differences in content. Others are called 'mid-market' and fall between these two extremes (see Table 10.1). The qualities (such as *The Times*) report national and international news in depth and analyse current events and the arts in editorials and articles. The populars (such as the *Sun*) deal with relatively few 'hard news' stories, tend to be superficial in their treatment of events and much of their material is sensationalized and trivialized. It cannot be said that the downmarket populars are instructive, or concerned with raising the critical consciousness of readers. But owners and editors argue that their readership demands particular styles, interests and attitudes. 'Mid-market' papers, such as the *Daily Mail* and *Express*, cater for intermediate groups.

Qualities and populars were also historically distinguished by their format. Populars were tabloid or small-sheet while qualities were broadsheet (large-sheet).

PLATE 10.2 National newspapers.
A selection of national tabloid newspapers. The *Independent* is a quality newspaper but changed to tabloid form in October 2003.
(*Ray Tang/Rex Features*)

This distinction has largely disappeared in recent years as more broadsheets have become tabloid or 'compact' in form. Some critics argue that the broadsheets have also become more 'tabloidized', sensationalist and superficial in content.

Sales of popular papers on weekdays and Sundays far exceed those of the qualities. Qualities are more expensive than populars and carry up-market advertising that generates essential finance. Populars carry less advertising and cater for more down-market material. However, the press as a whole takes much of the total finance (49 per cent in 2003) spent on advertising in Britain.

There is no state control or censorship of the British press, although it is subject to laws of publication and expression and there are forms of self-censorship, by which it supposedly regulates its own conduct. The press is also financially independent of the political parties and receives no funding from government (except for Welsh-language community papers).

It is argued that most newspapers are politically right-of-centre and sympathize with the Conservative Party. But their positions are arguably usually driven by readers' opinions and their standard biases in fact can vary considerably over time and under the influence of events. For example, the small-circulation leftist *Morning Star* has varied between Stalinist, Euro-Communist and Democratic Left views. Papers may have a political bias and support a specific party, particularly at election times, although this can change. A few, such as those of the Trinity Mirror group, consistently support the Labour Party, some

TABLE 10.1 Main national newspapers (average daily sales: May 2005)

Name	Founded	Sales	Owned/controlled by
Popular dailies			
Daily Mirror	1903	2,188,806	Trinity Mirror
Sun	1964	3,250,276	News International
Daily Star	1978	470,131	Express Newspapers
Mid-market dailies			
Daily Mail	1896	2,383,384	Associated Newspapers
Daily Express	1900	938,968	Express Newspapers
Quality Dailies			
The Times	1785	670,754	News International
Guardian	1821	367,033	Guardian Newspapers
Daily Telegraph	1855	907,095	Telegraph Group
Financial Times	1888	433,858	Financial Times Ltd
Independent	1986	258,505	Independent Newspapers
Popular Sundays			
News of the World	1843	3,693,741	News International
People	1881	953,263	Trinity Mirror
Sunday Mirror	1963	1,509,085	Trinity Mirror
Mid-market Sundays			
Mail on Sunday	1982	2,288,267	Associated Newspapers
Sunday Express	1918	1,014,828	Express Newspapers
Quality Sundays			
Observer	1791	444,195	Guardian Newspapers
Sunday Times	1822	1,398,296	News International
Sunday Telegraph	1961	719,086	Telegraph Group
Independent on Sunday	1990	209,472	Independent Newspapers

Source: Adapted from Audit Bureau of Circulations, 2005

such as *The Times* and the *Independent* consider themselves to be independent, others, like the *Guardian*, favour a left-of-centre position, while the *Daily Telegraph* supports the Conservative Party. It appears that the British public receive a reasonable variety of political views from their newspapers.

The press is dependent for its survival upon circulation figures; upon the advertising that it can attract; and upon financial help from its owners. A paper may face difficulties and fail if advertisers remove their business and all the media are currently experiencing difficulties in attracting advertising revenue. A high circulation does not necessarily guarantee the required advertising and consequent survival, because advertisers now tend to place their mass-appeal consumer products on television, where they will benefit from a larger audience. Most popular papers are in constant competition with their rivals to increase their sales. They attempt to do this by gimmicks such as bingo games and competitions, or by calculated (often sensationalist) editorial policies which are intended to catch the mass readership.

Many newspapers now have colour pages and daily and weekend supplements covering a wide range of interests which attempt to attract the newspaper public and appeal to advertisers. Owners, however, may refuse to rescue those papers which make continuous losses. A number of newspapers in the twentieth century ceased publication because of reduced circulation, loss of advertising revenue, refusals of further financial aid, or a combination of all three factors.

Despite a fall in hard-copy circulation, most national newspapers now have online Internet versions, which are often free (at least in outline format). They also offer subscription access to special features and longer articles. This rapidly expanding service provides an additional medium for information, communication and advertising revenue, as well as continuously updated news.

Regional and ethnic newspapers

Some 1,300 regional and local newspapers are published in towns and cities throughout Britain. They largely focus on local or regional news, but also contain national and international features; are supported financially by regional advertising; and may be daily morning or evening papers, Sundays or weeklies. Some nine out of ten adults read one or more of the different regional or local papers every week; 41 million regional papers were sold in the second half of 2003; and 75 per cent of local and regional newspapers also operate an Internet website.

Excluding its national newspaper industry, London has one paper (the *Evening Standard*) with daily sales of 346,265 in May 2005. But there are also about a hundred local weeklies, dailies and evening papers of various sizes and types which appear in the Greater London districts.

Quality daily regional (and national) papers, such as *The Scotsman* (Edinburgh), the *Glasgow Herald*, the *Western Mail* (Cardiff), and the *Yorkshire Post* (Leeds), have good reputations and sales outside their specific regions. Other high-selling Scottish papers are the *Daily Record*, the popular *Sunday Mail* (Glasgow) and the *Sunday Post* (Dundee). Northern Irish papers include the *Belfast Telegraph* and the *News Letter*.

There has also been a growth of 'free newspapers' throughout Britain, such as the daily *Metro* with a circulation of 450,000 in London (now widely available throughout the country in shops, train stations and at street stalls with a circulation of 1.2 million). Some 650 free papers, such as the *Manchester Metro News* and the *Glaswegian*, are published weekly on a local basis and are financed by local advertising, to such an extent that news is often outweighed by the advertisements. It is estimated that they have a weekly circulation of some 29 million. These are often delivered direct to homes, as well as being widely available elsewhere, and for which the consumer does not pay.

Britain's ethnic communities also produce their own newspapers and magazines, which are increasing in numbers, are available nationally in the larger cities and are improving in quality. Some, such as Muslim magazines, are becoming more mainstream in order to appeal to a younger Muslim and wider non-Muslim audience. There is a wide range of publications for Jewish, Asian, Afro-Caribbean, Chinese and Arabic readers, published on a daily or (more commonly) periodic basis, such as the *Asian Times* and Afro-Caribbean papers such as the *Gleaner*, the *Voice*, *New Nation* and *Caribbean Times*.

Periodicals and magazines

There are some 8,500 different periodicals and magazines in Britain, which are of a weekly, monthly or quarterly nature and are dependent upon sales and advertising (worth £1.8 billion in 2003) to survive. They are aimed at different markets and levels of sophistication and either cover trades, professions and business (read by 95 per cent of occupational groups) or are consumer titles dealing with sports, hobbies and interests (read by 80 per cent of adults).

Although the number of periodicals has expanded, it is still difficult to break into the established consumer market with a new product. Some attempts, which manage to find a gap in the market, succeed, but most usually fail. Others, which are initially successful, may also become victims of new fashions and trends.

The teenage and youth magazine market is fiercely fought for, but has suffered large sales losses recently. This is attributed to greater Internet and mobile phone usage. The men's general interest magazine market (some with a specifically 'laddish' appeal) is similarly volatile. Women's periodicals, such as *Take a Break*, *Woman* and *Woman's Own*, have large and wide circulations. But the best-selling publications are the weekly *Radio Times* and *What's on TV*, which contain feature stories and scheduled programmes for BBC and independent television and radio. Other magazines cover interests such as computers, rural pastimes, gardening, railways, cooking, a wide variety of sports, architecture and do-it-yourself skills.

Among the serious weekly journals are the *New Statesman and Society* (a left-wing political and social affairs magazine); *The Economist* (dealing with economic and political matters); the *Spectator* (a conservative journal); and *New Scientist*. *The Times* publishes influential weekly magazines, such as the *Educational Supplement*, the *Higher* (education supplement) and the *Literary Supplement*. The lighter side of the market is catered for by periodicals like *Private Eye*, which satirizes the shortcomings of British society.

The broadcasting media

The contemporary broadcasting media are still divided into what has traditionally been thought of as two sectors. The 'public sector' is the British Broadcasting Corporation (BBC) financed by the television licence fee (payable by anyone who owns a television set). The 'independent sector' consists of commercial stations or channels, which are funded mainly by advertising revenue. Both sectors cover radio, terrestrial television and cable/satellite television.

Since 2003, the Office of Communications (Ofcom) has replaced the roles and duties of former regulators in both public and independent sectors and is the single regulator for the broadcast media. But although the BBC is subject to Ofcom regulation on programme standards and economic management, its Board of Governors is responsible for managing its public service remit. Opinions differ as to the future of the BBC in its present role and the continuance of its funding by the licence fee. These developments have to be seen in a historical perspective.

Radio was the first broadcasting medium to appear in Britain. Experimental transmissions were made at the end of the nineteenth century and were developed further in the early twentieth century. After a period of limited availability, national radio was established in 1922 when the British Broadcasting Company was formed under John Reith.

In 1927 Reith became the first Director-General of the British Broadcasting Corporation (BBC) and set the tone and style for the BBC's development. The BBC was funded by the licence fee, had a monopoly in broadcasting and a paternalistic image. Reith insisted that it should be independent of government and commercial interests; strive for quality; and be a 'public service broadcaster' (defined as a serious-minded duty to inform, educate and entertain). On this basis, the BBC built a reputation for impartial news reporting and excellent programmes.

The BBC's broadcasting monopoly in radio and television (which started in 1936 for a limited audience) led to pressure from commercial and political interests to widen the scope of broadcasting. As a result, independent television financed by advertising and under the supervision of the Independent Television Authority (ITA) was created in 1954 and the first programmes were shown in 1955. The BBC's monopoly on radio broadcasting was also ended in 1972 and independent radio stations were established throughout the country, funded by advertising.

A duopoly (two organizations) covered broadcasting: the public service of the BBC and the independent service of the ITA. The latter was expanded as cable, satellite and other broadcasting services developed. The ITA then evolved into the IBA (Independent Broadcasting Authority) which was succeeded by the ITC (Independent Television Commission) and the Radio Authority. These were replaced in 2003 by Ofcom. British broadcasting has thus been conditioned by significant change and the competition between the BBC and independent organizations.

Substantial reforms to British broadcasting were made by Conservative governments in the 1980s and 1990s, which created more radio and television channels. A deregulation policy was supposed to promote competition among broadcasters and more choice for consumers. This process is being continued today as broadcasting services become expanded and digitalized. But digitalization has proceeded slowly because of initial technical problems, geographical availability and a limited consumer take-up due to scepticism of the new digital offerings. However, digitalization will potentially create many more radio and television channels as analogue systems are phased out (possibly by 2012). By 2004, 13.1 million (53 per cent) of British households were capable of accessing both terrestrial and digital transmitters.

These and earlier changes have been controversial and criticized for their apparent emphasis on competition and commercialism, rather than quality. A larger number of television and radio channels may not lead to greater real choice, but rather inferior programmes of the same trivial type as broadcasters chase bigger audiences. There is a finite number of people to watch television or listen to radio; advertisers' budgets cannot be stretched to cover all available broadcast offerings; and advertisers gravitate towards those programmes which attract large audiences and therefore profits. Television in 1995 accounted for 28 per cent of total advertising spending but this had dropped to 25 per cent by 2003.

The public service ethos, embodied in the BBC, is also now a statutory requirement for terrestrial independent channels, although opinions differ as to its application. Ofcom is concerned to maintain the quality of programmes by the terrestrial public service broadcasters (the BBC, ITV1, Channel 4, Five and SC4 – see below). Under recent legislation they must provide a minimum level of different types of programming. Ofcom has found that standards are dropping; that there is too much reliance on popular appeal programmes; and that the audience share for public service broadcasters is falling. Critics have echoed this view and condemned the 'dumbing down' of British broadcasting in general and television in particular and the proliferation of inferior offerings.

The BBC

The BBC is based at Broadcasting House in London, but has stations throughout the country, which provide regional networks for radio and television. It was created by Royal Charter and has a board of governors who are responsible for supervising its programmes and their suitability. They are appointed by the Crown on the advice of government ministers and are supposed to constitute an independent element in the organization of the BBC. Daily operations are controlled by the Director-General, chosen by the board of governors.

The BBC is financed by a grant from Parliament, which comes from the sale of television licences (£1.6 billion per year). These are payable by anyone who owns a television set and are relatively low in international terms (£121 annually for a colour set in 2004). The BBC also generates considerable income from selling its programmes abroad and from the sale of a programme guide (*Radio Times*), books, magazines, videos and DVDs.

The BBC in recent years has come under pressure from government to reform itself. It has struggled to maintain its position as a traditional public service broadcaster, funded by the licence fee, at a time of fierce competition with independent broadcasters. Internal reorganization has led to a slimmer and more efficient organization. But it has had to develop alternative forms of funding, such as subscription and pay services and must include independent productions in 25 per cent of its television schedules. Although its charter has been extended, it is likely that the retention of the licence fee could again be re-evaluated, thus posing questions about the future nature and role of the BBC.

The BBC's external services, which consist of radio broadcasts in English (the World Service) and 42 other languages abroad, were founded in 1932 and are funded by the Foreign Office. These have a reputation for objective news reporting and programmes. The BBC also began commercially-funded television pro-grammes in 1991 by cable to Europe and by satellite links to Africa and Asia, such as *BBC World* (news) now merged with the World Service and *BBC Prime* (entertainment).

The BBC is not a state organization, in the sense that it is controlled by the government. But it is not as independent of political pressures as many in Britain and overseas assume. Its charter has to be renewed by Parliament and by its terms government can, and does, intervene in the showing of programmes which are alleged to be controversial or against the public interest. The BBC governors, although independent, are in fact government appointees. Governments can also exert pressure upon the BBC when the licence fee comes up for renewal by Parliament. The BBC does try to be neutral in political matters, to such an extent that all political parties have periodically complained (as with the Labour government over the conduct of the Iraq war) that it is prejudiced against them, being either too liberal/critical or too conservative/establishment. The major parties have equal rights to broadcast on the BBC and independent television.

Historically, the BBC (with its monopoly on radio) was affected by the invention of television, which changed British entertainment and news habits. The BBC now has two main terrestrial television channels (BBC 1 and BBC 2). BBC 1 is a mass-appeal channel with an audience share of 28 per cent. Its programmes consist of news, plays and drama series, comedy, quiz shows, variety performances, sport and documentaries. BBC 2, with an audience share of 11 per cent, tends to show more serious items such as news analysis and discussion, documentaries, adaptations of novels into plays and series, operas, concerts and some sport. It is also provides Open University courses.

The Labour government from 2001 expanded BBC television services by the creation of digital BBC 3 (contemporary entertainment, comedy, music and drama) and BBC 4 (culture and the arts) as well as two channels for children under six and over. But audience figures for these channels have been initially low.

BBC Radio performs an important service, although some of its audiences have declined recently. There are five national channels (to be increased by five new digital channels); 39 local stations serving many districts in England; and regional and community services in Scotland, Wales and Northern Ireland. They all have to compete for listeners with independent stations but offer an alternative in news, debate and local information to pop-based local and national independent stations. The national channels specialize in different tastes. Radio 1 caters for pop music; Radio 2 has light music, news, and comedy; Radio 3 provides classical and modern serious music, talks, discussions and plays; Radio 4 concentrates on news reports, analysis, talks and plays; and Radio Five Live (established 1990) has sport and news programmes. The BBC national and local radio audience share amounted to 53.1 per cent in 2004 (as opposed to independent radio with 45 per cent).

Independent broadcasting (The Office of Communications – Ofcom)

Ofcom does not make or produce programmes itself. Its government-appointed board regulates the independent television and radio companies (including cable/satellite services). It grants licences to the transmitting companies who commission many of the programmes often made by independent producers shown on three advertising-financed terrestrial television channels (ITV 1, Channel 4 and Five).

Britain is divided for ITV 1 television purposes into 14 geographical regions and commercial TV companies are granted licences to supply programmes for these regions. The companies form a network which independently commissions and schedules television programmes, including a statutory requirement to provide regional programming. Since 2004, the merged Carlton Communications and Granada plc owns most of the regional ITV 1 licences and smaller companies own the rest.

The licences granted to ITV 1 companies are renewable every ten years and the companies have to compete with any other interested applicants. They receive nothing from the television licence fee, which applies only to the BBC. The companies are thus dependent upon the finance they receive from advertising and the sales of programmes, videos, DVDs, books, records and other publications.

ITV 1 (with 22 per cent of audience share) is the oldest independent television channel and once seemed only to provide popular programmes of a light-entertainment and sometimes trivial type. But its quality has improved and it now has a high standard of news reports, drama productions and documentaries. But critics argue that the hunt for audience ratings is once again producing inferior programmes. Channel 4 (with 11 per cent of audience share) was established in 1982 to create a commercial alternative to BBC 2. It is a public corporation, which is funded by selling its own advertising time. It was intended to offer something different and challenging in an appeal to minority tastes and provides programmes in Welsh in Wales (S4C). Channel 4 initially had serious problems with advertising and the quality of its programmes (commissioned or bought from independent producers), but has now developed a considerable reputation.

Five (with 9 per cent of audience share) became operative in 1997 after a 10-year licence was awarded to Channel 5 Broadcasting Limited. It is funded by advertising, subscription and sponsorship; covers 80 per cent of the population; but had a shaky start in terms of the attraction of its programmes. Some of its programmes still have a dubious reputation but it has increased its financial base.

It was argued that the former ITC did not always keep a close watch on independent broadcasting developments and lacked clear regulatory powers and consistent policies. There had been controversy over its system of awarding ITV 1 licences, which often went to the highest bidder with little apparent regard to quality and production efficiency. Ofcom is an attempt to improve on this structure.

Ofcom also regulates cable and satellite television. Television and its associated technological developments have become very attractive in Britain and a rich source of entertainment profits. At one stage, it was thought that cable television by subscription would considerably expand these possibilities. Cable television (with the main provider being ntl/Telewest) is growing steadily through digital technology (with its increased number of channels) and is potentially available to 12.5 million homes largely in urban and suburban areas, with 3.4 million subscribers in 2004. But it has been challenged by video and DVD sales and by satellite programmes.

Television broadcasting by satellite through subscription was established in Britain in 1989 by British Sky Broadcasting (BSkyB). The biggest UK satellite television programmer is now called Sky Digital (2004) with 7.8 million subscribers. Its channels provide news, light entertainment, sport and feature films. The choice of satellite channels is expanding steadily through digital technology with over 420 radio and television satellite servers providing programming in Britain.

Cable and satellite have a 15 per cent share of television viewing. This suggests that while they are increasing their market share, they still lag behind terrestrial ITV 1 (22 per cent) and BBC 1 (28 per cent).

Ofcom also controls independent radio (three national stations and 150 local and regional stations throughout the country). All are funded by advertising and revenue figures suggest that radio is the fastest growing medium in Britain.

The national radio stations were created by Conservative governments to expand radio broadcasting. The first licence was awarded in 1991 to Classic FM (popular classical music and news bulletins); the second in 1992 to Virgin 1215 (rock music); and the third in 1995 to Talk Radio UK (speech-based service). National independent stations accounted for 10.1 per cent of total radio audience share in 2004.

Local independent radio once seemed to provide mainly pop music, news flashes and some programmes of local interest. But expansion has occurred at city, local and community levels because broadcasting has been deregulated by the government in an attempt to increase the variety of radio and include more tastes and interests. Local independent stations accounted for 34.9 per cent of total radio audience share in 2004.

The role and influence of television

Television is an influential and dominant force in modern Britain, as well as a popular entertainment activity. Over 98 per cent of the population have television sets in their homes; 95 per cent of these are colour sets; and over 50 per cent of homes have two sets or more. Some people prefer to rent their sets instead of owning them because rented sets are repaired and maintained free of charge. However, reports in 2001 suggested that radio (independent and BBC) is now more popular than television, indicating that some people are deserting the latter because of its alleged superficiality and declining quality. Average television viewing time (2005) seems to have decreased to 25 hours per week, although some surveys suggest a lower figure of 18 hours.

A large number of the programmes shown on television are made in Britain, although there are also many imported American series. A few programmes come from other English-speaking countries, such as Australia, New Zealand and Canada. But there are relatively few foreign-language productions on British television and these are either dubbed or sub-titled.

The range of programmes shown is very considerable, but they also vary widely in quality. Although British television has a high reputation abroad, it does attract substantial criticism in Britain, either because of the standard of the programmes or because they are frequently repeated. News reports, documentaries and current-affairs analyses are generally of a high standard, as are dramatic, educational, sporting, natural history and cultural productions. But there is also a wide selection of series, soap operas, films, quizzes and variety shows which are of doubtful quality.

The recent addition of Reality-TV (like *Big Brother, Survivor* and their many successors) and genres such as makeover, decorating and house sales programmes have led to charges of a 'dumbing-down' of British television. Many of these programmes are calculated to appeal to a mass audience and high ratings. Independent television companies need such successful offerings in order to attract advertising and profit. The BBC needs them to justify its expenditure and financial existence.

Competition between the BBC and independent television is strong and the battle of the ratings (the number of people watching individual programmes) indicates the popularity (or otherwise) of offerings. But competition can mean that similar programmes are shown at the same time on the major channels, in order to appeal to specific markets and attract the biggest share of the audience. It is also argued that competition has reduced the quality of programmes overall and resulted in an appeal to the lowest common denominator in taste. The BBC in particular is criticized for its failure to provide quality arts, drama and news programmes with a slide into commercialism in the battle for ratings. It is argued that the BBC must maintain its public service obligations to quality and creativity in order to justify its universal licence fee.

Voices have been raised about the alleged levels of sex, vulgarity, violence and bad language which now seem to saturate British television, particularly before the 'watershed' of 9 p.m. in the evenings when young children may be watching. Some individuals have attempted to reform and influence the kind of programmes that are shown. Research suggests that some individuals can be morally harmed by the content of some television programmes and televisual images and speech are quickly imitated, particularly by children. The Conservative government considered that violence, sex and obscenity on television do affect viewers and can encourage copycat behaviour. It was concerned to 'clean up' television. A Broadcasting Standards Complaints Commission had previously monitored programmes, examined complaints, established codes of conduct for the broadcasting organizations and had tightened its rules concerning invasion of privacy by broadcasters. The Commission's role has now been taken over by Ofcom. The sale and rent of 'video nasties' (videos which portray extreme forms of violence and brutality) have been banned and rules for the sale of videos have been tightened. Some 69 per cent of homes now own at least one video-cassette recorder. But British Social Attitudes 2000–1 suggested that Britons are becoming more permissive about the portrayal of sex in the media if this is relevant to a plot, and even more liberal if it occurs outside a family context on adult channels, video and cinema.

Today, there is fierce competition among broadcasters to attract viewers and advertising revenue. But it is questionable whether an 'entertainments' expansion means more genuine choice or declining quality. Digital broadcasting will increase television channels and has transformed some media into interactive forces which combine the Internet and personalized programming in a single package. But broadcasters risk losing audiences and revenue as more people switch to DVD and the Internet itself as an alternative to television. In 2004, 53 per cent of British households had Internet access.

Media ownership and freedom of expression

The financial and ownership structures of the British media industry are complex and involve a range of media outlets, which include the press, radio and television. Sometimes an individual company will own a number of print products, such as newspapers and magazines, and will specialize in this area.

But this kind of traditional ownership is declining. Today it is more common for newspapers to be owned and controlled by corporations which are concerned with wide media interests, such as films, radio, television, magazines, and satellite and cable companies. Other newspaper- and media-owning groups have diversified their interests even further, and may be involved in a variety of non-media activities. In Britain, only a few newspapers like the *Guardian* and the *Morning Star* have avoided being controlled by multinational and multi-media commercial concerns.

This involvement of large enterprises in the media, and the resulting concentration of ownership in a few hands, such as newspapers controlled by News International and Trinity Mirror, has caused concern. Although these concentrations do not amount to a monopoly situation, there have been frequent enquiries into the questions of ownership and control. Some critics argue that the state should provide public subsidies to the media industries in order to prevent them being taken over by big-business groups. But this suggestion has not been adopted, and it is felt that there are potential dangers in allowing the state to gain any direct or indirect financial influence over the media.

Today the law is supposed to guard against the risks inherent in greatly concentrated ownership of the means of communication. The purchase of further newspapers by an existing owner is controlled by law and newspaper owners' shareholdings in independent radio and television stations are restricted. Further restrictions, such as independent directors of newspapers; guarantees of editorial independence from owners' interference; and trustee arrangements to allow newspapers to maintain their character and traditions are usually imposed. These arrangements are intended to prevent monopolies and undue influence by owners. But such safeguards do not always work satisfactorily in practice and takeovers of ITV 1 television companies by rival companies and multi-media corporations are now permitted within limits.

The question of free expression in the media continues to be of concern. Critics argue that the media do not have sufficient freedom to comment on matters of public interest. But the freedom of the media, as of individuals, to express themselves, is not absolute. Regulations are placed upon the general freedom in order to safeguard the legitimate interests of other individuals, organizations and the state, so that a balance between competing interests may be achieved.

There are several legal restraints upon media freedom of expression. The *sub judice* rule means that the media may not comments on court proceedings and must restrict themselves to reporting the court facts. The rule is intended to protect the individuals concerned, and if a media organization breaks the rule it may be found guilty of contempt of court and fined. Contempt of court proceedings may also be used by judges to obtain journalists' sources of information, or to prevent the media from publishing certain court details and documents. Some journalists have refused to disclose their sources and have gone to prison as a result.

The obtaining and publishing of state and official information is controlled tightly by the Official Secrets Act and by D-notices (directives to the media concerning information which should not be divulged). The media are also liable to court proceedings for libel and obscenity offences. Libel is the making of accusations which are proved to be false or harmful to a person's reputation. Obscenity covers any action that offends against public morality. In such cases, the media organization and all the individuals involved may be held responsible.

New legislation by the Labour government has media implications. The Human Rights Act (1998) is a two-edged sword in terms of free expression. On the one hand, it supposedly allows the media greater freedom of expression to comment on matters of public importance. On the other, it allows individuals to complain and seek compensation if their individual rights and privacy have allegedly been infringed (for example, by the media). The Labour government failed to introduce legislation in 2006 making incitement to religious hatred a criminal offence in England and Wales. This had been seen as an infringement on the media's and artists' rights to comment critically on religion and religious belief. Criminal legislation already exists to prohibit alleged incitement to racial hatred. The question becomes one of distinguishing between genuine critical comment and deliberate criminal behaviour, particularly if the test for a successful charge of incitement rests on the subjective or personal assessment of the complainant.

These restrictions prevent absolute media freedom of expression. It is argued that there is a need for reform if responsible investigative journalism and the media are to do their job adequately. Britain is a secretive society, and the Labour government's Freedom of Information Act (2000) may break down some of the secrecy and executive control. But, while the media have been able to use the Act successfully in some cases, reports in 2005 suggested that it is not working satisfactorily and that official bodies avoid giving the information requested.

On the other hand, the media can act irresponsibly, invade individual privacy, behave in unethical ways and sensationalize events for their own purposes. The media have won some libel cases brought against them and gained important victories for open information. But they have also lost other cases because of their methods. Some media practices do cause concern and the government may impose statutory restrictions on invasions of privacy unless the media reform themselves. But it is generally felt that freedom of expression could be less restricted than it is at present. .

PLATE 10.3 Paparazzi at a royal event.
Photographers waiting outside the Ritz Hotel, London, 1999 for the first joint appearance in public of Prince Charles and Camilla Parker Bowles.
(*Rex Features*)

A restraining media institution, the Press Complaints Commission (PCC), was created in 1990. It is financed by newspaper owners and is supposed to guard the freedom and independence of the press; maintain standards of journalism; and judge complaints by the public against newspapers. Some critics argue that the PCC is not fighting as hard as it might for press freedom. Others maintain that it is not strict enough with newspapers when complaints against them are proved. A fear that the government might legislate against media abuses has led to a tightening of the PCC's rules about privacy invasion, harassment by photographers and protection of children. Newspaper owners have also created an ombudsman system for each newspaper, through which public complaints can be made and investigated. It remains to be seen whether the PCC, editorial control and the ombudsman system will be truly effective.

It is sometimes argued that the concentrated ownership patterns of the media might limit freedom of journalistic expression by allowing owners undue influence over what is included in their products. Ex-journalists have claimed that there is proprietorial interference in some (if by no means all) of the media, which is not being curbed either by editorial guarantees or by legal and government restrictions. On the other hand, editors and journalists can be very independently-minded people, who will usually strongly object to any attempts at interference. Owners, in practice, seem to be careful not to tread on too many toes, because there are always competing media sources which are only too willing to publish the facts.

A further concern about limitations on media freedom has been the extent to which advertisers might dictate policy and content when they place their products. The question of advertisers' influence is complex and might today be more applicable to the mass-consumer market of radio and television than the press. Advertisers dealing with the press are more concerned with the type or status of readers rather than their numbers. Arguably, the media have not succumbed in a substantial degree to the direct manipulations of the advertising agencies, in spite of the media's dependence upon advertising revenue.

Attitudes to the media

Apart from the issues discussed above, opinion polls suggest that the media are not a source of great concern to most British people, who tend to accept them for what they are without any great illusions. Respondents are reasonably, if not overly, satisfied with the BBC and independent broadcasters. However, most are generally very sceptical of the press and journalists, and mistrustful of the content of newspapers.

It is difficult to evaluate absolutely whether the media play a dominant part in influencing public opinion on a range of political and other matters. The left-wing view assumes that they do and consequently disapproves of the alleged right-wing bias in the British media. But, while some people may have their attitudes directly shaped in these ways, it is argued that a majority of readers and viewers have already made up their own minds and react against blatant attempts at indoctrination. On certain occasions (such as general elections), the media may have an important effect on public opinion. But it is also likely that the media may merely follow popular trends and reflect changing political and social views among the public themselves.

Many people learn to read between the lines of newspapers and broadcasts and are conditioned early in life 'not to believe everything you read in the papers', or hear 'on the telly'. Since television in particular is often accused of being either right-wing or left-wing, depending on which government is in power, it would seem that the British people are receiving enough information from all sides of the political spectrum. In practice, most people make up their own minds, object to having politics and other concerns 'thrust down their throats' and many take a sceptical (and often cynical) attitude to such matters.

Given these attitudes, it is interesting to note that a MORI/British Council poll in 1999 found that only 28 per cent of overseas respondents (5 per cent for Germany) believed that the British media as a whole cannot be relied on to tell the truth. The British media were regarded as being more truthful than their counterparts in most of the overseas countries surveyed in the poll.

Exercises

Explain and examine the following terms:

media	circulation	'free newspapers'	'compacts'
press	tabloid	*Private Eye*	'hot metal'
advertising	broadsheet	ownership	libel
The Times	*Sun*	Rupert Murdoch	*sub-judice*
Fleet Street	John Reith	World Service	BBC 2
licence	Ofcom	Channel 4	dubbing
PCC	mid-market	newsboys (girls)	duopoly

Write short essays on the following topics:

1 Describe and comment critically on the structure of British broadcasting.

2 Examine the problems of media freedom of expression.

3 Discuss the division of British national newspapers into 'populars' and 'qualities'.

Further reading

1 Bignell, J., Lacey, S. and Macmurraugh-Cavanagh, M.K. (2000) *British Television Drama: Past, Present and Future* London: Macmillan/Palgrave

2 Briggs, A. and Cobley, O. (2002) *The Media: An Introduction* London: Pearson Longman

3 Curran, J. and Seaton, J. (2003) *Power without Responsibility: The Press and Broadcasting in Britain* Routledge: London

4 Franklin, B. (2001) *British Television Policy: A Reader* London: Routledge

5 Stokes, J. and Reading, A. (eds) (1999) *The Media in Britain: Current Debates and Developments* London: Palgrave/Macmillan

6 Wedell, G. and Luckham, B. (2000) *Television at the Crossrads* London: Macmillan/ Palgrave

Websites

Department of Culture, Media and Sport: www.culture.gov.uk
British Broadcasting Corporation (BBC): www.bbc.co.uk
ITV (Channel 3): www.itv.com
Channel Four: www.channel4.com
Five: www.channel5.co.uk
Office of Communications (Ofcom): www.ofcom.gov.uk
The Press Association: www.pad.press.net

Press Complaints Commission (PCC): www.pcc.org.uk
The Times: www.the-times.co.uk
The Guardian: www.guardian.co.uk
The Daily Telegraph: www.telegraph.co.uk

Chapter 11

Religion

- Religious history
- The Christian tradition
- The non-Christian tradition
- Cooperation among the faiths
- Religion in schools
- Religious identification
- Attitudes to religion and morality
- *Exercises*
- *Further reading*
- *Websites*

British religious history has been predominantly Christian. Following the Protestant Reformation, it was characterized by conflict between Roman Catholics and Protestants and by quarrels among Protestants which led to division into separate Nonconformist churches and sects. But this history has also included the appearance of non-Christian faiths, such as Judaism, and groups with humanist and special beliefs. Today, Britain still possesses a diversity of religious denominations (170), which have been added to over the years (particularly in the twentieth century) by immigrants and their religions, such as Islam, Hinduism, Buddhism and Sikhism.

Despite these features, commentators have long argued that there is a continuing decline in religious observance and that the country seems to be largely secular in terms of the low figures (13 per cent) for all types (Christian and non-Christian) of regular weekly attendance at religious services. Secularization (the movement from sacred to worldly concerns) is allegedly affecting most faiths, particularly Christianity. This leads to a decline in the attraction of organized religion represented by mainstream or traditional faiths. But a distinction has to be made between attendance at religious services and an apparent non-practising religious belief in the population.

Religion still arguably remains a factor in national life, whether for believers or as a background to the national culture. It is reflected in active adherence to specific denominations, in a nominal identification with different faiths and in a general ethical and moral behaviour. Formal religiosity is proportionally greater in Wales, Scotland and (particularly) Northern Ireland than in England.

Religious history

There is little evidence of organized religion in very early British history, beyond archaeological discoveries which suggest various forms of pagan belief. Some Christian influences had reached Britain during the Roman occupation, but opinions differ as to how widespread or permanent they were.

Missionaries and monks in Ireland, who represented a Celtic variant of the Roman Catholicism brought from Rome, had converted some of the pagan Gaelic kings to Christianity possibly as early as AD 300. This process continued and much of Ireland was converted from around AD 432 by St Patrick and others. Irish missionaries spread Christianity to Wales, Scotland and northern England, establishing religious centres, such as that of St Columba on the Scottish island of Iona. Opinions differ as to the extent of the Celtic Church's influence in England.

In AD 596–7 the Anglo-Saxons of Kent in southern England were further influenced by the Roman Catholic faith through St Augustine and other monks, who had been sent from Rome by Pope Gregory, and who also founded the ecclesiastical capital of Canterbury in AD 597. The spread of Christianity was encouraged by Anglo-Saxon kings, who thought that the hierarchical example of the Christian church would support their royal authority. The church also provided educated advisers and administrators, through whom the kings could control their kingdoms more efficiently. The connection between church and state was consequently established at an early stage in English history.

Southern English Christianity was based on the beliefs and practices of the Church of Rome. Although the faith of Ireland, Wales, Scotland and northern England was also founded on Roman doctrines, it had a more Celtic identification. Conflicts and divisions inevitably arose between the two branches of Christianity. But these were eventually resolved at the Synod (meeting) of Whitby in AD 664, where all the churches agreed to accept the Roman Catholic form of worship.

Christianity became a central and influential force in society. The church was based on a hierarchy of monks, priests, bishops and archbishops. It was a part not only of religious culture but also of administration, government and law. But it was increasingly accused of worldliness and materialism. It was thought to be corrupt and too concerned with politics at the expense of religion. However, monarchs maintained their allegiance to the Roman Catholic Church and the Pope in spiritual matters, some with more conviction than others.

But the relationship between England and Rome became difficult and by the sixteenth century was at breaking point. English monarchs were jealous of the wealth and power of the church and resented the influence of Rome in national affairs. Henry VIII argued in 1529 that as King of England he, not the Pope, was the supreme legal authority in the country and that the church and courts owed their allegiance to him.

In 1534 Henry broke away from Rome and declared himself head of the church in England. The immediate reason for this breach was the Pope's refusal to accept Henry's divorce from his queen, Katharine of Aragon, who had not produced a male heir to the throne. But Henry also wanted to curb the church's power and wealth. In 1536 he dissolved many monasteries and confiscated much of the church's property.

Although Henry had established a national church, that church was still Roman Catholic in its faith and practices. Henry did not regard himself as a Protestant, nor did he consider the English church to be part of the Protestant Reformation, which was affecting religious life in continental Europe. Indeed, Henry had defended the papacy against Martin Luther in 1521. The Pope rewarded him with the title of Fidei Defensor (Defender of the Faith), which British monarchs still bear today, and which can be seen on most British coins.

Nevertheless, the influence of the European Reformation caused the English, Scottish and Welsh churches to move away from Rome's doctrines. This development in England increased under Edward VI (1547–53), when practices and beliefs became more Protestant. John Knox in Scotland also accelerated the process by founding the separate Protestant Church of Scotland in 1560. Meanwhile, Ireland remained mostly Roman Catholic.

Conflicts between Catholics and Protestants began, which often involved violent persecution. Henry VIII's daughter, the Roman Catholic Mary Tudor, tried to restore the Roman Catholic faith during her reign (1553–8), but did not succeed. Her half-sister, the Protestant Elizabeth I (1558–1603), established the Protestant status of the Church of England by the terms of her Church Settlement. The Church's doctrine was stated in the Thirty-Nine Articles of Faith (1571) and its forms of church worship were contained in the Book of Common Prayer (both revised in later centuries). English replaced Latin in church documents and services and priests were later able to marry. The English church now occupied an intermediate position between Roman Catholicism and the Protestant churches of Europe.

However, the creation of the Protestant Church of England did not stop the religious arguments which were to affect Britain in later centuries. Many Protestants in the sixteenth and seventeenth centuries felt that the church had not distanced itself sufficiently from Rome. Some left to form their own religious organizations. Initially called Dissenters because they disagreed with the majority view, they were later known as Nonconformists and today are members of the Free Churches. Religious tension between adherents of various forms of Protestantism also occurred in the Civil War (1642–51) between Parliamentarians and Royalists, which led to the protectorate of Oliver Cromwell.

The collapse of Cromwell's narrowly puritan regime after his death, and the restoration of the Stuart monarchy under Charles II in 1660, did bring some religious moderation. But minority religions still suffered. The Roman Catholic Church underwent persecution and exclusion for 300 years after the Reformation, and Jews and Nonconformists also experienced discrimination. These religious groups were excluded from the universities, the House of Commons and public positions. It was not until the early nineteenth century that most restrictions placed on them were formally removed. Meanwhile, the Church of England solidified its dominant position in 1688, when the Protestant William III succeeded James II, the last English king to sympathize with the Catholic cause.

But further quarrels affected religious life in the eighteenth century, as groups reacted to rationalist developments in the Church of England. For example, the Methodists (founded 1739) stressed the emotional aspects of salvation and religion. They tried to work within the Church of England, but opposition to their views eventually forced them to separate. Nevertheless, an Evangelical wing within the Church was strongly affected by Methodism. The Evangelicals based their faith on a literal interpretation of the Bible and a humanitarian idealism. They accomplished many industrial and social reforms in nineteenth-century Britain. Today, the 'Low Church' wing of the Church of England is influenced by Evangelicalism.

Other groups reacted to the Church of England in the eighteenth and nineteenth centuries and founded a variety of Nonconformist sects, such as the Baptists. Nonconformists were (and are) particularly strong in Wales. On the other hand, the Oxford or Tractarian Movement, which developed in the 1830s, emphasized the Church of England's connections with Roman Catholicism. It followed Catholic doctrines and used elaborate ritual in its church services. It influenced succeeding generations and today is represented by the Anglo-Catholic or 'High Church' wing of the Church of England.

By the end of the nineteenth century the various Christian and non-Christian churches, such as Judaism, were scattered throughout Britain. In the twentieth century, immigrants have added further religious diversity. Muslim mosques, Sikh and Hindu temples, and West Indian churches, such as the Pentecostalists, are common in areas with large ethnic communities.

In Britain today the growth of Christian and non-Christian religious observance and vitality is found outside the big traditional Christian churches. The Evangelical movement continues to grow as a branch of Christianity and is characterized by a close relationship among members and a personal feeling between them and God, Christ and the Holy Spirit. It has basic Christian beliefs, but expresses them in different ways; breaks down the barriers of more traditional worship; places little reliance on church furniture; and has many different meeting places. The growth of fundamentalist faiths, 'enthusiastic' Christian churches and some 500 cults or religious movements have also increased the number of people active in religious life. Meanwhile non-Christian faiths, such as Islam, have expanded significantly.

There is religious freedom in contemporary Britain; a person may belong to any religion or none; and religious discrimination is unlawful. The Labour

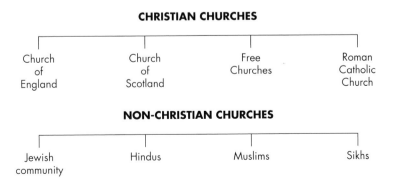

FIGURE 11.1 Main contemporary religious groups

government attempted, but failed, in 2006 to make incitement to religious hatred a criminal offence in England and Wales. There is no religious bar to the holding of public office, except that the monarch must be a member of the Church of England. None of the churches is tied to a political party and there are no religious parties as such in Parliament.

The Christian tradition

Christianity in Britain is represented mainly by the Church of England (Anglican) and the Roman Catholic Church (which are the largest), the Church of Scotland and the Free Churches. The Church of England attracts about a fifth of religiously active Britons and the Roman Catholic Church does only marginally better. It is argued that these two churches built too many buildings for too few people in the nineteenth century. They have since used resources to subsidize churches that should have been closed and poorly-attended services contribute to decline. Surveys suggest that traditional or mainstream Christian churches have lost their ability to attract the young and need a more contemporary image; 42 per cent of members of existing congregations consist of retired people and the average age of church-goers is over 70. People under 55 tend to opt for more evangelical forms of worship.

The Church of England

The Church of England is the established or national church in England. This means that its legal position in the state is confirmed by the Elizabethan Church Settlement and Parliament. The monarch is the head of the church; its arch-bishops, bishops and deans are appointed by the monarch on the advice of the Prime Minister; and Parliament has a voice in its organization and rituals. But it is not a state church because it receives no public financial aid, apart from salaries for non-clerical positions and help with church schools. The church therefore has a special relationship with the state, although there are calls for its disestablish-ment (cutting the connections between church and state) so that it has autonomy over its own affairs.

The church is based on an episcopal hierarchy, or rule by bishops. The two Archbishops of Canterbury and York, together with 24 senior bishops, sit in the House of Lords, take part in its proceedings and are the church's link to Parliament. Organizationally, the church is divided into the two provinces of Canterbury and York, each under the control of an archbishop. The Archbishop of Canterbury (called the Primate of All England) is the senior of the two and the professional head of the church. The two provinces are sub-divided into 44 dio-ceses, each under the control of a bishop. Most dioceses are very old and situated in ancient cathedral towns, such as Chichester, Lincoln, Durham and Salisbury.

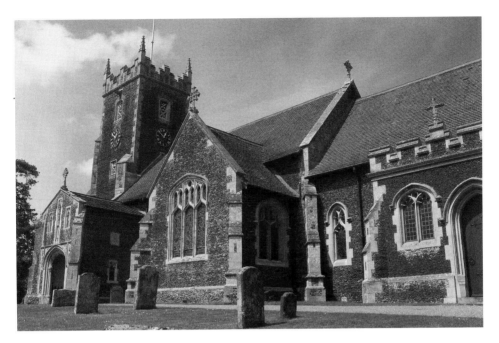

PLATE 11.1 The church of St Mary Magdalene, Sandringham, Norfolk.
Rural Anglican (Church of England) church with characteristic Norfolk pebble wall facings.
(*John Melhuish/Rex Features*)

The dioceses are divided into some 13,000 parishes and each is centred on a parish church. Most parishes, except for those in rural areas, have a priest (called either a vicar or a rector) in charge and a large parish may have additional assistant priests (curates). The priest occupies rent-free accommodation in a vicarage, but does not have a large salary, which is paid out of diocesan funds.

The main financial resources of the church come from its substantial property and investment holdings and it is the third largest landowner in Britain (after the Crown and the Forestry Commission). The assets of the church, which have been estimated at over £400 million, are administered by the Church Commissioners. This wealth has to finance many very expensive demands, such as pensions for the clergy and administrators, maintenance of churches and cathedrals and activities in Britain and abroad. In recent years the finances of the church were depleted because of investment failures and there are growing demands upon its capital finance.

The Church of England is considered to be a 'broad church' in which a variety of beliefs and practices coexist. Priests have freedom as to how they conduct their church services. These can vary from the elaborate ritual of High Church worship to the simple, functional presentation of Low Church services. The High Church or Anglo-Catholic wing (some 20 per cent of church membership) lays stress on church tradition and the historical influence of Roman Catholic practices and

PLATE 11.2 Westminster Abbey, London.
A large Gothic church in Westminster where most English kings since William I (the Conqueror) in 1066 have been crowned. Many famous people are buried or commemorated here.
(*Eye Ubiquitous/Rex Features*)

teaching. The Low Church or Evangelical wing (some 80 per cent of church membership) bases faith and practice on simplicity and often a literal interpretation of the Bible and is suspicious of Roman Catholic influences.

The two wings of the church do not always cooperate happily and between them there is a considerable variety of fashions. Some priests have introduced contemporary music and theatre into their services, in order to appeal to younger congregations and more modern concerns. The latest attempt to broaden the church's attraction is the establishment of an i-church (internet service), which may appeal to those unable or unwilling to attend the local church. Today priests have to deal with a wide variety of problems and pressures in their work, particularly in deprived and inner-city areas, and cannot easily be restricted to a purely religious role.

The membership of the Church of England is difficult to determine, because the church does not have adequate registers of members. Membership is assumed when a person (usually a baby) is baptized into the church. But only 40 per cent of the English population have been baptized. This membership may be confirmed at 'confirmation' at the age of 14 or 15. It is estimated that only a fifth of those baptized are confirmed and that 1.8 million people are formal members of the church. In terms of regular weekly observance at under 1 million, the Church is the second-largest Christian faith (after Roman Catholicism). But numbers continue to decline slowly as does the number of priests (owing to retirement and lack of recruitment). However, many other Britons may nominally identify themselves with the Church of England, even though they are not members.

Lay members of the parish are associated with church organization at the local level through parochial church councils. These send representatives to the local diocesan councils (or synods), where matters of common concern are discussed. Cases may then be sent to the General Synod, which is the national governing body of the Church. It has spiritual, legislative and administrative functions and makes decisions on subjects such as the ordination of women priests.

Women in the past served as deacons (an office below that of priest) and in women's religious orders, but could not be ordained as priests in the Church. Debate and conflict still surround this question, although the General Synod approved the ordination of women and the first women were ordained in 1994. There are now 1,262 full-time women priests (compared with 7,720 male clergy) and a small number have reached senior positions. The debate has split the church into factions, driven some members and clergy into the Roman Catholic Church, and there is significant hostility to women priests in many parishes and from male priests. Current controversial debate in this area is concerned with the question of whether women should be appointed as bishops in the Church, which at present is under discussion.

Another area of conflict is the question of whether priests should be openly gay or in practising gay relationships. At present, non-practising gays may become priests, but the issue raises fierce controversy. Splits have appeared in many parishes and the Church is finding it difficult to maintain an acceptable policy.

The Church of England is sometimes referred to as the 'Anglican Church', in the sense that it is part of a worldwide communion of churches whose practices and beliefs are very similar, and many of which descend from the Church of England. This Anglican Communion comprises some 90 million people in the British Isles (with Anglican churches in Wales, Scotland and Northern Ireland) and abroad, such as the Protestant Episcopal Church in the USA and others in Africa, South-East Asia, South America and Canada. Some of these churches have women priests and bishops, others do not. But the question of whether to accept practising gays as priests or bishops is also being debated in the Communion, with the danger of schism between conservative (African) and liberal provinces (North American). The Lambeth Conference (a meeting of Anglican bishops from all over the world) is held every ten years in London and is presided over by the Archbishop of Canterbury. It has great prestige and its deliberations on doctrine, relations with other churches and attitudes to political and social questions can be influential.

Today, much of the Church membership is middle- and upper-class, rural-based and ageing and it is identified with the ruling establishment and authority. There is conflict within the Church between traditionalists, who wish to maintain old forms and beliefs, and modernists, who want a more engaged and adventurous Church to attract a contemporary congregation.

In recent years, the Church of England has been more willing to enter into controversial arguments about social and political problems in contemporary Britain, such as the condition of people living in the inner cities, and has been critical of government policies. This brought it into conflict with the Conservative government and its popularity among politicians at present is not high. It has tended to avoid such issues in the past and has been described as 'the Conservative Party at prayer' because of its safe, establishment image. It is still widely felt that the Church, like the monarchy, should not involve itself in such questions and historically it has favoured compromise. However, some critics argue that the Church is mediocre, riven with squabbles, uncertain of its future and lacks both authority and charm. In this view, it must modernize its attitudes, organization and values if it is to continue as a vital force in British life.

The Church of Scotland

The Church of Scotland (commonly known as the Kirk) is the second established Protestant church in Britain and the largest in Scotland. Its position as the official national church in Scotland has been confirmed by successive legislation from 1707, which has asserted its freedom in spiritual matters and independence from all parliamentary supervision. The Church is separate from the Church of England, has its own organizational structures and decides its own doctrines and practices.

It was created in 1560 by John Knox. He was opposed to episcopal rule and considered that the Church of England had not moved sufficiently far from Roman Catholicism. The Scottish church followed the teachings of Calvin, a leading exponent of the European Reformation, and developed a rather severe form of Presbyterian Protestantism. Presbyterianism means government by ordained ministers and elected elders (who are lay members of the Church).

The Church has a democratic structure. Individual churches are governed locally by a Kirk Session, which consists of the minister and elders. Ministers (who include women) have equality with each other. The General Assembly is the supreme organizational body of the Church and comprises elected ministers and elders. It meets every year under the presidency of an elected Moderator, who serves for one year and is the leader of the church during the period of office. There are some 600,000 adult members of the church.

The Roman Catholic Church

The Roman Catholic Church in Britain experienced much persecution and discrimination after the Reformation and had difficulties in surviving. Although its hierarchy was restored and the worst suspicions abated by 1850, reservations about it still continued in some quarters.

Today Catholicism is widely practised throughout Britain and enjoys complete religious freedom, except for the fact that no Catholic can become monarch. There are seven Roman Catholic provinces in Great Britain (four in England, two in Scotland and one in Wales), each under the supervision of an archbishop; 30 dioceses each under the control of a bishop; and over 3,000 parishes. The head of the church in England is the Cardinal Archbishop of Westminster and the senior lay Catholic is the Duke of Norfolk. In Northern Ireland, there is one province with seven dioceses, some of which overlap with dioceses in the Irish Republic.

PLATE 11.3 Mass at Westminster Cathedral (Roman Catholic), London.
The cathedral is the centre of England's Roman Catholic faith and the seat of its premier Catholic cleric, the Cardinal Archbishop of Westminster.
(*Times Newspapers/Rex Features*)

It is estimated that there are five million nominal members of the Roman Catholic faith in Britain, although the number of active participants is 1.9 million. But regular weekly observance is just over a million, which makes it the single largest Christian church in Britain. Its membership is centred on the urban working class, settlers of Irish descent, a few prominent upper-class families and some middle-class people.

The church continues to emphasize the important role of education for its children and requires its members to try to raise their children in the Catholic faith. There are many voluntary schools which cater (if not exclusively today) for Catholic pupils and are sometimes partly staffed by members of religious orders, like the Jesuits and Marists. These and other orders also carry out social work, such as nursing, hospital duties, child care and looking after the elderly.

The Free Churches

The Free Churches are composed of those Nonconformist Protestant sects which are not established like the Churches of England and Scotland. Some broke away from the Church of England after the Reformation and others departed later. In general, they dissented from some of the Church's theological beliefs; refused to accept episcopal rule or hierarchical structures; and most have ordained women ministers. Their history has also been one of schism and separation among themselves, which has resulted in the formation of many different sects.

Their egalitarian beliefs are reflected in the historical association between political and religious dissent, which were important in the formation of the Labour Party and the radical wing of the old Liberal Party. They have developed their own convictions and practices, which are often mirrored in their simple church services, worship and buildings. The Free Churches tend to be strongest in northern England, Wales, Northern Ireland and Scotland and most of their membership has historically derived from the working class. The main Free Churches today are the Methodists, Baptists, the United Reformed Church, Pentecostalists and the Salvation Army.

The *Methodist Church* is the largest of the Free Churches, with 353,000 adult members and a community of 1.3 million. It was established in 1784 by John Wesley after Church of England opposition to his evangelical views obliged him to separate and form his own organization. Further arguments and division occurred within the Methodist Church in the nineteenth century, but most of the doctrinal and administrative disputes were settled in 1932. Today the Methodist Church in Britain is based on the 1932 union of most of the separate Methodist sects. But independent Methodist churches still exist in Britain and abroad, with a worldwide membership of many millions. Attempts were made in the 1960s and 1970s to unify the Methodists and the Church of England, but the proposals failed. In practice, however, some ministers of these denominations share their churches and services.

The *Baptists* (formed in the seventeenth century) are today grouped in associations of churches. Most of these belong to the Baptist Union of Great Britain and Ireland, which was formed in 1812 and has a total membership of some 145,000 people. There are also independent Baptist unions in Scotland, Wales and Ireland (bringing the total Baptists to some 240,000), in addition to a worldwide Baptist fellowship.

The ancient Congregational Church in England and Wales had its roots in sixteenth-century Puritanism. It merged with the Presbyterian Church in England (which was associated with Scottish Presbyterians) in 1972 to form the *United Reformed Church*, which now has some 96,500 members. Further mergers with existing sects occurred in 1982 and 2000.

The Salvation Army emphasises saving souls through a practical Christianity and social concern. It was founded in Britain by William Booth in 1865; now has some 55,000 active members; has spread to 89 other countries and has a worldwide strength of 2.5 million. The Salvation Army is an efficient organization and has centres nationwide to help the homeless, the abused, the poor, the sick and the needy. Its uniformed members may be frequently seen on the streets of British towns and cities, playing and singing religious music, collecting money, preaching and selling their magazine *War Cry*.

Other Christian churches

Although active membership of the large Christian churches is declining, there are a considerable number of smaller Free Church denominations throughout Britain. The dissenting tradition has led groups in very varied directions and they all value their independence and origins. For example, the *Religious Society of Friends* (Quakers) was founded in the seventeenth century. It has no ministers and its meetings for worship are somewhat unconventional. But the Quakers' pacifism and social work are influential and their membership has increased since the early twentieth century to about 17,000 people.

There has been a significant recent increase in 'enthusiastic' Christian churches. These are defined as independent Christian groups, which number half a million members and are characterized by their Pentecostalist or charismatic nature. They emphasize the miraculous and spiritual side of the New Testament rather than dogma, sin and salvation. Among them are churches, like the Assemblies of God and the Elim Pentecostal Church, which have many members of West Indian (Afro-Caribbean) descent. Fundamentalist evangelical groups have also been increasing. There are many other religious sects in Britain, such as the Seventh Day Adventists with a defined Christian ambience, and others such as Jehovah's Witnesses, the Mormon Church, Christian Scientists and Spiritualists which are Christian variants often deriving from the USA. Other immigrants to Britain over the centuries have established their own Christian denominations in the country (mainly in the large cities), of which the largest today is the Greek Orthodox Church.

This diversity of Christian groups produces a very varied religious life in Britain today, but one which is an important reality for significant numbers of people. Some of it illustrates a growth area in religious observance, marked by frustration or disenchantment with the heavy, formal and traditional style of the larger mainstream churches and a desire to embrace a more vital, less orthodox and more spontaneous form of Christianity and personal religious experience.

The non-Christian tradition

The non-Christian tradition in Britain is mainly associated with immigrants into the country over the centuries, such as the Jews and, more recently (from the nineteenth and particularly twentieth centuries), Muslims, Sikhs and Hindus, among many others.

The Jewish community

The first Jews came with the Norman Conquest and were involved in finance and commerce. The present community dates from the mid-seventeenth century, following its earlier expulsion in the thirteenth century. It now has some 283,000 members and is estimated to be the second largest Jewish population in Europe.

PLATE 11.4 Synagogue, Hackney, London.
Orthodox Jews leaving the Egerton Road Synagogue in Hackney, London, built in 1914. London contains the largest proportion of Jews in Britain.
(*Rex Features*)

The community is composed of the original Sephardim (from Spain, Portugal and north Africa) and the subsequent majority Ashkenazim (from Germany and central Europe).

In religious terms, the community is divided into the majority Orthodox faith (of which the main spokesman is the Chief Rabbi) and minority Reform and Liberal groups. The focus of religious life is the 300 local synagogues and Jewish schools are attended by one in three Jewish schoolchildren. The Board of Deputies of British Jews is the umbrella representative body and voice for all Jews. The majority of Jews live in London, where the East End has traditionally been a place of initial Jewish settlement, while others live mainly in urban areas outside London.

The community has declined in the past 20 years. This is due to a disenchantment with religion and growing secularism; an increase in civil and mixed marriages; considerable emigration by young Jews; a relatively low birth rate; and an ageing population of active practitioners. For some British Jews, their Jewishness is a matter of birth and they are tending to assimilate more with the wider society. For others, it involves deep religious beliefs and practice and this fundamentalism seems to be increasing. But the majority also have a larger global identity with Jewish history and experiences.

Other non-Christian religions

Immigration into Britain, particularly during the last 50 years, has resulted in a substantial growth of other non-Christian religions, such as Islam, Sikhism and Hinduism. The number of practitioners is growing because of relatively high birth rates in these groups and because of conversion to such faiths by young working-class non-whites and middle-class whites.

There are now some 1.6 million Muslims, of whom some 665,000 regularly attend the mosque. Most have origins in Pakistan and Bangladesh, but there are other groups from India, Arab countries, Cyprus, the Middle East and Eastern Europe. The Islamic Cultural Centre and its Central Mosque in London are the largest Muslim institutions in the West, and there are mosques (1,000) in virtually every British town with a concentration of Muslim people. The Muslim Council of Britain, formed in 1997, is the umbrella representative body for most British Muslims.

There are also active Sikh (400,000) and Hindu (165,000) religious adherents in Britain. Most of these come from India with a minority from East Africa and have many temples located around the country in areas of Asian settlement, with 200 Sikh and 143 Hindu temples. Various forms of Buddhism are also represented in the population, with about 50,000 active participants. All these faiths have their own representative bodies.

Non-Christian religions amount to some 1.4 million active or practising members and represent a significant growth area when compared to the Christian

PLATE 11.5 Muslim Friday prayers.
Muslims attend Friday prayers at Regents Park Mosque, London on 8 July 2005, following bombings in central London the previous day.
(*Lena Kara/Rex Features*)

PLATE 11.6 A Hindu wedding ceremony.
(*Rex Gardner/Rex Features*)

Churches. But these communities constitute a relatively small proportion of the total British population, 72 per cent of which remains nominally Christian despite the growth of agnostics, atheists and those who claim no denominational identity. Non-Christian groups have altered the religious face of British society and influenced employment conditions, since allowances have to be made for them to follow their religious observances and customs.

They have also become vocal in expressing their opinions on a range of matters, such as protests about British foreign policy in the Middle East and Iraq; a Muslim demand for their own schools supported by state funds; Muslim outrage against Salman Rushdie's novel *The Satanic Verses*, parts of which are considered to be blasphemous; and Muslim claims that British law discriminates against their religion.

Cooperation among the faiths

The earlier intolerance and bigotry of Christian denominations in Britain have gradually mellowed after centuries of hostility, restrictions and repression. There is now considerable cooperation between the churches, although this stops short of ecumenism (full unity). Discussions continue between the Roman Catholic Church and other Christian churches about closer ties and an Anglican-Roman Catholic Commission explores points of possible unity. The old enmity between Protestants and Catholics has been reduced. But tension continues in parts of Scotland and most demonstrably in Northern Ireland.

On other levels of cooperation, Churches Together in Britain and Ireland has representatives from the main Christian churches and works towards common action and Christian unity. The Free Church Federal Council does a similar job for the Free Churches. The Anglican and the main Free Churches also participate in the World Council of Churches, which attempts to promote worldwide cooperation and studies common problems. The Council of Christians and Jews works for better understanding among its members and the Council for Churches of Britain and Ireland has established a Committee for Relations with People of Other (non-Christian) Faiths. A recent creation, the Inter Faith Network for the UK consists of some 100 organizations and promotes good relations between the different faiths in the UK. The growth of inter-faith and multi-faith bodies since 2000 indicates both a desire and a need for such cooperation to solve some of Britain's current problems.

Such attempts at possible cooperation are seen by some as positive actions, which might break down barriers and hostility and promote a more inclusive Britain. Others see them as signs of weakness since denominations are forced to cooperate because of declining memberships and their lack of real influence in the contemporary world. Any movement towards Christian unity may also be threatened by the ordination of women priests in the Church of England, since the worldwide Anglican Communion accepts them, but the Roman Catholic Church is opposed.

Many church people at the grassroots level argue that the churches must adapt more to the requirements of modern life, or else decline in membership and influence. Religious life in Britain has become more evangelical and cooperative in order to reflect a diverse contemporary society and values. But some traditionalists wish to preserve the historical elements of religious belief and practice and the tension between them and modernists in all religious groups is likely to continue.

Religion in schools

Non-denominational Christian religious education is legally compulsory in state primary and secondary schools in England and Wales. The school day is supposed to start with an act of collective worship and religious lessons should be provided which concentrate on Christianity as the main religious tradition of the country but also include the other main faiths. However, if a pupil (or parent) has strong objections, the pupil need not take part in either the service or the lessons. Religious services and teaching are not compulsory in Scotland.

In practice, few secondary schools hold daily religious assemblies. Custom differs for the religious lessons, particularly in areas with large ethnic communities. The lessons can take many different forms and may not be tied to specific Christian themes. Frequent proposals are made that the legal compulsion in religious education should be removed, but it is still enshrined in legislation. Some people see religious education and collective worship as a way to raise moral standards and encourage social values. Others disagree. Many schools cannot meet their religious legal obligations and question the point of doing so.

Religion-based state schools at primary and secondary levels ('faith schools') have long existed in Britain and are now largely funded by the state. Most of them are Christian and emphasize the particular faith of the school, such as the Church of England, Roman Catholicism and Methodism. The Labour government wishes to increase the number of faith schools because of their academic records and discipline, as well as its wish to reflect social and religious diversity. The Church of England and the Methodists want to open more such schools and the first state-funded Islamic secondary school for girls opened in 2001. Independent religious schools (such as a few existing Muslim schools) are not funded by the state.

These developments are controversial. It is argued that single-faith schools will institutionalize segregation, lead to a 'balkanization' of British society rather than an embrace of pluralism, increase intolerance from inside and outside the schools, and children will grow up ignorant of other religious and social values. Experience in Northern Ireland illustrates the potential dangers of segregated religious schooling, although there has been a recent increase in integrated schools in the province.

Religious identification

Declining membership of the mainstream Christian churches and decreasing regular attendance in the twentieth century have continued. But expansion has occurred in some of the Free Churches, new or independent religious movements and, in particular, some of the non-Christian denominations.

Traditionally, it has been difficult to obtain precise information about religious observance and belief in Britain since denominations have their own methods of assessing membership and attendance figures. Estimates were based on internal registers, public opinion polls and research surveys, which could vary in their findings. A British Social Attitudes 2000–1 report found that 27 per cent of respondents considered themselves to be Church of England, 9 per cent were Roman Catholic, 4 per cent were Church of Scotland, 6 per cent were 'other Protestant', 10 per cent were 'other religion' and 44 per cent had no religion. These figures suggested a reduction in Church of England attendance, an increase in the number of people without a religion and a rise in the 'other religion' category. Secularization appeared to be increasing, but growth and pluralism was suggested by those with 'other religions' (many of which were non-Christian).

The report also found that only 13 per cent of all faiths attended a service once a week; 54 per cent never attended or practically never; 10 per cent attended at least twice a year; and 6 per cent at least once a year. These figures had remained constant over an eight-year period. But while church attendance outside special occasions, such as weddings, funerals and baptisms, was low, the degree of decline, though continuing, had been (perhaps surprisingly) slight. The figures suggest a large overall decline in church membership, but a smaller decline in actual church attendance. It seems that the majority of British people very rarely actually enter a religious building for observational or religious purposes.

These conclusions and statistics, which have been commonplace in Britain for many years now have to be placed in a newer context. More religious information for England, Wales and Scotland (Great Britain) became available from the 2001 census, which for the first time contained a question on religious identification and a choice from a number of specified religions. Response to the question was voluntary but 92 per cent answered. Some 77.2 per cent of the population reported that they identified with a religion or faith; 15.1 per cent said that they had no religion; and 7.8 per cent either did not state a religion or entered a non-specified faith.

Of those who identified with a religion, 71.8 per cent (41 million people) regarded themselves as Christian, making Christianity the main religion in Great Britain. This group included the Churches of England and Scotland, the Church in Wales, Protestant and other Christian denominations and the Roman Catholic Church.

Of the 3.1 million people (5.4 per cent of the population) who identified with a religion other than Christianity, 2.8 per cent (1.6 million people) were Muslims, with smaller percentages of Hindus (558,000 or 1 per cent), Sikhs 336,000 or 0.6 per cent), Jews (267,000 or 0.5 per cent) and Buddhists (149,000 or 0.3 per cent).

A religious question has been asked in Northern Ireland since 1926, although the 2001 census question was different from that for Great Britain. But the results showed that some 86 per cent identified themselves with a religion; 53 per cent identified with the Protestant community; 44 per cent with the Catholic; and 3 per cent had no or another religious identity.

All these figures suggest that secularism might not have advanced as much as is commonly thought. However, 'identification' does not necessarily translate into regular institutional observance, formal membership of a denomination or even allegiance to a given set of religious doctrines, practices and beliefs.

Attitudes to religion and morality

There are three opposed positions on religious life in modern Britain. The first suggests falling levels of involvement with the main Christian churches and a general decline of religious faith. Increasing secularization indicates that religious institutions and consciousness are losing their social and public significance. The second position indicates a religious renewal in some churches and an actual growth in others because of religious pluralism and a diversity of faiths. The third position is that while institutional membership of denominations or formal observance may no longer be popular in Britain, polls suggest that people still have religious beliefs on a personal level, which include belief in a God, sin, a soul, heaven, life after death, the devil and hell. In this view, religion has become privatized and fragmented.

When respondents to the British Social Attitudes 2000–1 survey were asked about belief in a God, it was found that there had been little change from 1991–8. The figures suggested that 52 per cent believed in a God, 22 per cent did not know and 25 per cent did not believe. Over time, this meant that there had been only a small decline in belief in a God.

It is argued that such results, which vary between polls, mean that people in modern Britain are becoming more individualistic and less dependent upon church authorities. They consequently adopt a more personal approach towards religion and no longer automatically follow the lead of organized religion. The statistics suggest that a distinction can be made between formal religious observance of an institutional or organized kind and the private individual sphere of religious or moral feeling. Despite the appearance of a secular state, religion in its various forms is still a factor in national life. Radio, television and the press concern themselves with religious and moral topics on a regular basis. Religious broadcasting on radio and television attracts large audience figures and a demand for more, despite the attempts of some broadcasters (such as the BBC) to cut religious programming.

On an institutional level, religion is also reflected in traditions and ceremonies, as well as being evident in national and individual morality. Religious denominations are relatively prominent in British life and are active in education, voluntary social work and community care. Religious leaders of all faiths publicly debate doctrine, social matters, political concerns and the moral questions of the day, not always necessarily within narrow church limits. They may frequently come into conflict with politicians and the authorities on issues such as Iraq and poverty in Britain.

But the large churches appear incapable of countering further institutional decline and, given their ageing congregations, this process seems likely to continue. At the level of public or civic behaviour and according to a Leeds University survey in 1997, many Britons do not trust other people and now see life as less predictable, more time-pressured, less secure, more materialistic and fast-moving, and their society as riddled with mistrust, cynicism and greed. Lacking traditional faith in conventional religion, more people appear to put their trust in materialism, physical appearance, fashion, trends, the celebrity circus and individualism.

Nevertheless, there also seems to be a longing for spirituality, other-worldly comfort and explanation, particularly among the 18–30 age group. This search can lead in different directions. Some people believe increasingly in mysticism, alternative spiritual disciplines, New Age practices, the paranormal, telepathy, second sight and astrology, as well as in smaller religious groups such as Spiritualists, Pagans, Wicca, Rastafarianism, Jain, Bahai and Zoroastrianism. It is argued that this need for spirituality is not being provided by the established or mainstream churches.

Such religious concerns seem also to influence matters of personal morality and civic responsibility. Although there are differences of emphasis between younger and older generations and between men and women, the British have strong views about right and wrong. But these are not necessarily tied to the teaching of any particular denomination. Polls suggest that a majority of people think, for example, that the following are morally wrong: hard drugs like heroin, scenes of explicit violence on television, adultery, pornography on the Internet, scientific experiments on human beings and scientific experiments on animals.

But the British have become more tolerant, for example, of sex in films, homosexuality, cohabitation outside marriage, soft drugs such as cannabis, alternative lifestyles and euthanasia (allowing a doctor to end a patient's life) if the person has a painful incurable illness. A majority also feel that it is worse to convict an innocent person (miscarriage of justice) than to let a guilty individual go free.

In terms of civic responsibility, polls suggest that attitudes to authority remain relatively conventional in some areas. A majority of respondents feel that children should be taught in the home environment to respect honesty, good manners and other people. Negative attitudes to an increasing 'yob culture' and teenage excess have increased. Feelings have hardened towards those individuals who reject society as presently constituted, who demonstrate and protest and who encourage disobedience in children. Most respondents agree that schools should teach children to obey authority. But the number of people who consider that the law should be obeyed without exception has fallen and more now believe that one should follow one's conscience, even if this means breaking the law.

These mixed views indicate that many British people now embrace an authoritarian posture in some questions of morals and social behaviour. 'Moral traditionalism', old values, a sense of 'what is right' and civic responsibility are still supported. But there is often a greater adherence to concepts of personal and social morality than those dictated by official, religious and legal restraints. This is also reflected in people's considerable concerns about drugs, law and order, violent crime, unprovoked violence and vandalism, and their preference for strong action to be taken in these areas. In other matters, there seems to be a growing liberalism.

Exercises

Explain and examine the following terms:

Canterbury	Henry VIII	'Low Church'	confirmation
bigotry	Iona	Free Churches	General Synod
St Patrick	episcopal	Church Settlement	John Knox
Whitby	Quakers	vicar	Salvation Army
baptism	ecumenism	denomination	evangelism

Write short essays on the following topics:

1   What does the term 'Christianity' mean in relation to British religious history?

2   Discuss religious membership and observance in contemporary British life.

3   Critically examine the role of the Church of England.

4   Examine the various public opinion polls in this chapter. What do they tell us about British society?

Further reading

1   Alderman, G. (1998) *Modern British Jewry* Oxford: Clarendon Press
2   Bebbington, D. (1988) *Evangelicalism in Modern Britain: A History from the 1730s to the 1980s* London: Routledge
3   Brown, C.G. (2000) *The Death of Christian Britain* London: Routledge

4   Bruce, S. (1995) *Religion in Modern Britain* Oxford: Oxford University Press
5   Davie, G. (1997) *Religion in Britain since 1945: Believing without Belonging* Oxford: Blackwell Publishers
6   Furlong, M. (2002) *C of E: The State It's In* London: Hodder and Stoughton
7   *Religion in England and Wales: Findings from the 2001 Home Office Citizenship Survey* (2004), London: Home Office Research Study 274
8   *Religion in the UK Directory, 2001–3* (2001) Religious Resource and Research Centre at the University of Derby and the Inter Faith Network of the UK
9   Sewell, D. (2001) *Catholics: Britain's Largest Minority* London: Viking
10 *UK Christian Handbook–Religious Trends 2003/2004, No. 4 (2004)* Christian Research

Websites

The Church of England: www.church-of-england.org
Church of Scotland: www.cofs.org.uk/3colcos.htm
Roman Catholic Church: www.tasc.ac.uk/cc and www.catholic.org.uk
United Synagogue: www.brijnet.org.uk
Judaism: www.jewish.co.uk
Islam: www.muslimdirectory.co.uk
Q-News (Muslim): www.aapi.co.uk/q-news
Churches Together in Britain and Ireland: www.ctbi.org.uk
Inter Faith Network for the UK: www.interfaith.org.uk
Office of the Deputy Prime Minister/Inner Cities Religious Council:
www.neighbourhood.gov.uk/faith_communities.asp
Church of England Internet parish: www.i-church.org
Office for National Statistics: www.statistics.gov.uk

Leisure, sports and the arts

The diversity of life in contemporary Britain is reflected in the ways the British organize their leisure, sporting and artistic interests. These features reveal a series of very different cultural habits, rather than a unified image, and are divided between participatory and spectator pastimes. Some are associated with national identities and others with minority participation. In many cases, they are also connected to social class, disposable income and the pressures on leisure time.

According to the authors of *We British* (Jacobs and Worcester 1990: 124), the rich variety of available leisure, arts and sporting activities disproves the notion of Britain as a country of philistines who prefer second-rate entertainment to the best. Yet there are frequent complaints from many quarters about a 'dumbing-down' of British cultural life in television programmes, films, the arts, literature, popular music and education, as well as reduced standards in sports and declining participation in exercise activities.

Nevertheless, public opinion polls in the 1990s and 2000s showed that Britain's cultural life on home and wider social levels was thriving, although there had been decreases in some activities and increases in others. A large number of people participate in a considerable variety of available pastimes, sometimes with surprising priorities. Reading and visits to the library, for example, hold their own with the most popular habits, such as watching television.

The authors of *We British* (1990: 133) reached conclusions which are still arguably valid today, although some critics might not agree:

> we can report that the nation is in no telly-induced trance. Its tastes mix watching and doing, 'high' and 'low' cultures, with a richness that contradicts the stereotypes of the British as divided between mindless lager louts and equally money-grubbing consumers. The mix we have found will not please everybody. Not enough football for some, not enough opera for others. But that is what we should expect in the culture of a whole nation.

Certain findings about 'leisure pursuits' and their social implications have been formulated by academics. On one level and since much leisure time in Britain is now spent within the home and/or family environment, there would seem to be a growing separation from the wider social context and a movement into individual and small group activity. On another level, the actual provision or production of most leisure needs is commercialized or profit-oriented and is therefore part of the consumer society. But access to leisure, sports and arts activities is unevenly distributed in the population, because it is dependent upon purchasing power and opportunity. Exclusionary factors operate against some participation, whether they be the cost of expensive musical equipment, the price of opera and football tickets or lack of time in very busy lives.

The creative and cultural industries which service some parts of the 'leisure market' (such as cinema, theatre, publishing, museums, the performing arts and popular and orchestral music) are an important part of Britain's social and economic life. According to a Department for Culture, Media and Sport (DCMS) survey in 2002, these industries generated substantial annual revenue and export earnings and employed 1.9 million people, amounting in total to over 8 per cent of the UK Gross Value Added (GVA) or some £73 billion.

The DCMS itself also spends considerable amounts of public money in supporting the arts and cultural life in Britain. For example, some areas of expenditure in 2003/4 were museums, galleries and libraries (£868 million); historic buildings in England (£347 million); the arts in England (£334 million) and tourism in the UK (£58 million).

Leisure activities

Leisure activities in earlier centuries, apart from some cultural interests exclusive to the metropolitan elite, were largely conditioned by the rural and agricultural nature of British life. Village communities were isolated and transport was either poor or non-existent. People were consequently restricted to their villages and obliged to create their own entertainments. Some of these participatory activities were home-based, while others were enjoyed by the whole village. They might be added to by itinerant players, who travelled the countryside and provided a range of alternative spectator entertainments, such as drama performances and musical events.

Improved transport and road conditions from the eighteenth century onwards enabled the rural population to travel to neighbouring towns where they took advantage of a variety of amusements and wider social opportunities. Spectator and participatory activities increased with the industrialization of the nineteenth century, as more of the population moved to the towns and cities and as theatre, the music halls and sports developed and became available to more people. The establishment of railway systems and the formation of bus companies initiated the pattern of cheap one-day trips around the country and to the seaside, which were to grow into the mass charter and package tours of contemporary Britain. The arrival of radio, films and television in the early twentieth century resulted in a hugely expanded professional entertainments industry. The variety of offerings and levels of participation again increased dramatically from the 1960s and coincided with more leisure time, greater disposable income and the weakening of 'high' and 'low' cultural barriers. In all these changes, the mixture of participatory, spectator, home-based and wider social leisure activities has continued.

Many contemporary pursuits have their roots in the cultural and social behaviour of the past, such as boxing, wrestling, cricket, football and a wide range of athletic sports. Dancing, amateur theatre and musical events were essential parts of rural life for all classes and were often associated with the changing agricultural seasons. The traditions of hunting, shooting and fishing have long been widely practised in British country life (not only by the aristocracy), as well as blood sports, such as dog and cock fighting and bear baiting, which are now illegal.

A feature of contemporary Britain is the continuing attempt to stop some kinds of rural activities like fishing and hunting. For example, a MORI poll in 1997 showed that two-thirds of respondents favoured a complete ban on fox hunting with horses and dogs. The countryside lobby opposed such action, but foxhunting was banned first in Scotland and then in England and Wales in 2005. However, a MORI poll in February 2005 found that the actual support for a foxhunting ban had fallen to about a half, with an increase in those respondents who said they were neutral on the issue. Animal activists have become more violent in their objections to and campaigns against what they see as the cruelty of many rural traditions as well as in their opposition to the use of animals in commercial and medical activities.

In addition to cultural and sporting pastimes, the British enjoy a variety of other leisure activities since many more opportunities are now available to them and, despite their long working hours and busy lives, more people have more free time. The problem is how to organize and prioritize their activities. Most workers have at least four weeks' holiday a year, in addition to public holidays like Christmas, Easter and Bank Holidays, although Britain has fewer public holidays than most other European countries. The growing number of pensioners (some, if by no means all, of whom are reasonably affluent) has created an economically rewarding leisure market which benefits the elderly. Unemployment means that some groups of people have more enforced spare time (if not always the finances to enjoy it in full).

Consumer patterns associated with leisure activities are also changing in Britain. These coincide with part-time and shift working and greater disposable incomes, particularly among young people. There is a demand for pubs, clubs, cinemas, shops, restaurants and a range of leisure services to be open and available for longer periods during the week and at weekends.

The most common leisure pastimes are social or home-based, such as visiting or entertaining friends, trips to the pub (public house), bars or clubs, visits to restaurants, gardening, watching television, videos and DVDs, reading books and magazines, listening to the radio, tapes, records and cassettes, taking trips away from home, Do-It-Yourself (DIY) home improvements, sport and exercise and visits to the theatre or cinema. According to public opinion polls, these activities reflect consistent patterns of behaviour in recent years.

PLATE 12.1 Night club, Newquay, Cornwall.
Some towns on the south-west English coast are popular locations for young people, particularly in the summer months.
(*Simon Rawles/Rex Features*)

The most popular non-sporting leisure activity for all people aged four and over is watching television (for 25 hours a week in 2005), and for men television viewing is apparently the single most popular pastime throughout the year. But according to some surveys (such as those from the Henley research centre), the British public now spends more time reading each year and less time listening to radio and television, with some reports suggesting that television declined to 18 hours a week in 2005. Although television still tops the popularity list, the apparent decrease in viewing hours may be due to a dissatisfaction with the quality of the programmes shown on British television, together with the growing challenge from DVDs and alternative pursuits. DVDs, however, tend to appeal more to the middle-aged and elderly who prefer them to both television and the cinema. It is suggested that film producers are increasingly catering for immediate DVD production rather than first using the traditional intermediate step of cinema showings.

In 2003, 12.6 per cent of total household expenditure was spent on leisure goods, services and recreation (more than on food, but a decrease from 1999). The British now occupy some two-thirds of their spare time using electronic equipment. A large amount of money is spent on items such as television sets (owned by some 98 per cent of households with 7.8 million subscriptions to satellite television and 3.5 million to cable television in 2004), radio equipment (listened to for some ten hours a week), video recorders (owned by nine in ten households in 2004), computers, compact disc players, DVD equipment and DVDs. Some 53 per cent of households had access to the Internet in 2004 and 58 per cent of adults had accessed it at some time. By 2004, increasing numbers of homes and businesses were using high-speed broadband connections and more people were using the Internet in preference to television.

In these examples, the home has become the chief place for family and individual entertainment and poses competition to other activities outside the home, such as the cinema, sports and theatre. Leisure activities for both males and females exclusively within the home include listening to the radio or music; watching television; studying; reading books and newspapers; relaxing; conversation; entertaining; and hobbies.

Despite the competition from television, the cinema and other electronic media, reading is still an important leisure activity for over half of men and women in Britain (with 40 per cent not reading books). There is a large variety of books and magazines to cater for all tastes and interests. In 2004, an estimated 160,000 new and revised books were published in the UK and in 2003 the value of books sold (home and export) amounted to £3,053 million. The best-selling books are romances, thrillers, modern popular novels, detective stories, science fiction and works of adventure and history. Classic literature is not widely read, although sales of older novels can benefit from adaptations on television. The tie-in of books (of all types) with videos, DVDs and television series is now a very lucrative business.

There are 5,000 public libraries in the UK which provide books, CDs, records, audio/visual cassettes, videos and DVDs on loan (for a small fee) to the public, together with information, computer and Internet facilities. Libraries in Great Britain are very well-used with 34 million people (60 per cent of the population) in 2003 being members of local libraries. Some 10 million people visited a library at least once every two weeks. In total, 361 million books and 42 million other library articles were borrowed in 2003. Only readers in Finland, Denmark and the Netherlands borrow more library books per head of population.

Do-it-yourself hobbies (DIY), such as house painting, decorating and gardening, are very popular and home repairs and improvements amount to a large item in the total household budget. The number of restaurants has increased and the practice of eating out is much more popular with expenditure on restaurants and hotels being 11.3 per cent of the household budget in 2003. There are a variety of so-called 'ethnic' restaurants (particularly Indian, Chinese, Italian and French) in most British high streets and fast-food outlets serving pizza, hamburgers, kebabs, chicken and fish and chips. The quality of food in British restaurants has continued to improve, as has the variety of available cuisines.

But visiting the pub is still a very important part of British life and more money is spent on drinking and other pub activities (3.9 per cent of household expenditure in 2003) than on any other single form of leisure. Some seven out of ten adults visit pubs and one-third go once or more a week. Research from Leeds

PLATE 12.2 An urban English pub, Nottingham.
The Trip to Jerusalem is reputed to be the oldest inn/pub in England (1189). Legend holds that Crusaders (or at least pilgrims) stayed here on their way to the Holy Land. Some of the pub's cellars and rooms are carved into the rock on which Nottingham Castle stands. (*Hardys and Hansons PLC*)

University in 2001 suggested that the pub was a psychological necessity for most men and visits were good for their health. They used the pub to bond, to recharge their batteries and as an emotional outlet. Almost half of the research sample said that they would still go to the pub if there was no alcohol.

But the pub, as a social institution, has changed over the years, although it still caters for a wide range of different groups and tastes. The pub is said to be Britain's most envied and imperfectly imitated institution, where people can gather on neutral ground and socialize on their own terms. However, falling custom, rising property prices, takeovers by chain ownership and restaurants, an obsession with trendiness, faddishness and quick profits have led to a decline in Britain's unique pub heritage. The UK's 56,000 pubs are being depleted by more than 20 a month and turned into gentrified eateries, clubs or bars in an attempt to emulate 'café society'. At worst, the premises are converted into huge palaces dedicated to vertical drinking with little of the traditional pub ambience.

Pub licensing hours, which apply to opening times for the sale of alcohol, have been liberalized and pubs from 2005 can open for extended drinking hours in the evening or into the early morning and in some cases for 24 hours a day. Most pubs may provide food in addition to drinks, and some, in more prosperous urban and rural areas, have restaurants attached to them. Attempts in 2006 to allow smoking in pubs which do not offer food were defeated in Parliament. Smoking is now banned in the workplace and public areas, such as pubs.

In recent years, there has been a mushrooming of wine bars, café bars, discos and nightclubs with extended opening hours. The growth and popularity of the club scene with its music, drink and appeal to the young offers considerable competition to the traditional pub trade, although people move between different venues during an evening. Such developments (together with late-hours pubs) have also led to a 'binge-drinking' phenomenon in city and town centres and an upsurge in anti-social behaviour on the streets, which is causing great concern.

British nightlife for most young people is varied and vibrant, with nightclubs, large-scale pop gigs at arenas and sports grounds, music festivals and controversial outdoor 'rave' parties. British bands and DJs are much admired throughout the world. Use of so-called recreational drugs such as cannabis, Ecstasy (despite well-publicized deaths from its usage) and cocaine has become so widespread that there have been calls for decriminalization of some hard and soft drugs. There is also a thriving lesbian and gay scene, more developed than in some other European countries.

Holidays and where to spend them have also become an important part of British life and have been accompanied by more leisure time and money for the majority of the people. They represent the second major leisure cost (after pub drinking). Some Britons take their holidays in Britain itself (27 million in 2002), where the south-west English coastal resorts and Scotland are very popular in

PLATE 12.3 Canary Islands, Spain.
Spain is the most popular holiday destination for British tourists.
(*Steve Brown/Rex Features*)

summer. But much larger numbers now also go abroad in both winter or summer or both, and the great days of the British (particularly seaside) resorts have declined. The number of long holidays taken abroad by the British amounted to 59 million in 2002, with Spain, France, Ireland, the USA, Italy and Greece being the main attractions for holidaymakers, who buy relatively cheap package tours. But the British seem to have become more adventurous and are now travelling widely outside Europe to Asia and Africa on a variety of holidays.

Many people prefer to organize their own holidays and make use of the good air and sea communications between Britain and the continent. In Britain itself, different forms of holiday exist, from the traditional 'bed and breakfast' at a seaside boarding house, to hotels, caravan sites and camping. Increased car ownership has allowed greater travel possibilities, with day trips in Britain for example amounting to 31 million in 2002. Today, more than seven out of ten households have the use of at least one car and 27 per cent have two or more.

Sports

There is a wide variety of sports in Britain today, which cater for large numbers of spectators and participants (the latter at different levels of competence). Some of these are minority or class-based sports (such as yachting and rugby league respectively), while others appeal to majority tastes (like football). The number of people participating in sports had increased in the 1990s. This coincided with a greater awareness of health needs and the importance of exercise, particularly at a time when many Britons are overweight and increasing numbers are obese. Expenditure on playing and watching sports, and buying sports equipment, amount to a considerable part of the household budget. But it is argued that Britain has inadequate sporting facilities and leisure centres in both the public and private sectors and that sports participation has again declined in recent years.

The 2002 General Household Survey reported that 59 per cent of adults over 16 participate in outdoor and indoor sports or forms of exercise (an overall decrease for both men and women since 2001). The most popular participatory sporting activity for both men (36 per cent) and women (34 per cent) is walking (including rambling and hiking). Billiards/snooker/pool (15 per cent) are the next most popular for men, followed by cycling (12 per cent), indoor swimming (12 per cent), football (10 per cent) and golf (9 per cent). Keep fit/yoga (16 per cent) is the next most popular sport for women, followed by indoor swimming (15 per cent), cycling (6 per cent) and snooker/pool/billiards (3 per cent). Fishing is the most popular country sport. But most of these percentages have declined from figures reported in 2001, despite government efforts to increase the exercise rates and to counter obesity.

Amateur and professional football (soccer) is played throughout most of the year and also at international level. It is the most watched sport and today transcends its earlier working-class associations. The professional game has developed into a large, family-oriented organization, but has suffered from hooliganism, high ticket prices, declining attendances and financial crises. However, enforced changes in recent years such as all-seater stadiums, greater security, improved facilities and lucrative tie-ins with television coverage (such as Sky-Sport and ITV1) have improved this situation. Many of the top professional football clubs in the English Premier League have become public companies quoted on the Stock Exchange and football is now big business.

But there is a widening gulf between these clubs and others in the lower divisions. Some 80 per cent of England's soccer clubs in 2001 were losing money despite television income, which goes largely to the 20 clubs in the Premiership. Most football clubs (even in the Premiership) are in a precarious financial position despite increased income, with only a few making a profit and many losing control over their costs. It is argued that this situation is due to poor club organization, bad business sense, huge salaries for players, inflated transfer fees and lack of success on the pitch and in European competition.

Rugby football is a popular winter pastime and is widely watched and played. It is divided into two codes. Rugby union was once confined to amateur clubs and was an exclusively middle-class and public school-influenced game. But it

PLATE 12.4 A Premier League football match.
Played at Highbury Stadium between Arsenal and Fulham in the 2005–06 season. Arsenal will move from Highbury to the newly constructed Emirates Stadium in 2006.
(*Andrew Couldridge/Rex Features*)

PLATE 12.5 Village cricket match.
Villages are often regarded as quintessential locations for cricket, with matches played by local amateur teams.
(*Rex Features*)

became professional in 1995 (at least for the top clubs), now covers a wider social spectrum and received a boost when England won the World Cup in 2003. Rugby league is played by professional teams, mainly in the north of England and still tends to be a working-class sport in terms of participation and support. Both types of rugby are also played internationally.

Cricket is a summer sport in Britain, but the England team also plays in the winter months in Commonwealth countries. It is both an amateur and professional game. The senior game is professional and is largely confined to the English and Welsh county sides which play in the County Championship. Attendance at county cricket matches continues to decline (although one-day games attract spectators) and the contemporary game has lost some of its attractiveness as it has moved in overly-professional and money-dominated directions. It was in danger of becoming a minority sport. But it regained popularity in the summer of 2005 when England gained victory over the visiting Australians in the Ashes Test Match series.

There are many other sports which reflect the diversity of interests in British life. Among these are golf, horse racing, hunting, riding, fishing, shooting, tennis, hockey, bowls, darts, snooker, athletics, swimming, sailing, mountaineering, walking, ice sports, motor-car and motor-cycle racing and rally driving. American football and basketball are increasingly popular owing to television exposure. These sports may be either amateur or professional, and spectator- or participator-based, with car and motor-cycle competitions, greyhound racing and horse racing being the most watched.

The professional sporting industry is now very lucrative, and is closely associated with sponsorship schemes, television income, brand merchandizing and non-sport sales. Gambling or betting on sporting and other events has always been a popular, if somewhat disreputable, pastime in Britain, and is now much more in the open and acceptable. Most gambling (through betting shops or bookmakers) is associated with horse and greyhound racing, but can involve other sports. Weekly football pools (betting on match results) are very popular and can result in large financial wins.

The new-found acceptability of gambling in Britain was reflected in the estab-lishment of a National Lottery in 1994. It is similar to lotteries in other European countries and considerable amounts of money can be won. Some of its income has also funded artistic, community, leisure and sports activities which are in need of finance to survive. But falling ticket sales and profits in 2001 meant that the lottery could no longer guarantee financial support for all these 'good causes'.

A National Centre for Social Research survey in June 2000 found that 72 per cent of British adults gamble at least once a year (if only on the annual Grand National horse race). The National Lottery came top (65 per cent) followed by scratchcards (22 per cent), fruit machines (14 per cent), horse racing (13 per cent), private bets with friends or workmates (11 per cent), football pools (9 per cent), bingo (7 per cent) and casino gambling (3 per cent). The Labour government has also controversially opened up the possibility for more large casinos in some big cities.

Many sports have contributed to institutionalized features of British life and provide a certain degree of national identity. For example, Wimbledon is tennis; the Football Association Cup Final is football in England (at the old Wembley Stadium, now being rebuilt); St Andrews is golf in Scotland; Twickenham in England, Murrayfield in Scotland, and the Millennium Stadium in Cardiff, Wales are rugby union; Lords Cricket Ground in London is cricket; the Derby at Epsom is flat horse racing, the Grand National in Liverpool is steeplechasing; Henley Regatta is rowing; Cowes Week off the Isle of Wight is yachting; Ascot is horse racing; and the British Grand Prix is Formula One motor racing. Some of these sports may appeal only to certain sections of the population, while others may still be equated more with wealth and social position.

Although tobacco sponsorship of most sporting events has now been banned by the Labour government, some people feel that the professionalization and commercialization of sport in Britain has tended to weaken the traditional sporting image of the amateur and the old emphasis upon playing the game for its own sake. But these values still exist to some degree, in spite of greater financial rewards for professional sport, the influences of sponsorship and advertising and more cases of unethical behaviour in all sports. Football players, in particular, have been accused of increasing boorish behaviour on the field.

British governments have only recently taken an active political interest in sport. They are now more concerned to promote sport at all levels and there are Ministers for Sport in England, Scotland, Wales and Northern Ireland, who are supposed to coordinate sporting activities throughout the country. The Labour government is concerned to improve sporting facilities in Britain by setting up sports councils, colleges, funds and action zones, operating on a regional basis. However, nationally-funded provisions for sport in Britain are still inadequate and there is a lack of professional coaches, capital investment and sporting facilities compared with other countries. Local authority sports and leisure centres, particularly in inner city areas, continue to be sold off, despite the Labour government's attempt to focus more money on playing fields and open spaces in deprived areas.

The sporting notion of 'a healthy mind in a healthy body' has long been a principle of British education. All schools are supposed to provide physical recreation and a reasonable range of sports is usually available for schoolchildren. Schools may play soccer, rugby, hockey or netball during the winter months, and cricket, tennis, swimming and athletics during the summer. Some schools may be better provided with sporting facilities than others and offer a wider range of activities.

However, there are frequent complaints from parents that physical education classes, team games and competitive sports are declining in state schools and that there is a lack of professionally-trained teachers. School reorganization and the creation of large comprehensives have reduced the amount of inter-school competition, which used to be a feature of education; some left-wing councils are opposed to competitive activities; there is a shortage of playing fields; and a lack of adequate equipment and coaching facilities. The position is particularly acute in the inner city areas, and is of concern to those parents who feel that their children are being prevented from expressing their normal physical natures. They maintain that the state school system is failing to provide sporting provision for children and some parents turn to the independent sector, which is usually well-provided with sports facilities. The Labour government is now exerting pressure on independent schools to share these with local state schools.

The Labour government has also promised more aid in an attempt to improve the availability and standards of state school sports. In a reversal of previous ideology, it has tried to address the lack of sporting facilities and recent achievement in Britain by embracing the notion of competition between schoolchildren and creating databases of sporting facilities, since none were available at school or local government level. Nevertheless, 70 per cent of the most talented youngsters drop out of sport between the ages of 14 and 17, as opposed to 20 per cent in countries such as France. But better facilities in themselves may not be enough and critics maintain that some schools and local areas are in fact reasonably good in terms of provision. It is argued that more people of all ages should be encouraged to take up sport and that there should be greater cooperation between schools and local communities in the use of facilities and coaching.

The arts

The 'arts' once had a somewhat precious and exclusive image associated with notions of high culture, which were usually the province of the urban and privileged metropolitan middle and upper classes. This attitude has lessened to some degree since the Second World War under the impetus of increased educational opportunities and the gradual relaxation of social barriers. The growth of mass and popular culture has increased the potential audience for a wider range of cultural activities, and the availability and scope of different varieties of the arts has spread to greater numbers of people. These activities may be amateur or professional and continue the mixture of participatory, spectator and home-based entertainment.

It is argued that the genuine vitality and innovation of the British arts are to be found in the millions of people across the country who are engaged in amateur music, art and theatre, rather than in the professional and commercial arts world. Virtually every town, suburb and village has an amateur group, whether it be a choir, music group, orchestra, string quartet, pipe band, brass band, choral group, opera group or dramatic club. In addition, there are some 500 professional arts and cultural festivals held each year throughout Britain, many of which are of a very high standard and appeal to diverse tastes. These range from the Glastonbury (pop and rock) Festival to the Glyndebourne Opera Festival in East Sussex.

The funding of the mainstream arts in Britain is precarious and involves the private and public sectors. The public sector is divided between local authorities and the regional Arts Councils. Local authorities raise money from the council (property) tax to fund artistic activities in their areas, but the amounts spent vary considerably between different areas of the country and local authorities are attacked for either spending too much or too little on cultural activities.

Members of the regional Arts Councils in England, Scotland, Wales and Northern Ireland are appointed by the Secretary of State for Culture, Media and Sport. They are responsible for dividing up an annual government grant to the arts and the finance has to be shared among theatres, orchestras, opera and ballet companies, art galleries, museums and a variety of other cultural organizations. The division of limited funds has inevitably attracted much criticism. It means that many artistic institutions are often dependent upon the private sector to supply donations, sponsorship and funding, in addition to their state and local government money, in order to survive and provide a service. But some cultural organizations, such as the Royal Opera and museums, have received much-needed finance from the National Lottery.

British theatre can be lively and innovative and has a deserved international reputation. There are some 300 commercial or professional theatres, in addition to a large number of amateur dramatic clubs, fringe and pub theatres throughout the country. London and its suburbs have about 100 theatres, but the dominant influence is the London 'West End'. The majority of the West End theatres are commercial, in that they are organized for profit and receive no public funds. They provide a range of light entertainment offerings from musicals to plays and comedies.

However, some of the other London theatres are subsidized from grants supplied by the Arts Council, such as the National Theatre, the Royal Shakespeare Company (as well as at Stratford-upon-Avon) and the English Stage Company. These cater for a variety of plays from the classics to modern drama. The subsidized theatres in both London and the regions constantly plead for more state financial aid, which the government is loath to give. The government subsidy is considerably less than that given to most comparable theatres in continental Europe. But there is a feeling in some quarters that these theatres should be more competitive and commercially-minded like the West End, although Arts Council grants have been recently increased.

Many of the theatres in the regions outside London are repertory theatres, which means that they provide a number of plays in a given season and have a resident theatre company and organization. The repertory companies have traditionally been the training ground for British actors and actresses. They present a specific number of classical and innovative plays and a variety of other artistic offerings in a season.

Most theatres in London and elsewhere have had difficult times in recent years in attracting audiences and in remaining solvent, although the West End theatres bring considerable finance into the British economy. They have had to cope with increased competition from alternative and new entertainment activities. New commercial theatres in some cities are proving popular and are taking audiences away from the established repertory companies. These commercial theatres provide a wide range of popular entertainment, shows and drama, as well as plays prior to a London run. There are now signs that audience figures for all types of theatres are picking up again.

Opera in Britain occupies a similar position to that of the theatres and is divided into subsidized, commercial and amateur companies. The Royal Opera in London provides London seasons and occasional regional tours while the English National Opera Company supplies a similar service at its base at the London Coliseum. The Royal Opera operates from the reburbished facilities of the Covent Garden Theatre. There is a range of other opera companies, both in London and the regions, such as the English Opera Group, the Welsh National Opera and the Scottish Opera Company. There are also several light opera groups, and ballet companies such as the Ballet Rambert, the London Festival Ballet, the Scottish Theatre Ballet and the Royal Ballet, the latter of which operates in London and Birmingham. A number of contemporary dance companies have also been formed in recent years.

Britain has many quality orchestras, although most of them are based in London, such as the London Symphony Orchestra, the London Philharmonic and the BBC Symphony Orchestra. There are regional symphony orchestras of high quality, such as the Hallé in Manchester, the City of Birmingham Symphony, the Ulster Orchestra, the BBC National Orchestra of Wales and the Royal Scottish National Orchestra and a number of chamber groups in London and the regions. Most of the opera, ballet and orchestra activities have their greatest appeal in London and still cater only for a minority of the people. But more popular forms, such as brass bands, choral singing and light music have a large following. The more exclusive entertainments are heavily dependent upon Arts Council subsidies, local government grants and private donations. The country's operatic, dance and classical music offerings can compete against international rivals.

The history of the cinema in Britain has shown a big decline since its early days as a very popular form of mass entertainment and from 1946 when annual visits reached a total of 1.6 billion. The domestic film industry had virtually ceased to exist, because of lack of investment and government help, although British films with British actors continued to be made abroad and in Britain with foreign financial backing. Although some government and National Lottery finance has recently been provided to support British film making, relatively few British films are being made in Britain, and the film industry has been criticized for making too many indifferent films.

In 1960 there were over 3,000 cinemas in Britain. But many have now either gone out of business, or changed to other activities such as dancing and bingo. But

PLATE 12.6 Odeon cinema, Shaftesbury Avenue, London.
Shaftesbury Avenue, a street in central London near Piccadilly Circus, is regarded as the centre of West End theatre and has many theatres.
(*Paul Brown/Rex Features*)

new screens have been built since 1996 and today there are 2,954 cinema screens situated either in single buildings or in multiplexes with five or more screens. Annual audience figures dropped from some 501 million in 1960 to 193 million in 1970. This decline was hastened by the arrival of television and continued as new forms of home entertainment, such as videos and DVDs, increased. Annual admissions sank to 55 million by 1984. But there was an increase to 142 million in 2000 and 176 million in 2002 before declining again to 167 million in 2003. Some improvement in audience figures since 1984 has been encouraged by cheaper tickets, a wider range of films (beyond the usual blockbuster fare), responses to competition, appeal to younger people and the provision of an alternative leisure activity within more modern surroundings. Latest figures in 2005 suggest increased audience figures are due in part to the success of British-based films aimed at the younger generation (such as the Harry Potter films). But more than 30 per cent of the population never go to the cinema and 47 per cent of those aged over 35 never go.

The percentage of the population which attends various types of cultural event has remained fairly stable since the early 1990s. A Target Group Index (BRMB International) poll in 2003–4 found that attendances at 'cultural events' of the population over 15 in Britain were increasing (despite variable figures for film) and were 61 per cent for cinema, followed by theatre (25 per cent), art galleries/exhibitions (24 per cent), classical music (13 per cent), ballet (8 per cent), opera (8 per cent) and contemporary dance (6 per cent). Some polls include other institutions in this category, such as museums, pantomime, football matches, heritage sites, libraries and pop concerts.

British popular music increased hugely and influentially in Britain and led the world from the 1960s and was both an economic and cultural phenomenon. Since the Beatles and early Rolling Stones, the domestic market for music sales has multiplied more than sixfold. However, in recent years, there has been a stale-ness in the popular field which has affected mainstream genres, hip hop, rap, avant-garde and 'ethnic' music alike. Some critics attribute this to commercial manipulation, overly packaged offerings and standardized bands, and others to a lack of substantial and consistent talent. Old-guard pop stars complain about the inadequacy of contemporary British pop music with its bland, vacuous material and ephemeral boy and girl bands, which have difficulty breaking into the global (and particularly the American) market.

But British popular and rock music today still has a domestic and international following, is again slowly becoming attractive to the home and overseas youth market and constitutes a considerable industry. Music was worth £2 billion a year in 2003 (down in value since 2000) and the industry employed some 125,000 people. UK record sales in 2003 saw an increase to 236 million pop record albums, but a decrease to 36 million pop singles. The increase in albums and decline in singles has been marked in recent years. Sales of classical albums have tended to increase steadily. But all these sales have been negatively affected by widespread

PLATE 12.7 The Tate Modern, London.
A gallery and exhibition hall on the south bank of the River Thames (created in 2000 from a disused power station), which specializes in contemporary art and sculpture.
(*Alisdair MacDonald/Rex Features*)

downloading of music from various sources and the development of equipment which bypasses the traditional record (and even CD). But the music business still constitutes a sizeable amount of British exports in the form of recordings, concert tours, clothing and books. Polls suggest that 81 per cent of Britons between 16 and 24 spend their leisure time listening to CDs, tapes or records at least once a week and more people attend live music performances than football matches.

There is a wide range of museums and art galleries in Britain (some 1,860), which provide for a variety of tastes. Most of them are financed and controlled by local authorities, although some are commercial ventures and others, such as national institutions like the British Museum and the National Gallery in London, are the province of the Secretary of State for Culture. Entry to most of the public museums and art galleries is now free of charge, after a period when entrance fees were levied for some institutions. But museums and art galleries are finding it difficult to operate on limited funds and are dependent upon local government grants, Arts Council subsidies and National Lottery donations. Museum and art gallery attendance in England rose from 25 million in 2000 to 34.7 million in 2003–4 and there were proportional increases in Wales, Scotland and Northern Ireland.

As in sport, certain arts activities and their associated buildings have become virtual institutions, such as the West End, repertory companies, the Last Night of the Proms, the Albert Hall, the Royal Festival Hall, the National Theatre, the Tate Gallery (now called Tate Britain), the National Gallery and the Royal Shakespeare Theatre at Stratford-upon-Avon. These have been added to in recent years by buildings, such as Tate Modern which is associated with often controversial prizes such as the Turner Prize. They reflect Britain's lively (and internationally important) contemporary art scene.

Exercises

Explain and examine the following terms:

Do-It-Yourself	the pub	rugby football
package tour	National Lottery	sponsorship
bear baiting	casinos	'bed and breakfast'
high culture	cricket	the Arts Council
'West End'	brass bands	repertory theatres
football pools	ethnic restaurants	multiplexes

Write short essays on the following topics:

1   What impression do you gain of the British people, based on their leisure, sporting and artistic activities?

2   How would you account for the fluctuations in cinema attendance in Britain in the twentieth century?

Further reading

1   Bennett, A. (2000) *Popular Music and Youth Culture: Music, Identity and Place* London: Palgrave/Macmillan
2   Christopher, D. (1999) *British Culture: An Introduction* London: Routledge
3   Fowler, D. (2005) *Youth Culture in the Twentieth Century* London: Palgrave/Macmillan
4   Hill, J. (2002) *Sport, Leisure and Culture in Twentieth-Century Britain* London: Palgrave/ Macmillan
5   Holt, R. and Mason, T. (2000) *Sport in Britain 1945–2000* Oxford: Blackwell
6   Jacobs, E. and Worcester, R. (1990) *We British: Britain under the Moriscope* London: Weidenfeld and Nicolson
7   Monk, C. and Sargeant, A. (2002) *British Historical Cinema* London: Routledge
8   Polley, M. (1998) *Moving the Goalposts: A History of Sport and Society Since 1945* London: Routledge

Websites

Department for Culture, Media and Sport: www.culture.gov.uk
UK Sport: www.uksport.gov.uk
Sport England: www.english.sports.gov.uk
The FA Premiership: www.fa-premier.com
Rugby Football Union: www.rfu.com
Artsonline: www.artsonline.com
The Arts Council (England): www.artscouncil.org.uk
Arts Council of Wales: www.ccc-acw.org.uk
Scottish Arts Council: www.sac.or.uk
Arts Council of Northern Ireland: www.artscouncil-ni.org
National Lottery Commission: www.natlotcomm.gov.uk
BBC: www.bbc.co.uk
ITC: www.itc.org.uk

Index